故宫陶瓷馆
卷五·专题

故宫博物院 编
故宫出版社

Ceramics Gallery of the Palace Museum
Vol. V Theme

Compiled by the Palace Museum
The Forbidden City Publishing House

红旗
让理想飞扬
图录由"中国一汽 红旗品牌"支持出版
With Support of Hongqi, FAW Group

目 录

Contents

序

陶瓷是中华传统文化瑰宝，其历史源远流长、内涵博大精深。从上万年前的朴拙陶器到晋代“缥瓷”，从隋唐的“南青北白”到宋代的“五大名窑”，从元之青花到明之五彩、清之珐琅彩，百花齐放、争奇斗艳。既传承有序又别具一格的各时代陶瓷珍品，是历史留给我们不可多得的财富，是巨大的知识和艺术智慧之源。

故宫博物院是中国最大的古代艺术品宝库，其186万多件丰厚藏品中，陶瓷器约占36万件，收藏有清宫旧藏的汝、官、哥、定、钧窑“五大名窑”瓷器和明、清两代御器（窑）厂烧造的御用瓷器（俗称“官窑瓷器”）。1949年后，通过国家拨交、私人捐赠以及流散文物征集等渠道，故宫博物院所藏陶瓷器得以不断充实。除此之外，故宫还收藏有3800多件古陶瓷实物资料、7万多片从全国各地陶瓷窑址采集的陶瓷残片标本等。故宫博物院收藏陶瓷作品上自新石器时代、下迄近现代，几乎涵盖中国陶瓷发展史上所有品种，较全面地反映了中国陶瓷8000年连绵不断的历史，其流传有序、品类齐全、数量庞大、质量精湛，为国内外诸多收藏机构所无法比拟。

2020年，是紫禁城建成600年，也是故宫博物院建院95周年，值此良机，故宫博物院“陶瓷馆”从文华殿来到武英殿，以崭新的姿态与观众朋友见面。陶瓷馆始创于1952年，旨在依托故宫博物院藏品优势，全面展示中国陶瓷艺术数千年延绵不断的传承发展。此后，随时代发展和研究深入，陶瓷馆不断在“进化”，展览内容不断丰富，展出条件不断优化，展示手段不断升级。现在我们所看到的新陶瓷馆，无论展品数量、内容设计还是展陈形式等，都堪称前所未有。展品数量从原来的400多件增加至1000多件；展示内容由之前的11个主题增加到17个主题，特别增加了“等级森然”“承续烧造”“喜庆吉祥”“富丽华贵”“敬天法祖”“庄严法相”等主题展示，还首次集中展示了民国瓷器，可谓类皆精品。相信通过丰富的展品、精心的设计，辅之以高科技的展陈手段，一定会带给公众高品质的观展体验，引领大家走进陶瓷的殿堂，尽情品味陶瓷文化艺术的流光溢彩。

衷心祝愿每一位驻足在此的观众朋友，可以通过古朴典雅的史前陶器、商至两汉原始青瓷，透过绚丽斑斓的唐三彩、“千峰翠色”的越窑青瓷、“类银似雪”的邢窑白瓷、色泽优雅的元明青花瓷、色彩缤纷的明清御窑五彩瓷……感悟陶之古朴、瓷之华美，并启迪思考、与时偕行。让我们一道携手同行、继往开来，传承弘扬中国陶瓷文化艺术，发扬光大中华优秀传统文化，使其在新的时代绽放新的光彩！

故宫博物院院长

Preface

Ceramics is one of the most important forms of ancient Chinese art and one of the greatest achievements of human inventiveness. Throughout a long history of over thousands of years, a vast range of types of Chinese ceramics from crude pottery to painted earthenware, from jadelike early celadon to elaborate hard porcelain with monochrome or polychrome, under or over glaze decorations have been created, leaving a great cultural legacy of China to the world and exerting profound influence on the advancement of global civilization.

As one of the leading museums in China, the Palace Museum permanently houses the finest imperial collections of over 1.86 million objects, including one of the largest and the most comprehensive Chinese ceramics collections in the world. Comprised of approximately 360,000 heirloom pieces or sets, the Museum's Chinese ceramics collection is based on the Qing rulers' collections that had been brought together and handed down for successive generations. Among the collection's treasures are an outstanding array of a distinguished assemblage of the invaluable Five Great Wares including Ru, Ge, Guan, Jun and Ding wares of the Song Dynasty, the prestigious Jingdezhen official wares made at the Imperial Kilns of the Ming and Qing Dynasties, and the finest collection of prehistory earthenware, early celadon, Tang tri-colour pottery, Yue celadon with mountain-verdant glaze, Xing porcelain with silvery white glaze, Yuan porcelain with elegant blue-and-white designs and the Ming and Qing famille-verte porcelain. Over 70,000 shards and more than 3,800 individual pieces of ancient pottery and porcelain collected by the Museum's research staff from the sites of historic kilns around China as well as transferred government holdings, private donations and retrieved items have also enriched the entire collection since 1949. From the earliest products by humankind in the Stone Age to works by contemporary artists, this incomparable collection encompasses the most representative objects in the history of ceramics production in China spanning over 8,000 years.

For the celebration of the 600th anniversary of the completion of Forbidden City and the 95 year history of the Palace Museum, a new Ceramics Gallery will be opened to the public in 2020. Found in 1952, the Ceramics Gallery initially featured the most extraordinary examples from the collection that reflects the continuous development of Chinese ceramics in the past. Several substantial changes have been made since the Gallery opened in order to improve the visitor experience, including updating the Gallery's showcase by incorporating the latest findings of international researches plus new digital platforms. New and refurbished exhibition spaces, refined settings and decorations as well as varying exhibits have usually been provided. The renovation undergoing this year emphasizes on the relocation of the Gallery from the Hall of Literary Brilliance to the magnificent Hall of Military Prowess, along with the area of exhibition space expanded and the number of exhibits increasing from 400 to over 1,000. Six new thematic displays of the most exquisite pieces or sets from the Ming and Qing imperial collections titled *Rigid Hierarchical Structure, Successor of Firing Technology, For Joyous and Auspicious Moment, Luxurious Splendor, In Reverence of Heaven and Worship of Ancestors* and *Solemn Appearance* as well as a selection of porcelain collection of the Republican Period of China will be presented for the first time in the new space. These new displays together with the permanent exhibitions in the Gallery will provide the visitors a broad perspective on the grand history of Chinese ceramics.

We sincerely hope the new Gallery of Ceramics becomes a showcase of our superb collection that delights and inspires the visitors of today. And we look forward that our fine traditions of Chinese ceramics bring energy to this new era of cultural prosperity.

Wang Xudong
Director of the Palace Museum

前言

中国是享誉世界的文明古国，在悠久的历史长河中，创造了灿烂的物质和精神文化，陶瓷堪称其中最重要的标志之一。

早在距今约两万年前，我们的祖先就发明了制陶术，使我国成为世界上最早制作和使用陶器的国家之一。在距今约三四千年前的夏、商时期，我国已能烧造原始瓷器；到了距今 1800 多年前的东汉时期，又发明了真正意义上的瓷器，这是我们祖先在人类文明史上写下的光辉一页。从红陶、灰陶、彩陶、黑陶、白陶到原始瓷、青瓷、黑瓷、白瓷以及五光十色的颜色釉瓷和色彩缤纷的釉下彩、釉上彩瓷等，体现出中国陶瓷绵延不断的发展历程，堪称世界工艺史上一大奇迹。

中国陶瓷自唐代以来即大量远销海外，其卓越的制瓷技术和辉煌的艺术成就，对世界上许多国家的陶瓷生产均产生过广泛而深远的影响，极大地推动了世界陶瓷文化的发展，充分证明中国无愧于“瓷国”之称号。

故宫博物院是在明、清两代皇宫建筑及其收藏品基础上建立的中国最大的综合类博物馆，在所收藏 186 万多件文物中，陶瓷类文物完整器约占 36 万件，而且绝大部分属于清代宫廷旧藏，可谓自成体系，流传有序。特别是经过几代专家的研究鉴定，使故宫博物院的陶瓷藏品具备较高的真实性和可靠性。

本次改陈我们从中遴选出约 1000 多件具有代表性的藏品，按时代发展顺序和使用功能分 17 个主题予以展示，力求反映中国陶瓷约 8000 年绵延不断的历史和博大精深的文化内涵，供观众朋友欣赏、研究。

Foreword

China, one of the cradles of world's earliest civilizations, has created a splendid culture with her accumulated treasure of age. Throughout a long history over thousands of years, Chinese ceramics has been one of the most important forms of ancient Chinese art and exerted profound influence on the advancement of world civilization.

Pottery was first used and made by the ancestors of Chinese from nearly 20,000 years ago. The earliest Chinese proto-porcelain was dated to the Xia and Shang Dynasties, prior to the development of ceramics that matured and transited to true porcelain in the East Han Period. Regarded as one of the most marvelous achievements of human inventiveness, Chinese ceramics slowly develops over the last years, covering a vast range of types from crude pottery to painted earthenware, from proto-porcelain to hard porcelain with monochrome or polychrome, under or over glaze decorations.

Chinese ceramics was exported overseas from the Tang Dynasty (618-907) onwards. Its advanced workmanship and immense beauty tremendously urged the development of global ceramics industry. Praised as "the Cradle of Porcelain", China took enormous pride in the true porcelain (china) she bore, raised and sent abroad.

The Palace Museum, located in the imperial palace complex of the Ming and Qing Dynasties, is one of the world's leading museums that open to visitors from across the globe. It permanently houses many of the finest imperial collections of over 1.86 million objects, including one of the largest and the most comprehensive Chinese ceramics collections in the world. Comprised of approximately 360,000 individual intact pieces in total, the Chinese ceramics collection at the Museum has a majority assembled by the Qing court and handed down for generations. The authenticity and provenance of these objects has been confirmed by experts from one generation to the next after decades of research.

The new selection for the refurbished Ceramics Gallery is based on the insight of history and function of objects. It features over 1,000 representative items with chronologies and 17 showcases with different themes and settings, encompassing a history of ceramics production spanning over 8,000 years in China. We hope our magnificent collection can enlighten and inspire the visitors of today.

图版目录

List of Plates

图版

Plates

主题十一

蜚声海外

中国陶瓷的外销

中国陶瓷生产有大约两万年绵延不断的历史，堪称世界工艺史上的一大奇迹，为人类文明发展做出过杰出贡献。

在适应国内市场需求的基础上，至迟从唐代开始，中国陶瓷已被作为一种特产而大量销往海外。宋、元时期外销陶瓷的烧造进一步兴盛，窑场遍布东南沿海。明、清两代外销陶瓷的烧造呈现繁荣景象，其中最主要的产地是江西景德镇和浙江龙泉，其他还有福建漳州、德化等。

明代中期以前，中国陶瓷主要销往亚、非地区，此后开始大量销往欧、美地区。特别是 17 世纪以来，欧洲的一些国家相继成立由政府授权与东方进行贸易的东印度公司，例如 1600 年成立的英国东印度公司（1600 ～ 1874 年）、1602 年成立的荷兰东印度公司（1602 ～ 1799 年）、1616 年成立的丹麦东印度公司（1616 ～ 1729 年）、1628 年成立的葡萄牙东印度公司（1628 ～ 1633 年）、1664 年成立的法国东印度公司（1664 ～ 1769 年）、1731 年成立的瑞典东印度公司（1731 ～ 1813 年）、1775 年成立的奥地利东印度公司（1775 ～ 1785 年）等。它们曾将大量中国茶叶、丝绸、陶瓷器和藤编制品等特产运往欧洲，瓷器是其中的大宗商品。

在漫长的历史进程中，中国陶瓷作为物质载体曾满载中华民族的深情厚谊，传遍亚洲、非洲、欧洲和美洲，每到一地，既带去了中华文明，也载回世界各国的文明。因此，中国陶瓷被誉为文明交往的使者和东西方文化交流的桥梁和纽带。

人类文化凭借各地域文化的相互交流才得以不断发展、异彩纷呈。由于陶瓷是土与火的艺术，具有耐腐蚀、抗高温、历久弥新等特质，因此，那些留存至今的中国外销陶瓷，对于深入研究历史上各国、各地区人类文化的交流互鉴具有重要意义。

Theme 11

Renowned Abroad

Chinese Export Ceramics

China's ceramics production can be traced back to about 20,000 years ago. It is a miracle in the history of craft, and has made outstanding contributions to the development of human civilization.

It is widely believed that China already began to export ceramics during the Tang Dynasty. Having developed in the Song and Yuan Dynasties, the export market of Chinese ceramics boomed in the Ming and Qing Dynasties. Among numerous kilns in China, export ceramics were mostly produced at Jingdezhen in Jiangxi, Longquan in Zhejiang, Zhangzhou and Dehua in Fujian.

Chinese ceramics were first transported to Asia and Africa. In the middle Ming Dynasty, Chinese ceramics finally arrived in Europe and America. Between the 17th and 18th centuries, several European countries set up trading institutions that were authorized by government, namely the East India Company. These include the British East India Company (1600-1874), the Dutch East India Company (1602-1799), the Danish East India Company (1616-1729), the Portuguese East India Company (1628-1633), the French East India Company (1664-1769), the Swedish East India Company (1731-1813), the Austrian East India Company (1775-1785), etc. The East India Company mainly imported Chinese tea, silk, cane products and the most principal commodity among all — ceramics.

In the long course of history, Chinese ceramics, being a carrier, spread profound friendship of the Chinese nation as well as its civilization throughout Asia, Africa, Europe and America, from where it brought back local civilization in turn. Chinese ceramics are regarded as ambassador for exchanging civilization, playing a bridging role between the East and the West.

Human civilization has been constantly evolving through cultural exchange. Ceramics — resistant to corrosion and fire as well as timeless in value — is art of clay and fire. It is Chinese export ceramics that play a vital role on cultural exchange between countries and regions throughout history.

风靡全球的中国外销陶瓷

中国陶瓷唐代已大量销往海外，如果以明代正德朝（1506 ～ 1521 年）为界限，大致可分为前后两个阶段：前一阶段主要销往亚洲、非洲诸国，后一阶段除继续销往这些地区外，开始直接与欧洲各国进行大规模瓷器贸易，而且销量猛增。有学者统计过，从明代万历三十年（1602 年）至清代康熙二十一年（1682 年）的 80 年间，仅荷兰东印度公司贩运到欧洲的中国瓷器就达约 1200 万件。18 世纪前期，欧洲很多国家获许在广州开设贸易机构，最早获得这一权利的是英国东印度公司（1715 年）。随后，法国于 1728 年、荷兰于 1729 年、丹麦于 1731 年、瑞典于 1732 年也都先后在广州设立了贸易机构，进一步促进了中国瓷器的外销，销售地域也进而扩展到美洲各国。仅在 18 世纪初，英国东印度公司即把约 2500 万件至 3000 万件中国瓷器运往欧洲各国，并在 18 世纪 30 年代后占据了欧洲各国对华瓷器贸易的首位。中国陶瓷贸易的运输路线，被当代考古学者称为“陶瓷之路”。

World-Famous Chinese Export Ceramics

Export of Chinese ceramics in large quantities can be traced back to the Tang Dynasty at the latest. If taking Zhengde Period, Ming Dynasty (1506-1521) as a dividing point, the export history can be roughly divided into two phases: in the first phase, ceramics had been traded mainly in Asia and Africa; and in the second phase, apart from those traditional trade areas, the export trade began in large-scale in Europe and showed a rapid sale growth there. Based on some statistics collected by scholars, within 80 years, beginning from the 30th year of Wanli Period, Ming Dynasty (1602) and ending in the 21st year of Kangxi Period, Qing Dynasty (1682), around 12 million pieces of porcelains were transported to Europe merely by the Dutch East India Company. In the early 18th century, many European countries were allowed to establish trading institutions in Guangzhou. Among them, the British East India Company was the first one to obtain the trading approval (in 1715), followed by France in 1728, the Netherlands in 1729, Denmark in 1731 and Sweden in 1732. The establishment of trading institutions further promoted the export of Chinese porcelain, and the sales area thereby expanded to the Americas. In the early 18th century alone, around 25 to 30 million pieces of Chinese porcelains were transported to Europe by the British East India Company, of which trade volumes remained the top place among European countries after the 1830s. The transport route of Chinese ceramics trade is thus called “the Ceramics Road” by contemporary archaeologists.

001 长沙窑褐绿彩枕

唐

高 7.2 厘米　面横 15.4 厘米　面纵 9.2 厘米

底横 13.1 厘米　底纵 8.0 厘米

枕面呈圆角长方体形，面略大于底。除底面露胎外，其余各面均施釉。枕面以绿色彩点围绕褐色圆圈组成有规律的图案，枕壁以绿彩描绘花叶纹。造型简洁规整，釉面剥落较为严重。

褐绿彩装饰是长沙窑产品中较为常见的装饰方法，而且也是早期釉下彩装饰的代表。以绿彩装饰联珠纹的做法，当与伊斯兰文化有关。考古发现表明，长沙窑瓷器是唐代外销瓷中最重要的品种之一，在产品大量外销的同时，自身也受到外来文化影响，别具一格。（唐雪梅）

Changsha Ware Pillow Decorated in Green and Brown Enamels

Tang Dynasty, H: 7.2cm; L(at top): 15.4cm; W(at top): 9.2cm; L(at base): 13.1cm; W(at base): 8.0cm

002 西村窑青白釉凤首壶

北宋

高 17.8 厘米　口横 4.8 厘米　口纵 3.5 厘米

腹径 13.0 厘米　足径 8.5 厘米

壶顶部为凤首形，高冠、大眼、曲喙，凤顶花冠为注水口。长颈上凸起 3 道弦纹，圆腹丰满，圈足较宽。壶体一侧置弯流，另一侧置曲柄。通体施青白釉，釉层较薄。腹上部刻划缠枝花纹、下部刻划蕉叶纹。

此壶为广州西村窑产品，系故宫博物院古陶瓷研究专家冯先铭、李辉柄先生于 1981 年从菲律宾带回。西村窑瓷器主要用于外销，在东南亚一带特别是菲律宾曾有大量出土。此件凤首壶的造型源于隋唐时期受波斯文化风格影响的器物，但腹部又有自己的独特风格。（赵小春）

Xicun Ware Bluish-White Glazed Phoenix-Head Ewer

Northern Sony Dynasty, H: 17. 8cm; L(at mouth): 4.8cm; W(at mouth): 3.5cm; Diam.(at belly): 13.0cm; Diam.(at foot): 8.5cm

003 西村窑青白釉褐斑刻划凤纹碗

北宋

高 8.9 厘米　口径 33.3 厘米　足径 9.5 厘米

碗敞口、折沿、弧腹、圈足。通体施青白釉。内底刻划凤纹，并有规律地涂点由 5 个褐色斑点组成的 5 朵花；内壁刻划缠枝花纹，随意涂点褐色斑点。碗外光素无纹饰。

此碗形体大而规整，釉下刻花纹饰与釉上点彩相互衬托，繁而不乱，属于西村窑为外销东南亚国家而烧造瓷器中颇具代表性的作品。系 1981 年故宫博物院古陶瓷研究专家冯先铭、李辉柄先生从菲律宾带回。（赵小春）

Xicun Bluish-White Glazed Bowl with Incised Design of Phoenix and Brown Enamels

Northern Song Dynasty, H: 8.9cm; Diam.(at mouth): 33.3cm; Diam.(at foot): 9.5cm

004 青花花卉纹瓜棱瓶

明万历

高 31.0 厘米　口径 6.3 厘米　足径 11.5 厘米

瓶撇口、长颈、垂腹、圈足。口部镶银，腹部呈瓜棱形。胎体略厚，釉面莹亮。通体青花装饰。颈部绘丛竹纹，腹部瓜棱形开光内均绘折枝花纹，近足处绘朵云纹。

此瓶属于明代万历时期专门为东南亚各国烧造的外销瓷，当时备受异域人士喜爱，他们经常在瓷器的口、流部镶以各种美丽的银质边饰。通过这样的二次加工，不仅保护瓷器口、流免于磕碰（有的器物系因原有磕伤而镶金属），也起到了很好的装饰作用，致使外销瓷的面貌有所改观，体现异国情调。（董健丽）

Blue-and-White Lobed Bottle with Floral Design

Wanli Period, Ming Dynasty, H: 31.0cm; Diam.(at mouth): 6.3cm; Diam.(at foot): 11.5cm

005 青花开光花卉草虫纹盘

明万历

高 6.3 厘米　口径 36.0 厘米　足径 20.0 厘米

盘敞口、宽折沿、浅弧腹、圈足。盘内、外和圈足内均施白釉。内外青花装饰。内壁饰大、小相间排列的开光各 8 个，依次在开光内绘相间排列的折枝花纹、杂宝纹。内底绘八角形开光，开光内绘怪石花卉草虫小景。外壁绘 8 个圆圈，以双竖线中间加一短粗线相隔。

这种瓷器被称作“克拉克”瓷，系明末清初景德镇观音阁等处民窑烧造的主要用于外销的瓷器。“克拉克”青花瓷盘的装饰风格大体相同，均图案满密，且多在盘内底绘花鸟图，内壁绘 16 组开光图案。“克拉克”瓷自明代万历时期开始大量外销至东亚、南亚、中东、欧洲等地，葡萄牙、荷兰、日本、墨西哥、秘鲁等国家均有收藏。（郑宏）

Blue-and-White Plate with Panelled Design of Insect-Among-Grass

Wanli Period, Ming Dynasty, H: 6.3cm; Diam.(at mouth): 36.0cm; Diam.(at foot): 20.0cm

006 漳州窑青花开光花草纹盘

明万历

高 3.0 厘米　口径 21.2 厘米　足径 11.2 厘米

盘敞口、宽折沿、浅弧腹、圈足。盘内、外和圈足内均施白釉，足端无釉。内壁饰 8 个莲瓣形开光，开光内绘花果和杂宝纹。内底绘 8 个连弧组成的开光，开光外绘鱼鳞纹、莲瓣纹等，开光内绘花草纹。外壁绘潦草的圆圈与竖线间隔排列的纹饰。

此盘属于“克拉克”风格的外销瓷，这是一种在 16 世纪末至 17 世纪风靡东南亚和欧洲的瓷器，产地主要有江西景德镇、福建漳州和日本有田。与此盘风格相似的青花盘在 2004 年至 2005 年打捞的沉没于马来西亚东海岸附近的“万历号”沉船中也有发现。万历号船是往返于中国澳门、菲律宾马六甲、马尼拉和印度果阿之间的葡萄牙商船，因爆炸而沉没。打捞出水瓷器中 60% 为盘、碟等生活用瓷。

漳州窑中心窑场位于今福建省漳州市平和县的五寨乡和南胜乡。清康熙五十四年（1715 年）《漳州府志》卷二十七“物产”条载：“瓷器出南胜窑，殊胜他邑，然亦不甚工巧。”（唐雪梅）

Zhangzhou Ware Blue-and-White Plate with Panelled Design of Flowers

Wanli Period, Ming Dynasty, H: 3.0cm; Diam.(at mouth): 21.2cm; Diam.(at foot): 11.2cm

007 漳州窑青花开光人物天马纹盘

明万历

高 8.0 厘米　口径 39.0 厘米　足径 19.0 厘米

盘敞口、弧腹、圈足。盘内、外和圈足内均施白釉。盘内青花装饰。内壁均匀分布以花草相隔的 8 个扇形区域，每个扇形区域内均有一圆形开光，开光内依次相间饰人物纹和阿拉伯文。内底中心圆形区域内绘仙人骑凤图；圆形区域外环绕 5 个扇形开光，每个开光内均绘一匹飞奔的天马。外底有粘砂。

此盘属于明代万历时期漳州窑烧造的用于外销的“克拉克”瓷。（赵小春）

Zhangzhou Ware Blue-and-White Plate with Panelled Design of Sage-Riding-on-Phoenix and Winged-Horse

Wanli Period, Ming Dynasty, H: 8.0cm; Diam.(at mouth): 39.0cm; Diam.(at foot): 19.0cm

008 漳州窑红绿彩花卉纹盘

明万历

高 7.5 厘米　口径 36.5 厘米　足径 18.0 厘米

盘撇口、弧腹、圈足。内、外施白釉，外壁近足至底部不施釉。胎质较粗。圈足粘砂严重。盘内以红、绿彩描绘纹饰。口沿处画一道红彩弦线，其下以绿彩和黑彩描绘几何纹边饰。内壁以红、绿彩锦地开光装饰，4 组开光内均绘折枝花纹。内底 5 道红彩弦线内绘红、绿彩花卉纹。（王照宇）

Zhangzhou Ware Polychrome Plate with Floral Design

Wanli Period, Ming Dynasty, H: 7.5cm; Diam.(at mouth): 36.5cm; Diam.(at foot): 18.0cm

009 漳州窑红绿彩鱼藻罗经纹盘

明万历

高 8.5 厘米　口径 37.5 厘米　足径 17.5 厘米

盘撇口、弧腹、圈足。内、外施白釉，外底涩胎有釉斑且有粘砂。胎质较粗。盘内以红、绿彩描绘纹饰。近口沿处以绿彩和黑彩描绘几何纹边饰。内壁以红彩、绿彩、黑彩描绘 5 组鱼藻纹，鱼呈昂首腾跃状。内底数条红彩弦线内以红彩、绿彩描绘两层纹饰，中心以矾红彩竖写“天”“一”二字，外圈以矾红彩环写 24 字，顺时针依次为“子、癸、丑、艮、寅、甲、卯、乙、辰、巽、巳、丙、午、丁、未、坤、申、庚、酉、辛、戌、乾、亥、壬”，包括天干 8 字、地支 12 字、八卦 4 字。（王照宇）

Zhangzhou Ware Polychrome Plate with Design of Fish, Water-Weed and Diagram of Chinese Compass

Wanli Period, Ming Dynasty, H: 8.5cm; Diam.(at mouth): 37.5cm; Diam.(at foot): 17.5cm

010 青花团花纹瓜棱军持

明

高 19.0 厘米　口径 3.0 厘米　足径 6.5 厘米

军持直口、口下出相轮、长颈、6 瓣瓜棱腹，肩、腹之间置乳状流，圈足。通体施白釉，以青花装饰，足端无釉。颈、肩部自上而下装饰蕉叶纹、朵花纹、钱纹，腹部 6 面各画不同的团状花卉。外底青花双圈内绘兔形花押。

瓷器上非文字的图案落款一般统称“花押款”，常见于民窑产品。“花押”本意是在文书契约上的签字或代替签字的符号，被用作取信于人的凭记。花押款瓷器在明清时期广为流行，常见花押图案有：佛教图案，如轮、螺、伞、盖、花、罐、鱼、肠等；道教图案，如还魂扇、宝剑、葫芦、花篮、渔鼓、笛子、荷花等；动植物图案，如龙、凤、鹿、龟、鹤、松、竹、梅、灵芝、瑞草、艾叶等；博古图案，如八卦、太极、八宝、琴棋书画等；“豆腐干”图案，即在双重方框内绘横竖相间的线条；“四朵花”图案，即在双重圆圈内绘 4 个似字非字的图案或 4 朵花。（韩倩）

Blue-and-White Kendi with Design of Floral Medallion

Ming Dynasty, H: 19.0cm; Diam.(at mouth): 3.0cm; Diam.(at foot): 6.5cm

011 青花灵芝花卉纹军持

明万历

高 20.5 厘米　口径 3.3 厘米　足径 9.5 厘米

军持直口、口下起相轮、长颈、圆腹，肩、腹之间置乳状流，流口镶银，圈足。通体施白釉，以青花装饰，足端无釉。腹部主题图案以竖线分为 6 个区域，依次在区域内相间描绘折枝灵芝、花卉纹。（韩倩）

Blue-and-White Kendi with Design of *Lingzhi* Fungus and Floral

Wanli Period, Ming Dynasty, H: 20.5cm; Diam.(at mouth): 3.3cm; Diam.(at foot): 9.5cm

012 青花缠枝莲纹军持

清康熙

高 21.0 厘米　口径 6.3 厘米　足径 9.2 厘米

军持有残缺，剩下部分撇口、束颈、圆腹、浅圈足。肩部置乳状流，其口部及流口均镶银。军持内、外和圈足内均施白釉，足端不施釉。通体绘青花缠枝莲纹，构图繁密。（王照宇）

Blue-and-White Kendi with Design of Lotus Scrolls

Kangxi Period, Qing Dynasty, H: 21.0cm; Diam.(at mouth): 6.3cm; Diam.(at foot): 9.2cm

013 青花凸莲瓣花卉纹军持

清康熙

通高 26.8 厘米　口径 7.5 厘米　足径 9.3 厘米

军持口微撇、束颈、圆腹、浅圈足。肩部置乳状流。军持内、外和圈足内均施白釉。外底中心有凸起，无款识。颈部的上半部及乳状流之口部均镶银。腹部交错凸起两层莲瓣，上层 8 个大莲瓣内绘梅花、菊花、牡丹花、荷花等四季花卉，近足处 16 个小莲瓣承托器身。乳状流也凸起莲瓣，内绘四季花纹。通体纹饰布局满密，但繁而不乱。（董健丽）

Blue-and-White Kendi Moulded in the Form of Lotus Petals with Floral Design

Kangxi Period, Qing Dynasty, H(with cover): 26.8cm; Diam.(at mouth): 7.5cm; Diam.(at foot): 9.3cm

014 青花缠枝莲纹长颈瓶

清康熙

高 15.0 厘米　口径 2.6 厘米　足径 4.5 厘米

瓶直口、长颈、圆鼓腹、圈足。通体青花装饰。颈上半部饰蕉叶纹，下半部及腹部满绘缠枝莲纹。（唐雪梅）

Blue-and-White Long-Necked Vase with Design of Lotus Scrolls

Kangxi Period, Qing Dynasty, H: 15.0cm; Diam.(at mouth): 2.6cm; Diam.(at foot): 4.5cm

015 青花蕉叶纹嵌壁菊瓣式饮水器

清雍正

高 36.0 厘米　口横 9.5 厘米　足横 13.0 厘米　足纵 9.5 厘米

器呈剖开的半瓶式。唇口、垂腹，腹下部饰兽形出水孔，圈足。通体青花装饰，颈及腹部饰上下相对的变形蕉叶纹，近足处饰莲瓣纹。无款识。

此器胎体厚重，青花色泽蓝中泛灰，纹饰描绘略显粗率。属于当时欧洲人在中国订烧的嵌在墙壁上使用的饮水器，出水孔处可安装铜质水龙头。同样造型的器物在康熙时已有烧造，传世见有五彩品种，不但有盖，而且还有与之配套使用的菊瓣式承盆。此器也应有盖和配套使用的菊瓣承盆，惜均已佚。（高晓然）

Blue-and-White Wall Waterpot Moulded in the Form of Chrysanthemum Petals with Design of Plantain Leaf

Yongzheng Period, Qing Dynasty, H: 36.0cm; L(at mouth): 9.5cm; L(at foot): 13.0cm; W(at foot): 9.5cm

016 青花花卉纹四足汤盆

清雍正

高 15.5 厘米　口横 32.0 厘米　口纵 18.2 厘米

底横 11.0 厘米　底纵 10.0 厘米

汤盆撇口、深腹、平底。口沿两侧对称置向下弯曲的柄，底部下承翻卷的 4 个兽蹄形足。胎体略厚。通体青花花卉纹装饰。

这种器物是 18 世纪欧洲人在中国订制的外销瓷，其造型和纹饰均按欧洲银鎏金汤盆制作而成，成型和烧成难度均较大。（赵小春）

Blue-and-White Four-Legged Tureen with Floral Design

Yongzheng Period, Qing Dynasty, H: 15.5cm; L(at mouth): 32.0cm; W(at mouth): 18.2cm; L(at base): 11.0cm; W(at base): 10.0cm

017 广彩开光花卉人物图折沿盆

清乾隆

高 12.8 厘米　口径 40.8 厘米　足径 20.6 厘米

盆敞口、折沿、深弧腹、圈足。盆内、外和圈足内均施白釉，足端无釉。盆内以多层开光表现丰富的人物、花鸟图案。内折沿上饰 6 个花边开光，开光内均绘花鸟图，开光之间满绘百花蝴蝶纹，隙地描金。内壁亦饰 6 个扇形开光，其中 3 个绘庭院人物图，相隔 3 个绘折枝花鸟伴蝴蝶图，开光外满绘绿色卷草纹。内底绘 4 个扇形开光环绕中心的圆形开光，扇形开光内相间描绘庭院人物图和花鸟图，开光之间满绘绿色卷草纹，隙地描金。中心圆形开光内绘花鸟蝴蝶图。外壁绘 3 朵对称的折枝花。（冀洛源）

Basin with Everted Rim and Panelled Design of Human Figures in Cantonese Enamels

Qianlong Period, Qing Dynasty, H: 12.8cm; Diam.(at mouth): 40.8cm; Diam.(at foot): 20.6cm

018 广彩徽章折枝花纹盘

清乾隆

高 3.2 厘米　口径 14.0 厘米　足径 8.8 厘米

盘敞口、浅弧腹、圈足。通体施白釉。外壁光素，盘内图案主要采用黑彩描绘。口沿描绘金边，其下用黑彩描绘花草纹边饰，内壁以黑彩加金彩描绘四枝折枝花纹，内底中心以黑彩加金彩描绘徽章，上边窄带上写有拉丁文“AMAT VICTORIA CURAM”，翻译成中文意思是“机会总是垂青有准备的人”。

此盘胎体轻薄，纹饰简洁明快。经查，盘心所绘徽章系英国诺里奇 · 克拉克家族徽章。克拉克家族有多名成员曾在英国东印度公司工作。其中汤玛斯 · 克拉克少校出生于 1761 年，曾供职于英国东印度公司；其弟罗伯特 · 克拉克出生于 1763 年，后来成为英国东印度公司董事。装饰这种徽章的瓷器系 18 世纪英国克拉克家族在中国景德镇专门订烧的家族用瓷。

广彩是由广东陶瓷商人在江西景德镇购买素白瓷，依照外国商人提供的装饰纹样，在广东当地雇工将纹饰描画在素白瓷上，然后，入炭炉经 800℃左右焙烧而成。产品经广东港口海运输往国外。（赵聪月）

Plate with the Arms of the English Family Clark and Design of Floral Sprays in Cantonese Enamels

Qianlong Period, Qing Dynasty, H: 3.2cm; Diam.(at mouth): 14.0cm; Diam.(at foot): 8.8cm

019 广彩徽章折枝花纹盘

清乾隆

高 3.1 厘米　口径 14.0 厘米　足径 8.4 厘米

盘敞口、浅弧腹、圈足。内、外和圈足内均施白釉，足端无釉。图案采用广彩中的黑彩绘画。盘口沿描绘金边，盘内口沿下绘花草纹边饰，内壁装饰 4 朵小花，内底绘徽章纹。外壁光素。

此盘纹饰简单明快，以英国诺里奇·克拉克家族徽章作为盘心图案。克拉克家族有多名成员在英国东印度公司工作。这件瓷盘的主人可能是图版 18 所述克拉克兄弟中的一位，也可能是家族的其他成员。（赵聪月）

Plate with the Arms of the English Family Clark and Design of Floral Sprays in Cantonese Enamels

Qianlong Period, Qing Dynasty, H: 3.1cm; Diam.(at mouth): 14.0cm; Diam.(at foot): 8.4cm

020 广彩徽章纹盘

清乾隆

高 2.8 厘米　口径 12.1 厘米　足径 7.3 厘米

盘敞口、浅弧腹、圈足。外光素，内广彩装饰。内口沿饰青花蓝地金彩朵花纹边饰。内壁绘 4 组折枝花纹。内底绘徽章纹，经考证系荷兰范 · 斯宾家族（Van Spaen）与范 · 霍根多普家族（Van Hogendorp）的徽章。这两个家族都是具有悠久历史的荷兰贵族。瓷盘的主人是范 · 斯宾男爵（1746 ~ 1827 年）与其妻萨拉 · 琼安娜（1755 ~ 1828 年），可能是 1785 年夫妇二人为庆祝铜婚纪念而在中国订制的带有家族徽章的瓷器。（黄卫文）

Plate with the Arms of Two Dutch Families in Cantonese Enamels

Qianlong Period, Qing Dynasty, H: 2.8cm; Diam.(at mouth): 12.1cm; Diam.(at foot): 7.3cm

021 ## 广彩徽章纹盘

清乾隆

高 3.2 厘米　口径 14.1 厘米　足径 8.1 厘米

盘敞口、浅弧腹、矮圈足。通体施白釉。口沿描金。内壁画一道较粗的金线，绕以绿色带状纹，并在对称位置作蝴蝶结。内底绘一只展翅白鸽，口衔红色打结丝带，其下挂一心形饰物，其内以金彩书写英文姓名首字母，外以花草环饰，下坠红花。圈足底部斜削，露出白色胎。外底微下塌。

此盘边饰简洁，突出内底主题徽章装饰，属于 18 世纪欧洲人在中国订烧徽章瓷的典型作品。（冀洛源）

Plate with the Arms of Family in Cantonese Enamels

Qianlong Period, Qing Dynasty, H: 3.2cm; Diam.(at mouth): 14.1cm; Diam.(at foot): 8.1cm

022 广彩西洋仕女图盘

清乾隆

高 2.7 厘米　口径 12.6 厘米　足径 7.3 厘米

盘敞口、浅弧腹、圈足。内、外和圈足内均施白釉。外壁光素，盘内广彩装饰。内壁近口沿以红彩加金彩描绘二方连续边饰，其下以紫彩描绘连珠纹，近底处以胭脂红彩和绿彩交错描绘连珠纹。内底在一周矾红彩加紫彩描绘的圆形挂饰内，以各种色彩描绘一欧洲妇女半身肖像。绘画笔触细腻，人物形象生动、色彩逼真，具有较强立体感和油画效果。（赵聪月）

Plate with Design of a Western Lady in Cantonese Enamels

Qianlong Period, Qing Dynasty, H: 2.7cm; Diam.(at mouth): 12.6cm; Diam.(at foot): 7.3cm

023 ## 广彩花鸟图盘

清乾隆

高 4.1 厘米　口径 25.2 厘米　足径 15.0 厘米

盘敞口、浅弧腹、圈足。内、外和圈足内均施白釉。外壁光素，盘内以广彩装饰。口部以矾红彩加金彩描绘边饰，内壁以青花描绘蝴蝶花卉纹，内底以各种彩料描绘两只凤凰戏于洞石花卉中。造型规整，设色华丽，纹饰布局疏朗，堪称乾隆朝广彩瓷中的精品。（赵聪月）

Plate with Design of Flowers and Birds in Cantonese Enamels

Qianlong Period, Qing Dynasty, H: 4.1cm; Diam.(at mouth): 25.2cm; Diam.(at foot): 15.0cm

024 广彩人物图碗

清乾隆

高 11.0 厘米　口径 25.7 厘米　足径 13.1 厘米

碗敞口、深弧腹、圈足。外壁以金彩折枝花纹为地，在花边开光内绘人物、山水花鸟图。其中有两组较大的开光。一组绘水岸上休闲的满族贵人，画面中有人倚桌而坐，有人旁立，有人树下交谈；有人手持烟杆，似在打理烟灰，另一人在旁观望；桌上的水丞、厅堂的小狗、远山近水、殿堂房舍等，尽入画中。第二组描绘一长者坐于椅上，侍者端茶立旁；树下一人手持长烟杆，另一人在旁凝望其手中烟杆。持烟杆人矮小的身体与长长的烟杆形成鲜明对比。碗内底绘两位满族装束者坐于山间戏鹰。一人抬起的左手臂上落一鹰，另一人坐在石凳上观看。两组大开光间各点缀两个小花叶形开光，开光内分别绘花鸟、山水图。

此碗所绘人物图反映了清代满族贵族子弟吸烟、喝茶、戏鹰等休闲生活场景，绘画受西方“洛可可”风格影响，纹饰多用金彩，纹饰满密，色彩艳丽华贵。采用透视绘画技法，以西方人视角来诠释清代满族贵族的生活状态和休闲、娱乐场景，是中西文化相互影响的写照和反映。（郑宏）

Bowl with Design of Human Figures in Cantonese Enamels

Qianlong Period, Qing Dynasty, H: 11.0cm; Diam.(at mouth): 25.7cm; Diam.(at foot): 13.1cm

025 青花加广彩花卉图双耳杯

清乾隆

高 9.6 厘米　口径 8.7 厘米　足径 5.0 厘米

杯撇口、深弧腹、外撇圈足。外壁两侧对称置龙形柄。内口边饰青花地留白朵花纹。外壁青花蓝地开光装饰。正反两面各有一较大开光，开光内绘折枝花纹；左右对称分布 3 组较小开光，其中上、下蝴蝶形开光内均刻划蝴蝶羽翅纹。开光外青花蓝地上排列繁密的珠点状装饰。圈足外墙饰青花折枝花纹。

此杯采用多个开光装饰，属于广彩瓷器上常见的构图方法。（郑宏）

Cup with Two Ears and Design of Flower Branches in Cantonese Enamels on Blue-and-White Ground

Qianlong Period, Qing Dynasty, H: 9.6cm; Diam.(at mouth): 8.7cm; Diam.(at foot): 5.0cm

026 青花山水楼阁图菱花式盘

清嘉庆

高 1.7 厘米　口径 14.3 厘米　底径 11.8 厘米

盘呈 6 瓣菱花式，撇口、浅弧腹、平底。内外施白釉，外底无釉。内壁绘青花锦纹，内底绘青花山水西洋楼阁图。此盘造型符合西方人的餐饮习惯，花纹中西合璧，青花色泽较深，纹饰布局疏密有致，属于嘉庆年间比较精细的外销瓷。

18 世纪以后，景德镇贸易瓷风格变化较大，以瓷盘而言，花口、长方形、菱花形等造型大量增多，这是根据西方人餐饮生活习惯而改变的现象。根据欧洲商家的订制要求，烧造不同造型的西方餐具，使中国瓷器尤其是景德镇瓷器造型更加多样化。（董健丽）

Blue-and-White Plate with Barbed Rim and Landscape Design

Jiaqing Period, Qing Dynasty, H: 1.7cm; Diam.(at mouth): 14.3cm; Diam.(at base): 11.8cm

027 广彩开光徽章纹盘

清嘉庆

高 2.1 厘米　口径 11.0 厘米　足径 5.5 厘米

盘敞口、折沿、浅弧腹、圈足。内、外和圈足内均施白釉。盘外光素，盘内广彩装饰。从里向外共有 3 层纹饰，内底描绘以虎象支撑并书写文字之徽章。内壁绘 4 个稍大扇形开光，间以 4 个稍小青花蓝地扇形开光。4 个稍大扇形开光内以矾红彩加金彩描绘菊花纹，4 个较小开光内均以金彩描绘钱纹锦地托矾红彩朵菊纹。近口沿处绘缠枝花纹。此盘纹饰色彩鲜艳夺目，装饰繁缛华丽，尤其突出金彩、蓝彩、红彩等。金彩的使用，在视觉上给人以富丽堂皇之感。（董健丽）

Plate with Panelled Design and the Arms of Family in Cantonese Enamels

Jiaqing Period, Qing Dynasty, H: 2.1cm; Diam.(at mouth): 11.0cm; Diam.(at foot): 5.5cm

028 广彩开光人物图胆式瓶

清道光

高 19.5 厘米　口径 1.5 厘米　足径 5.1 厘米

瓶小口、细长颈、垂腹、圈足。瓶内、外和圈足内均施白釉。通体以广彩装饰。颈部绘折枝花纹；腹部前后两面开光，开光内均绘人物图。此瓶用色以鲜艳的橘黄为主，间以黄、绿、蓝、白等色彩，绘画工艺精细，花纹满密，体现出广彩瓷器独特的装饰风格。（董健丽）

Gall-Bladder Vase with Panelled Design of Human Figures in Cantonese Enamels

Daoguang Period, Qing Dynasty, H: 19.5cm; Diam.(at mouth): 1.5cm; Diam.(at foot): 5.1cm

029 广彩缠枝牡丹团花纹盘

清同治

高 2.7 厘米　口径 15.5 厘米　足径 9.0 厘米

盘敞口、折沿、浅弧腹、圈足。外壁光素，内壁广彩装饰。内底绘 5 组“十”字状分布的蓝地金彩朵花；内壁以粉红彩、绿彩描绘缠枝牡丹纹；折沿上以青花蓝地描金花卉、网格纹装饰。（黄卫文）

Plate with Design of Peony Scrolls and Floral Medallions in Cantonese Enamels

Tongzhi Period, Qing Dynasty, H: 2.7cm; Diam.(at mouth): 15.5cm; Diam.(at foot): 9.9cm

030 广彩缠枝牡丹团花纹盘

清同治

高 2.9 厘米　口径 11.0 厘米　足径 5.2 厘米

盘敞口、折沿、浅弧腹、圈足。内壁折沿上以青花蓝地描金锦地开光花卉纹装饰；内底以相同手法绘 5 朵团花，四周环绕缠枝牡丹纹。

此盘从造型、装饰到纹饰，均显示出这一时期典型的外销瓷风格。（唐雪梅）

Plate with Design of Peony Scrolls and Floral Medallions in Cantonese Enamels

Tongzhi Period, Qing Dynasty, H: 2.9cm; Diam.(at mouth): 11.0cm; Diam.(at foot): 5.2cm

031 ## 广彩缠枝花纹盘

清同治

高 3.0 厘米　口径 14.5 厘米　足径 7.5 厘米

盘敞口、折沿、浅弧腹、圈足。盘内广彩装饰。内底绘朵花纹，内壁下部绘缠枝花纹，折沿绘锦地开光花卉纹。

此盘造型规整、釉面光洁，主要以胭脂红彩和淡绿彩描绘纹饰，色彩显得鲜艳娇嫩。（黄卫文）

Plate with Design of Floral Scrolls in Cantonese Enamels

Tongzhi Period, Qing Dynasty, H: 3.0cm; Diam.(at mouth): 14.5cm; Diam.(at foot): 7.5cm

032 广彩缠枝花纹盘

清同治

高 2.5 厘米　口径 11.0 厘米　足径 6.0 厘米

盘敞口、折沿、浅弧腹、圈足。盘外光素，盘内广彩装饰。内底饰青花蓝地金彩朵花纹；内壁以粉红彩和绿彩描绘缠枝花纹，折沿青花蓝地上饰以描金锦地开光花卉纹。

此盘造型规整，釉面光润，纹饰色彩艳丽。尤其蓝地金彩装饰，使画面更显富丽。（黄卫文）

Plate with Design of Floral Scrolls in Cantonese Enamels

Tongzhi Period, Qing Dynasty, H: 2.5cm; Diam.(at mouth): 11.0cm; Diam.(at foot): 6.0cm

属于世界的中国陶瓷

中国陶瓷深受世界各国人民喜爱，至迟自唐代开始大量销往国外以后，即不断被仿制。尤其是到了17世纪中叶至18世纪，世界上许多国家为了探寻中国瓷器的秘密，节约因从中国进口大量瓷器所需的巨额资金，纷纷因地制宜，仿烧中国陶瓷，如亚洲的日本、朝鲜、越南、泰国、缅甸、伊朗等，欧洲的荷兰、德国、西班牙、英国、意大利、法国、奥地利等。这些国家在模仿中国陶瓷的基础上，又结合各自文化不断创造出具有异域特色的陶瓷产品，共同将世界陶瓷百花园装点得绚丽多姿。

Chinese Porcelain-Art Belonging to the World

The world-renowned Chinese porcelain has been imitated soon after its first appearance abroad since the Tang Dynasty. In particular from the mid-17th century to the 18th century, many countries such as Japan, Korea, Vietnam, Thailand, Burma, Iran in Asia or the Netherlands, Germany, Spain, Britain, Italy, France and Austria in Europe, endeavoring to reveal the secret of Chinese porcelains and save enormous financial amounts spent on importing them, began to imitate Chinese porcelains by adapting techniques according to their local conditions. On the basis of their imitation, those countries splendidly enriched the world's ceramic treasure by creating ceramics with exotic features with cultural distinctions.

033 五彩麒麟图瓜棱执壶

清乾隆

通高 13.5 厘米　口径 4.5 厘米　足径 10.C 厘米

壶通体起瓜棱。直口、溜肩、垂腹、平底，底下置三足。附伞形盖，盖顶置圆珠钮。一侧置曲柄，另一侧本置有弯流，但流已残佚，遂被安装银流。通体五彩装饰。腹部绘坡地花草栏杆及麒麟，口部绘矾红彩回纹，柄上以红、绿彩描绘云纹。

此种造型的茶壶多见于清代乾隆时期的外销瓷。其银质壶流非中国风格，或为欧洲镶嵌二艺。（孙悦）

Polychrome Lobed Teapot and Cover with Design of *Qilin*

Qianlong Period, Qing Dynasty, H(with cover): 13.5cm; Diam.(at mouth): 4.5cm; Diam.(at foot): 10.0cm

034 粉彩描金徽章纹单柄壶

清乾隆

通高 19.0 厘米　口径 7.0 厘米　足径 10.4 厘米

壶体呈深罐形。直口、单柄、曲流。柄与流位置并非对应，而是呈 90 度角。附伞形盖，盖钮为寿桃状。通体施白釉。口沿和盖边缘饰青花地描金星形纹。壶身中心部位以釉上彩描绘徽章纹。徽章轮廓为盾形，盾中央为字母“S”，代表订制者姓名缩写。盾牌外围饰下垂幔帐纹。

此壶为典型清代外销瓷样式，造型模仿西方银执壶，在西方一般用于盛热巧克力，因此被称作巧克力壶，系 18 世纪流行于欧洲的新造型。

此壶身所绘徽章并非欧洲传统贵族的家族标识，而是 18 世纪欧洲订制的“伪徽章瓷”（Pseudo-armorial porcelain）。这类徽章瓷不是按照徽章学规定设计，也没经过徽章院审核，而是新兴的富裕中产阶级想拥有一套带有个人标识的中国瓷器而订制。这类纹章瓷一般选取一个简单的纹饰模板作为标识，再配上自己姓名的首字母。美国华盛顿与李大学里夫斯中心 (Reeves center collection at Washington and Lee University) 藏有一件与此执壶造型、纹章式样均相同的巧克力壶，其盾形徽章中央字母为“JEA”，可知是另外的订购人使用同一纹章模板而订制。（孙悦）

Ewer and Cover with Pseudo-Armorial Design in *Famille Rose* and Gilt

Qianlong Period, Qing Dynasty, H(with cover): 19.0cm; Diam.(at mouth): 7.0cm; Diam.(at foot): 10.4cm

035 粉彩孔雀牡丹图椭圆形汤盆及托盘（一套）

清乾隆

汤盆：高 24.5 厘米　口横 25.0 厘米　口纵 20.5 厘米

足横 18.5 厘米　足纵 14.0 厘米　通长 26.4 厘米

托盘：高 5.0 厘米　口横 38.0 厘米　口纵 31.5 厘米

足横 26.0 厘米　足纵 20.0 厘米

汤盆呈椭圆体形。直口、溜肩、深弧腹，外侈圈足。盆内外和圈足内均施白釉，足底无釉。盆两侧对称置把手。通体粉彩装饰。腹部绘孔雀牡丹图，左侧绘两只孔雀立于山石上，右侧绘牡丹花。圈足外墙饰箭镞形纹饰。口沿处饰锦地 4 开光，开光内均绘青花花卉纹。把手涂矾红彩。盆附盖，盖面绘 4 组花卉纹，口沿处饰锦地 4 开光，开光内均绘青花花卉纹。盖钮涂矾红彩。

托盘敞口、折沿，浅弧腹、平底。内、外施白釉，外底无釉。内底以粉彩描绘孔雀牡丹图。画面左侧绘两只孔雀立于山石上，右侧绘牡丹花。内底边沿绘箭镞形边饰。折沿上描绘 4 组花卉纹，近口沿处饰锦地 4 开光，开光内均绘青花花卉纹。

此套汤盆和托盘上所绘箭镞形边饰，多流行于18世纪50 ~ 70年代，常见于外销欧洲的盘、碗类器物上。（孙悦）

Set of *Famille Rose* Tureen, Cover and Saucer with Design of Peacock-and-Peony

Qianlong Period, Qing Dynasty, Tureen: H: 24.5cm; L: 26.4cm; L(at mouth): 25.0cm; W(at mouth): 20.5cm; L(at foot): 18.5cm; W(at foot): 14.0cm, Saucer: H: 5.0cm; L(at mouth): 38.0cm; W(at mouth): 31.5cm; L(at foot): 26.0cm; W(at foot): 20.0cm

036 粉彩描金徽章纹杯及托盘（一套）

清乾隆

杯：高 6.8 厘米　口径 6.5 厘米　足径 4.4 厘米

托盘：高 3.2 厘米　口径 13.9 厘米　足径 8.4 厘米

杯敞口、直腹、圈足，一侧置耳状柄。托盘敞口、浅弧腹、圈足。

这是一套 18 世纪瑞典皇室喝咖啡用的杯和托盘。杯、托盘口沿均描金，盘内和杯外壁均描绘徽章纹，配以粉彩折枝花纹。外底均以黑彩书写“1776”。徽章以蓝彩和金彩描绘而成，上为以蓝彩和金彩描绘而成的带十字架的皇冠，皇冠下一圆形蓝地衬托一金彩字母“G”，圆形蓝地被月桂树花枝环绕，花枝上以黑彩书写英文日期“ D：19AUG：1772”。

杯、盘上的徽章属于瑞典皇室徽章。这套杯、托盘系瑞典国王古斯塔夫三世（1746 ~ 1792 年）在中国所订制，以纪念 1772 年 8 月 19 日古斯塔夫三世发动的一场他所称的“荣誉革命”，并将这些瓷器赠送给其忠实的追随者。徽章上的字母“G”，应为“Gustaf Ⅲ”（古斯塔夫三世）的首字母。王冠上绘有十字架，体现出订制者的基督信仰。

以皇冠作为徽章标识，在 18 世纪欧洲皇室颇为流行。（孙悦）

Set of Cup and Saucer with the Arms of Gustaf III, the King of Sweden, in *Famille Rose* and Gilt

Qianlong Period, Qing Dynasty, Cup: H: 6.8cm; Diam.(at mouth): 6.5cm; Diam.(at foot): 4.4cm, Saucer: H: 3.2cm; Diam.(at mouth): 13.9cm; Diam.(at foot): 8.4cm

037 粉彩描金徽章纹盘

清乾隆

高 6.8 厘米　口径 45.0 厘米　足径 26.0 厘米

盘敞口、浅弧腹、圈足。通体内、外和圈足内均施白釉。盘外光素，盘内粉彩装饰。内壁绘以两两对称的花草绕成的字母和由花草托着的插有瑞典国旗的堡垒。堡垒上的彩带内书写瑞典语“PLACIDO ROBORE”，译成汉语即“安宁和平静”。内底中心饰以用竹枝做成的花环，花环内书写三行拉丁文，摘自古罗马诗人朱维纳利斯（Juvenalis，60 ~ 127 年）的讽刺诗。

内壁对称花草组成的字母为“AEP”“JVU”，系安娜 · 伊丽莎白 · 皮克和雅克布 · 杰森 · 冯厄特夫尔（1715 ~ 1791 年）姓名的缩写。后者曾在 1736 ~ 1745 年随瑞典东印度公司的商船 4 次远航到达广州，两次作为船长助手、两次任船长。内底花环是 1765 年雅克布为庆贺自己 50 岁生日所设计。（赵小春）

Plate with the Arms of Two Swedish Families in *Famille Rose* and Gilt

Qianlong Period, Qing Dynasty, H: 6.8cm; Diam.(at mouth): 45.0cm, Diam.(at foot): 26.0cm

PLACIDO ROBORE
Quis ferat istas
Luxuriæ sordes? Quanta est gula!
O animal ad convivia natum!
PLACIDO ROBORE

038 青花山水人物图花口折沿椭圆托盘

清乾隆

高 6.5 厘米　口横 28.0 厘米　口纵 19.7 厘米

底横 21.7 厘米　底纵 13.0 厘米

此托盘属于汤盆的托盘。菱花口、折沿、浅弧腹、平底。盘外光素，盘内青花装饰。折沿上绘花草纹，内壁绘锦纹，内底绘海景风情画。渔船上一位带狗女子正用竹竿撑船摆渡。

托盘造型模仿 18 世纪欧洲流行的洛可可风格银盘，内底纹饰具有中国风情，因此，这种装饰的托盘，堪称 18 世纪中、西文化合璧的产物。盘背面镶有金属片和活环，使此盘可用作挂盘，悬挂在墙上供人观赏。（唐雪梅）

Blue-and-White Oval Plate with Everted Barbed Rim and Design of Human Figures-in-Landscape

Qianlong Period, Qing Dynasty, H: 6.5cm; L(at mouth): 28.0cm; W(at mouth): 19.7cm; L(at base): 21.7cm; W(at base): 13.0cm

039 广彩描金花卉纹碗

清乾隆

高 13.6 厘米　口径 31.5 厘米　足径 15.0 厘米

碗敞口、深弧腹、圈足。内、外和圈足内均施白釉。外壁以黑彩描绘两组花卉图。内底以黑彩书写字母文字，并暗刻两枚圆形印章。内口沿处有以金彩描绘的箭镞形边饰。

此类箭镞形边饰多流行于 18 世纪 50 ~ 70 年代，可作为此碗的断代依据。(孙悦)

Bowl with Floral Design in Cantonese Enamels and Gilt

Qianlong Period, Qing Dynasty, H: 13.6cm; Diam.(at mouth): 31.5cm; Diam.(at foot): 15.0cm

主题十二

等级森然

清代宫廷进膳用瓷

清代宫廷称吃饭为“用膳”或“进膳”。对不同身份的使用者进膳所用器皿品种，均有严格规定，以辨等级、明尊卑。乾隆三十四年（1769年）成书的《国朝宫史》“铺宫”条记载了皇太后、皇后、皇贵妃、贵妃、妃、嫔、贵人、常在、答应、皇子福晋、皇子侧室福晋等所用御窑瓷器的品种和数量。品种方面的大致情况如下：

皇太后——黄瓷盘、碟、碗、钟，各色瓷盘、碟、碗、钟、杯，瓷渣斗。

皇后——黄瓷盘、碟、碗、钟，各色瓷盘、碟、碗、钟、杯，瓷渣斗。

皇贵妃——白里黄瓷盘、碟、碗、钟，各色瓷盘、碟、碗、钟，瓷缸。

贵妃——黄地绿龙瓷盘、碟、碗、钟，各色瓷盘、碟、碗、钟，瓷缸。

妃——黄地绿龙瓷盘、碟、碗、钟，各色瓷盘、碟、碗、钟，瓷缸。

嫔——蓝地黄龙瓷盘、碟、碗、钟，各色瓷盘、碟、碗、钟，瓷缸。

贵人——绿地紫龙瓷盘、碟、碗、钟，各色瓷盘、碟、碗、钟。

常在——五彩红龙瓷盘、碟、碗、钟，各色瓷盘、碟、碗、钟。

答应——各色瓷盘、碟、碗、钟。

皇子福晋——各色瓷盘、碟、碗、钟、罐。

皇子侧福晋——各色瓷盘、碟、碗、钟。

由此可见，清代乾隆年间规定后宫除了皇太后、皇后可使用里外黄釉瓷外，其他皇贵妃、贵妃、妃、贵人、常在、答应以及皇子福晋、侧福晋等，均不得使用纯黄釉瓷。清代御窑瓷器以黄釉瓷等级最高，其中又以全黄釉（即器里、外皆黄釉）瓷最为尊贵，顺理成章成为皇帝、皇后专用品。半黄（即器外黄釉、里白釉）者次之，黄地加其他色彩者又次之，其他地色加黄龙者再次之。

清代里外黄釉、外黄釉里白釉、黄地绿龙纹、蓝地黄龙纹、绿地紫龙纹、五彩红龙纹瓷器等，自康熙至宣统朝一直延续烧造。

Theme 12

Rigid Hierarchical Structure

Imperial Porcelain Dinner Services in the Qing Dynasty

The imperial family of the Qing Dynasty originated from the Manchu in Northeast China. Therefore, it kept the eating habits of the Manchu tradition. The imperial court had strict regulations on the use of porcelain dinner services for different rankings: porcelain glazed in yellow both inside and outside were exclusively for Emperor, Empress and Empress Dowager.

Historical records show that yellow became the imperial colour in the Qing Dynasty. Therefore, it stands to reason that yellow-glazed porcelain was exclusively for emperors. Porcelain glazed in yellow both inside and outside was the most precious, followed in a descending order by porcelain glazed in yellow outside and white inside, porcelain decorated in other enamels on yellow ground, and then porcelain decorated with dragon in yellow on other colour ground.

Throughout the history of the Qing Dynasty, different varieties of porcelain dinner services never ceased to be produced, such as porcelain glazed in yellow inside and outside, porcelain glazed in yellow outside and white inside, porcelain with dragon design in green on yellow ground, porcelain with dragon design in yellow on blue ground, porcelain with dragon design in purple on green ground and porcelain with dragon design in red on polychrome ground.

碗均敞口、深弧腹、圈足。内、外施黄釉，圈足内施白釉。外壁锥拱海水云龙纹，口、足处均刻划弦纹。外底分别署青花各朝年款。

饰有锥拱海水云龙纹的浇黄釉碗在清代自康熙朝开始烧造，后来历朝均有烧造，碗的造型有多种，如敞口、撇口、墩式等。清代宫廷规定，里外浇黄釉碗只有皇帝、皇后和皇太后可以使用。（赵聪月）

宣统
光绪
咸丰
同治
乾隆

040 里外浇黄釉锥拱海水云龙纹碗

清康熙

高 6.2 厘米　口径 12.7 厘米　足径 5.1 厘米

Bright-Yellow-Glazed Bowl with Incised Design of Dragon-among-Cloud and Waves

Kangxi Period, Qing Dynasty, H: 6.2cm; Diam.(at mouth): 12.7cm; Diam.(at foot): 5.1cm

041 里外浇黄釉锥拱海水云龙纹碗

清雍正

高 6.0 厘米　口径 12.9 厘米　足径 4.8 厘米

Bright-Yellow-Glazed Bowl with Incised Design of Dragon-among-Cloud and Waves

Yongzheng Period, Qing Dynasty, H: 6.0cm; Diam.(at mouth): 12.9cm; Diam.(at foot): 4.8cm

042 里外浇黄釉锥拱海水云龙纹碗

清乾隆

高 6.4 厘米　口径 12.5 厘米　足径 4.8 厘米

Bright-Yellow-Glazed Bowl with Incised Design of Dragon-among-Cloud and Waves

Qianlong Period, Qing Dynasty, H: 6.4cm; Diam.(at mouth): 12.5cm; Diam.(at foot): 4.8cm

043 里外浇黄釉锥拱海水云龙纹碗

清嘉庆

高 6.2 厘米　口径 12.2 厘米　足径 4.5 厘米

Bright-Yellow-Glazed Bowl with Incised Design of Dragon-among-Cloud and Waves

Jianqing Period, Qing Dynasty, H: 6.2cm; Diam.(at mouth): 12.2cm; Diam.(at foot): 4.5cm

044 里外浇黄釉锥拱海水云龙纹碗

清道光

高 6.2 厘米　口径 12.2 厘米　足径 4.5 厘米

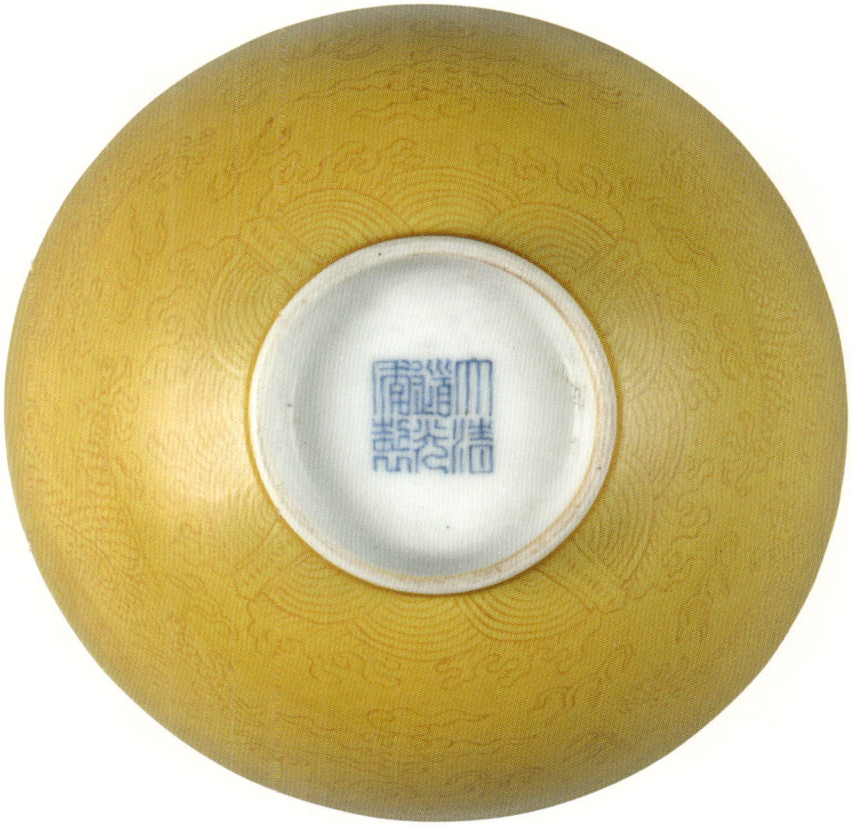

Bright-Yellow-Glazed Bowl with Incised Design of Dragon-among-Cloud and Waves

Daoguang Period, Qing Dynasty, H: 6.2cm; Diam.(at mouth): 12.2cm; Diam.(at foot): 4.5cm

045 里外浇黄釉锥拱海水云龙纹碗

清咸丰

高 6.2 厘米　口径 12.2 厘米　足径 4.5 厘米

Bright-Yellow-Glazed Bowl with Incised Design of Dragon-among-Cloud and Waves

Xianfeng Period, Qing Dynasty, H: 6.2cm; Diam.(at mouth): 12.2cm; Diam.(at foot): 4.5cm

046 里外浇黄釉锥拱海水云龙纹碗

清同治

高 5.0 厘米　口径 12.5 厘米　足径 5.2 厘米

Bright-Yellow-Glazed Bowl with Incised Design of Dragon-among-Cloud and Waves

Tongzhi Period, Qing Dynasty, H: 5.0cm; Diam.(at mouth): 12.5cm; Diam.(at foot): 5.2cm

047 里外浇黄釉锥拱海水云龙纹碗

清光绪

高 5.5 厘米　口径 12.6 厘米　足径 4.8 厘米

Bright-Yellow-Glazed Bowl with Incised Design of Dragon-among-Cloud and Waves

Guangxu Period, Qing Dynasty, H: 5.5cm; Diam.(at mouth): 12.6cm; Diam.(at foot): 4.8cm

048 里外浇黄釉锥拱海水云龙纹碗

清宣统

高 6.0 厘米　口径 14.3 厘米　足径 5.2 厘米

Bright-Yellow-Glazed Bowl with Incised Design of Dragon-among-Cloud and Waves
Xuantong Period, Qing Dynasty, H: 6.0cm; Diam.(at mouth): 14.3cm; Diam.(at foot): 5.2cm

纹。外底分别著青花各朝年款。

这种里白釉外浇黄釉锥拱海水云龙纹碗在清代自康熙朝开始烧造，后来历朝均有烧造。

（赵聪月）

光绪
咸丰
宣统

049 里白釉外浇黄釉锥拱海水云龙纹碗

清康熙

高 6.0 厘米　口径 12.0 厘米　足径 4.6 厘米

Bowl with Incised Design of Dragon-among-Cloud and Waves in Bright-Yellow Glaze Outside and White Glaze Inside

Kangxi Period, Qing Dynasty, H: 6.0cm; Diam.(at mouth): 12.0cm; Diam.(at foot): 4.6cm

050 里白釉外浇黄釉锥拱海水云龙纹碗

清雍正

高 6.0 厘米　口径 12.1 厘米　足径 5.1 厘米

Bowl with Incised Design of Dragon-among-Cloud and Waves in Bright-Yellow Glaze Outsice and White Glaze Inside

Yongzheng Period, Qing Dynasty, H: 6.0cm; D am.(at mouth): 12.1cm; Diam.(at foot): 5.1cm

051 里白釉外浇黄釉锥拱海水云龙纹碗

清乾隆

高 6.1 厘米　口径 13.3 厘米　足径 4.9 厘米

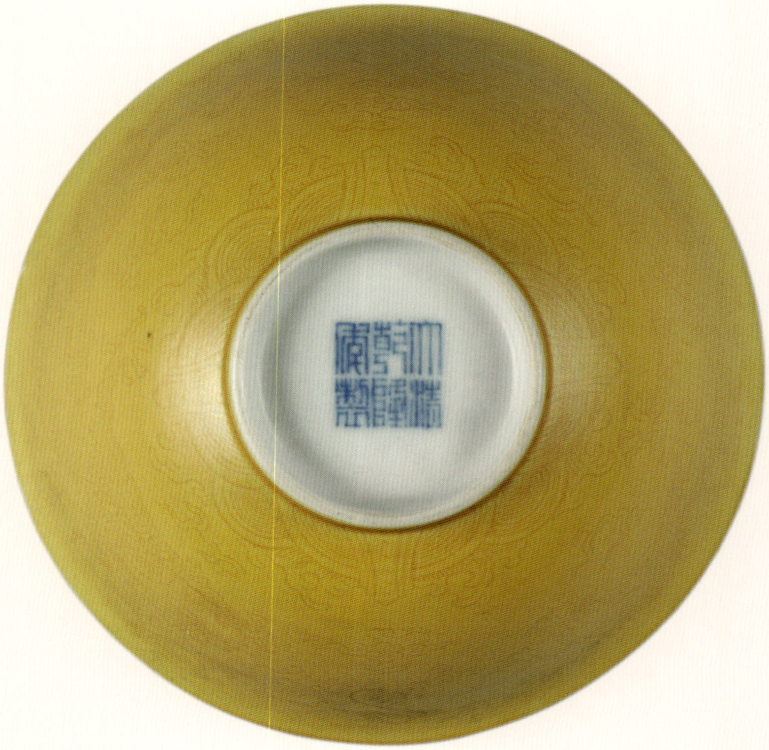

Bowl with Incised Design of Dragon-among-Cloud and Waves in Bright-Yellow Glaze Outside and White Glaze Inside

Qianlong Period, Qing Dynasty, H: 6.1cm; Diam.(at mouth): 13.3cm; Diam.(at foot): 4.9cm

052 里白釉外浇黄釉锥拱海水云龙纹碗

清嘉庆

高 5.1 厘米　口径 13.0 厘米　足径 4.5 厘米

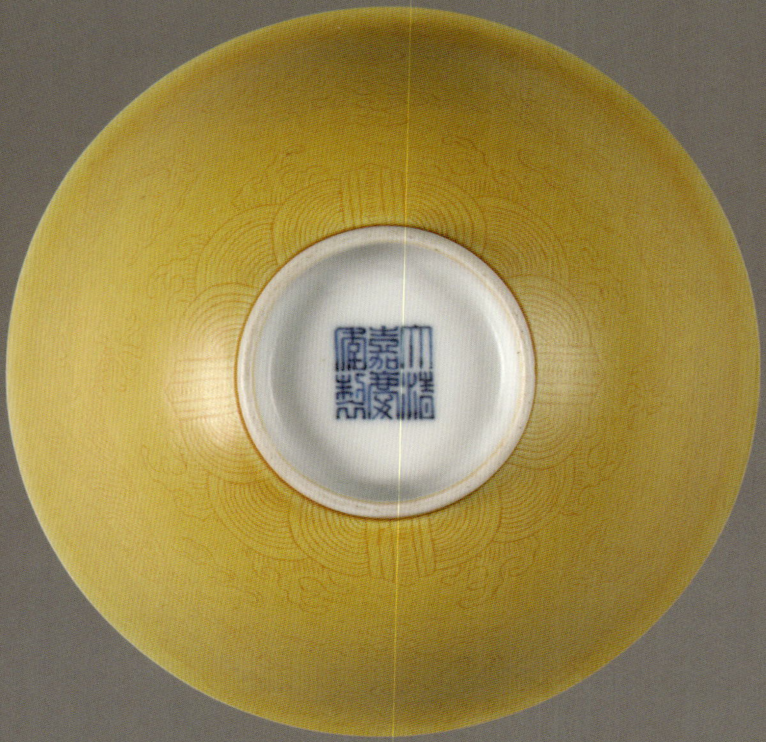

Bowl with Incised Design of Dragon-among-Cloud and Waves in Bright-Yellow Glaze Outside and White Glaze Inside

Jiaqing Period, Qing Dynasty, H: 5.1cm; Diam.(at mouth): 13.0cm; Diam.(at foot): 4.5cm

053 里白釉外浇黄釉锥拱海水云龙纹碗

清道光

高 6.0 厘米　口径 12.0 厘米　足径 4.8 厘米

Bowl with Incised Design of Dragon-among-Cloud and Waves in Bright-Yellow Glaze Outside and White Glaze Inside

Daoguang Period, Qing Dynasty, H: 6.0cm; Diam.(at mouth): 12.0cm; Diam.(at foot): 4.8cm

054 里白釉外浇黄釉锥拱海水云龙纹碗

清咸丰

高 6.0 厘米　口径 13.0 厘米　足径 4.8 厘米

Bowl with Incised Design of Dragon-among-Cloud and Waves in Bright-Yellow Glaze Outside and White Glaze Inside

Xianfeng Period, Qing Dynasty, H: 6.0cm; Diam.(at mouth): 13.0cm; Diam.(at foot): 4.8cm

055 里白釉外浇黄釉锥拱海水云龙纹碗

清同治

高 6.0 厘米　口径 12.9 厘米　足径 4.6 厘米

Bowl with Incised Design of Dragon-among-Cloud and Waves in Bright-Yellow Glaze Outside and White Glaze Inside

Tongzhi Period, Qing Dynasty, H: 6.0cm; Diam.(at mouth): 12.9cm; Diam.(foot): 4.6cm

056 里白釉外浇黄釉锥拱海水云龙纹碗

清光绪

高 6.1 厘米　口径 12.5 厘米　足径 4.7 厘米

Bowl with Incised Design of Dragon-among-Cloud and Waves in Bright-Yellow Glaze Outside and White Glaze Inside
Guangxu Period, Qing Dynasty, H: 6.1cm; Diam.(at mouth): 12.5cm; Diam.(at foot): 4.7cm

057 里白釉外浇黄釉锥拱海水云龙纹碗

清宣统

高 6.0 厘米　口径 12.9 厘米　足径 4.9 厘米

Bowl with Incised Design of Dragon-among-Cloud and Waves in Bright-Yellow Glaze Outside and White Glaze Inside

Xuantong Period, Qing Dynasty, H: 6.0cm; Diam.(at mouth): 12.9cm; Diam.(at foot): 4.9cm

光绪
嘉庆
康熙
雍正

道光

乾隆

058 浇黄地绿彩锥拱海水云龙纹碗

清康熙

高 6.5 厘米　口径 14.6 厘米　足径 5.6 厘米

Bowl with Incised Design of Dragon-among-Cloud in Green Enamel on Bright-Yellow Ground

Kangxi Period, Qing Dynasty, H: 6.5cm; Diam.(at mouth): 14.6cm; Diam.(at foot): 5.6cm

059 浇黄地绿彩锥拱海水云龙纹碗

清雍正

高 6.4 厘米　口径 14.7 厘米　足径 6.0 厘米

Bowl with Incised Design of Dragon-among-Cloud in Green Enamel on Bright-Yellow Ground

Yongzheng Period, Qing Dynasty, H: 6.4cm; Diam.(at mouth): 14.7cm; Diam.(at foot): 6.0cm

060 浇黄地绿彩锥拱海水云龙纹碗

清乾隆

高 6.6 厘米　口径 14.4 厘米　足径 6.3 厘米

Bowl with Incised Design of Dragon-among-Cloud in Green Enamel on Bright-Yellow Ground

Qianlong Period, Qing Dynasty, H: 6.6cm; Diam.(at mouth): 14.4cm; Diam.(at foot): 6.3cm

061 浇黄地绿彩锥拱海水云龙纹碗

清嘉庆

高 6.5 厘米　口径 15.2 厘米　足径 6.3 厘米

Bowl with Incised Design of Dragon-among-Cloud in Green Enamel on Bright-Yellow Ground

Jiaqing Period, Qing Dynasty, H: 6.5cm; Diam.(at mouth): 15.2cm; Diam.(at foot): 6.3cm

062 浇黄地绿彩锥拱海水云龙纹碗

清道光

高 6.5 厘米　口径 15.2 厘米　足径 6.0 厘米

Bowl with Incised Design of Dragon-among-Cloud in Green Enamel on Bright-Yellow Ground

Daoguang Period, Qing Dynasty, H: 6.5cm; Diam.(at mouth): 15.2cm; Diam.(at foot): 6.0cm

063 浇黄地绿彩锥拱海水云龙纹碗

清光绪

高 6.7 厘米　口径 15.3 厘米　足径 6.0 厘米

Bowl with Incised Design of Dragon-among-Cloud in Green Enamel on Bright-Yellow Ground

Guangxu Period, Qing Dynasty, H: 6.7cm; Diam.(at mouth): 15.3cm; Diam.(at foot): 6.0cm

064 浇黄地绿彩锥拱海水云龙纹碗

清宣统

高 6.6 厘米　口径 14.7 厘米　足径 5.6 厘米

Bowl with Incised Design of Dragon-among-Cloud in Green Enamel on Bright-Yellow Ground

Xuantong Period, Qing Dynasty, H: 6.6cm; Diam.(at mouth): 14.7cm; Diam.(at foot): 5.6cm

碗均撇口、深弧腹、圈足。碗内底和外壁均以青花地黄彩云龙纹装饰。内底绘一正面云龙纹；外壁绘两条云龙纹，近足处绘变形莲瓣纹。外底分别署青花各朝年款。

清代宫廷档案称这种尺寸的青花地黄彩云龙纹碗为“仿成窑蓝地黄云龙茶圆”，在故宫博物院藏品中，从康熙朝至宣统朝产品齐全，仅缺雍正朝制品。但在雍正朝制品中见有口径 13.5 厘米的青花地黄彩云龙纹汤碗。经过比对可以发现，各朝烧造的青花地黄彩云龙纹碗，在装饰风格方面有细微变化。如康熙朝制品上所绘龙身较细，黄彩较薄；而从乾隆朝开始，所绘龙身加粗，黄彩亦变厚，致使黄彩明显变得色重；至同治、光绪、宣统朝，由于黄釉施得过厚，几乎看不到龙身上以青料描绘的龙鳞。另有一细节变化，即从道光朝开始，碗的圈足外墙多出一道青花弦线（同治朝除外）。（赵聪月）

咸丰

康熙

乾隆

光绪
同治
宣统
嘉庆
道光

065 青花地黄彩云龙纹碗

清康熙

高 5.2 厘米　口径 10.3 厘米　足径 5.0 厘米

Bowl with Design of Dragon-among-Cloud in Yellow Enamel on Blue-and-White Ground

Kangxi Period, Qing Dynasty, H: 5.2cm; Diam.(at mouth): 10.3cm; Diam.(at foot): 5.0cm

066 青花地黄彩云龙纹碗

清乾隆

高 5.4 厘米　口径 10.4 厘米　足径 5.0 厘米

Bowl with Design of Dragon-among-Cloud in Yellow Enamel on Blue-and-White Ground

Qianlong Period, Qing Dynasty, H: 5.4cm; Diam.(at mouth): 10.4cm; Diam.(at foot): 5.0cm

067 青花地黄彩云龙纹碗

清嘉庆

高 5.3 厘米　口径 10.5 厘米　足径 4.9 厘米

Bowl with Design of Dragon-among-Cloud in Yellow Enamel on Blue-and-White Ground

Jiaqing Period, Qing Dynasty, H: 5.3cm; Diam.(at mouth): 10.5cm; Diam.(at foot): 4.9cm

068 青花地黄彩云龙纹碗

清道光

高 5.2 厘米　口径 10.3 厘米　足径 4.8 厘米

Bowl with Design of Dragon-among-Cloud in Yellow Enamel on Blue-and-White Ground

Daoguang Period, Qing Dynasty, H: 5.2cm; Diam.(at mouth): 10.3cm; Diam.(at foot): 4.8cm

069 青花地黄彩云龙纹碗

清咸丰

高 5.2 厘米　口径 10.3 厘米　足径 4.9 厘米

Bowl with Design of Dragon-among-Cloud in Yellow Enamel on Blue-and-White Ground

Xianfeng Period, Qing Dynasty, H: 5.2cm; Diam.(at mouth): 10.3cm; Diam.(at foot): 4.9cm

070 青花地黄彩云龙纹碗

清同治

高 5.2 厘米　口径 10.2 厘米　足径 4.7 厘米

Bowl with Design of Dragon-among-Cloud in Yellow Enamel on Blue-and-White Ground

Tongzhi Period, Qing Dynasty, H: 5.2cm; Diam.(at mouth): 10.2cm; Diam.(at foot): 4.7cm

071 青花地黄彩云龙纹碗

清光绪

高 5.3 厘米　口径 10.3 厘米　足径 4.6 厘米

Bowl with Design of Dragon-among-Cloud in Yellow Enamel on Blue-and-White Ground

Guangxu Period, Qing Dynasty, H: 5.3cm; Diam.(at mouth): 10.3cm; Diam.(at foot): 4.6cm

072 青花地黄彩云龙纹碗

清宣统

高 5.3 厘米　口径 10.4 厘米　足径 4.8 厘米

Bowl with Design of Dragon-among-Cloud in Yellow Enamel on Blue-and-White Ground

Xuantong Period, Qing Dynasty, H: 5.3cm; Diam.(at mouth): 10.4cm; Diam.(at foot): 4.8cm

嘉庆
康熙

道光

乾隆

073　绿地紫彩锥拱云龙纹碗

清康熙

高 6.3 厘米　口径 15.0 厘米　足径 5.5 厘米

Eowl with Incised Design of Dragon-among-Cloud in Purple Enamel on Green Ground

Kangxi Period, Qing Dynasty, H: 6.3cm; Diam.(at mouth): 15.0cm; Diam.(at foot): 5.5cm

074 绿地紫彩锥拱云龙纹碗

清雍正

高 6.2 厘米　口径 15.4 厘米　足径 5.5 厘米

Bowl with Incised Design of Dragon-among-Cloud in Purple Enamel on Green Ground

Yongzheng Period, Qing Dynasty, H: 6.2cm; Diam.(at mouth): 15.4cm; Diam.(at foot): 5.5cm

075 绿地紫彩锥拱云龙纹碗

清乾隆

高 7.0 厘米　口径 15.0 厘米　足径 6.3 厘米

Bowl with Incised Design of Dragon-among-Cloud in Purple Enamel on Green Ground

Qianlong Period, Qing Dynasty, H: 7.0cm; Diam.(at mouth): 15.0cm; Diam.(at foot): 6.3cm

076 绿地紫彩锥拱云龙纹碗

清嘉庆

高 6.8 厘米　口径 14.9 厘米　足径 6.4 厘米

Bowl with Incised Design of Dragon-among-Cloud in Purple Enamel on Green Ground

Jiaqing Period, Qing Dynasty, H: 6.8cm; Diam.(at mouth): 14.9cm; Diam.(at foot): 6.4cm

077 绿地紫彩锥拱云龙纹碗

清道光

高 7.0 厘米　口径 14.6 厘米　足径 6.1 厘米

Bowl with Incised Design of Dragon-among-Cloud in Purple Enamel on Green Ground

Daoguang Period, Qing Dynasty, H: 7.0cm; Diam.(at mouth): 14.6cm; Diam.(at foot): 6.1cm

078 绿地紫彩锥拱云龙纹碗

清光绪

高 7.0 厘米　口径 15.1 厘米　足径 6.3 厘米

Bowl with Incised Design of Dragon-among-Cloud in Purple Enamel on Green Ground

Guangxu Period, Qing Dynasty, H: 7.0cm; Ciam.(at mouth): 15.1cm; Diam.(at foot): 6.3cm

五彩龙凤穿花纹碗（一组）

碗均撇口、深弧腹、圈足。碗内底和外壁均以五彩装饰。内底绘云龙纹。外壁口部绘八吉祥纹，腹部绘龙凤穿花纹，二龙、二凤相间排列。外底分别署青花各朝年款。

清代这种五彩龙凤穿花纹碗自康熙朝开始至宣统朝为止，历朝均有烧造。这里刊出的是康熙、乾隆、嘉庆、道光 4 朝产品。仔细观察，可以发现各朝产品的绘画风格有所不同。如康熙、乾隆朝制品上的龙身作翻滚状，而嘉庆朝制品上的龙身改作卷曲状。嘉庆朝制品上的绿龙毛发使用了黑彩，龙爪的方向与其他 3 朝也不相同。清代宫廷档案称这种尺寸的五彩龙凤穿花纹碗为“仿成窑五彩龙凤穿花汤碗”。（赵聪月）

乾隆

康熙

道光
嘉庆

079 五彩龙凤穿花纹碗

清康熙

高 6.4 厘米　口径 13.0 厘米　足径 6.0 厘米

Polychrome Bowl with Design of Dragon and Pheonix Flying among Flowers

Kangxi Period, Qing Dynasty, H: 6.4cm; Diam.(at mouth): 13.0cm; Diam.(at foot): 6.0cm

080 五彩龙凤穿花纹碗

清乾隆

高 6.3 厘米　口径 12.8 厘米　足径 6.2 厘米

Polychrome Bowl with Design of Dragon and Pheonix Flying among Flowers

Qianlong Period, Qing Dynasty, H: 6.3cm; Diam.(at mouth): 12.8cm; Diam.(at foot): 6.2cm

081 五彩龙凤穿花纹碗

清嘉庆

高 6.1 厘米　口径 13.0 厘米　足径 6.0 厘米

Polychrome Bowl with Design of Dragon and Pheonix Flying among Flowers

Jiaqing Period, Qing Dynasty, H: 6.1cm; Diam.(at mouth): 13.0cm; Diam.(at foot): 6.0cm

082 五彩龙凤穿花纹碗

清道光

高 6.5 厘米　口径 12.9 厘米　足径 6.0 厘米

Polychrome Bowl with Design of Dragon and Pheonix Flying among Flowers

Daoguang Period, Qing Dynasty, H: 6.5cm; Diam.(at mouth): 12.9cm; Diam.(at foot): 6.0cm

斗彩莲池鸳鸯图碗（一组）

碗均撇口、深弧腹、圈足。内底和外壁均以斗彩技法装饰。内、外近口沿处均画青花双弦线，内底绘一对鸳鸯游于 4 组荷莲之中，外壁绘 4 组鸳鸯荷莲纹。外底分别署青花各朝年款。

清代宫廷档案称这种斗彩莲池鸳鸯图碗为“仿成窑五彩鸳鸯荷花茶圆”。其实绘有这种纹饰的五彩碗、盘，最早可上溯至宣德御窑产品，正统至万历朝延续。元、明时期文献将织绣和器物上所饰莲池水景称作“满池娇”。

清代此种斗彩莲池鸳鸯图碗始烧于乾隆朝、终烧于宣统朝。仔细观察各朝产品可以发现，纹饰布局虽变化不大，但从早期到晚期绘画技法却逐渐呈现由精细到粗率的变化。母鸳鸯背毛所使用的黄彩装饰也有些许变化，乾隆朝至同治朝制品黄彩鲜亮，光绪朝制品黄彩变得浅淡，宣统朝制品则以矾红彩取代黄彩。（赵聪月）

同治

咸丰

乾隆

嘉庆

光绪
宣统
道光

083 斗彩莲池鸳鸯图碗

清乾隆

高 5.0 厘米　口径 10.1 厘米　足径 4.2 厘米

Doucai Bowl with Design of Mandarin Ducks on Lotus

Qianlong Period, Qing Dynasty, H: 5.0cm; Diam.(at mouth): 10.1cm; Diam.(at foot): 4.2cm

084 斗彩莲池鸳鸯图碗

清嘉庆

高 5.0 厘米　口径 10.2 厘米　足径 4.2 厘米

Doucai Bowl with Design of Mandarin Ducks on Lotus

Jiaqing Period, Qing Dynasty, H: 5.0cm; Diam.(at mouth): 10.2cm; Diam.(at foot): 4.2cm

085 斗彩莲池鸳鸯图碗

清道光

高 5.2 厘米　口径 10.4 厘米　足径 4.2 厘米

***Doucai* Bowl with Design of Mandarin Ducks on Lotus**

Daoguang Period, Qing Dynasty, H: 5.2cm; Diam.(at mouth): 10.4cm; Diam.(at foot): 4.2cm

086 斗彩莲池鸳鸯图碗

清咸丰

高 5.1 厘米　口径 10.3 厘米　足径 4.2 厘米

Doucai Bowl with Design of Mandarin Ducks on Lotus

Xianfeng Period, Qing Dynasty, H: 5.1cm; Diam.(at mouth): 10.3cm; Diam.(at foot): 4.2cm

087 斗彩莲池鸳鸯图碗

清同治

高 5.0 厘米　口径 10.3 厘米　足径 4.0 厘米

Doucai Bowl with Design of Mandarin Ducks on Lotus

Tongzhi Period, Qing Dynasty, H: 5.0cm; Diam.(at mouth): 10.3cm; Diam.(at foot): 4.0cm

088 斗彩莲池鸳鸯图碗

清光绪

高 5.2 厘米　口径 10.4 厘米　足径 4.1 厘米

Doucai Bowl with Design of Mandarin Ducks on Lotus

Guangxu Period, Qing Dynasty, H: 5.2cm; Diam.(at mouth): 10.4cm; Diam.(at foot): 4.1cm

089 斗彩莲池鸳鸯图碗

清宣统

高 5.3 厘米　口径 10.4 厘米　足径 4.1 厘米

Doucai Bowl with Design of Mandarin Ducks on Lotus

Xuantong Period, Qing Dynasty, H: 5.3cm; Diam.(at mouth): 10.4cm; Diam.(at foot): 4.1cm

主题十三

承续烧造

清代宫廷陈设赏赐用瓷

清代宫廷陈设和赏赐用瓷以瓶类器最为多见。瓶属于琢器，既是清代宫廷陈设用器，也是皇帝在年节或举行重大典礼活动时赏赐王公、大臣的礼物。这在清宫档案中有明确记载，其中又以玉堂春瓶最具代表性。例如光绪十年（1884 年）万寿赏用瓷瓶有五彩百蝶玉堂春瓶、青花起线玉堂春瓶、天青釉金皮球玉堂春瓶等。根据烧造清单可统计出清代用于赏赐的瓷瓶共有 8 种样式，即祭蓝釉象首衔环琮式瓶、窑变釉杏圆贯耳瓶、仿哥釉杏圆贯耳瓶、仿哥釉凸刻八卦纹琮式瓶、厂官釉直颈瓶、祭红釉玉壶春瓶、青花缠枝莲纹玉堂春瓶、青花竹石芭蕉图玉壶春瓶等。

清代沿袭明代制度，亦在景德镇设御窑专门烧造宫廷用瓷，其供应形式大致分为三种情况，即大运、传办和进贡等。所谓大运瓷器，从字义上解释是指大批运输的瓷器，从实际烧造情况看，系指御窑厂每年底在宫廷内务府奏销，按年例不用皇帝另外降旨、按固定式样烧造且统一运至京城、交付宫廷瓷器库收储的瓷器。大运瓷器可分为琢器和圆器两大类，琢器造型主要源自宋、元、明代瓷器，个别为清代新创，其中颜色釉瓷器造型多沿用明代瓷器。据档案记载，清代大批量烧造宫廷御用瓷器始于康熙朝。但大运瓷器真正形成固定式样并按例烧造，则始于乾隆十二年（1747 年）。当年十二月二十一日，乾隆皇帝旨令督陶官唐英，此后都要按照从宫中藏瓷中选定的 52 件琢器、164 件圆器样品烧造。琢器的样式、尺寸不许更改，颜色、花纹可酌量相互更换；圆器的样式、尺寸、颜色、花纹都不许更换。

乾隆时期，由于经济强盛加之乾隆皇帝对瓷器烧造的重视，景德镇御窑创烧出许多新的瓷器品种。统观清代大运瓷器中的琢器品种，以乾隆朝为最多，共计 52 种，以后各朝烧造品种每况愈下，嘉庆朝 37 种，咸丰朝至宣统朝则仅保留其中的 8 种瓶式。

Theme 13

Successor of Firing Technology

Porcelains used for Display and Reward in the Qing Imperial Court

Vases fall under the category of *Zhuo Qi* (carved vessel), which were used as display in the Qing Imperial Court as well as reward from emperors to imperial relatives or officers during festivals and ceremonies. A typical example was the *Yu Tang Chun* Vase documented in imperial court archives, which record that various types of *Yu Tang Chun* vases were manufactured for festivals as rewards in the 10th year of Guangxu (1884). Based on statistics, it can be inferred that eight types of porcelain vases altogether were manufactured as rewards in the Qing Dynasty.

Inheriting the system of the Ming Dynasty, the Qing Dynasty set up imperial kiln factories in *Jingdezhen* to fire imperial porcelain for three usages: *Da Yun (for mass production), Chuan Ban (by special orders)* or Tributes sent by kiln supervisors. Alhough the so-called "*Da Yun* porcelain" literally means porcelain transported in large-volume, in reality, it refers to porcelain fired annually according to fixed models and transported to the capital city without the Emperor's approval. Some archives from the imperial court recorded that mass production of imperial porcelain in the Qing Dynasty began from Kangxi. Two categories fall under *Da Yun* Porcelain: carved vessels *Zhuo Qi* and round vessels *Yuan Qi*. The shapes of carved vessels *Zhuo Qi* mainly inherited the tradition of the Song, Yuan, Ming Dynasty, though some were innovated in the Qing Dynasty. The colour and glaze mostly followed the distinctive style of the Ming Dynasty. However, it was not untill the 12th year of Qianlong in the Qing Dynasty (1747) that *Da Yun* porcelain was regularly fired in fixed pattern.

Two main factors resulted in creating and firing new varieties of porcelain during the Qianlong period: the booming economy and the priority given by the Qianlong Emperor to porcelain firing. The latter can be proved by statistics: the Qianlong Period was the forerunner of firing various types of *Da Yun* carved vessels, contributing fifty-two in total. Since then the Qing Dynasty experienced a decrease in varieties, with thirty-seven types in total in the Jiaqing Period, and only eight types of vase during the period from Xianfeng to Xuantong.

祭蓝釉象首衔环琮式瓶（一组）

瓶仿新石器时代玉琮造型。均呈四方体形，圆口、短颈、平肩、圈足。器身上方两侧对称置象首衔环耳。通体内、外和圈足内均施祭蓝釉。外底分别署青花各朝年款。

故宫博物院收藏的乾隆朝至宣统朝祭蓝釉象首衔环耳琮式瓶，除无咸丰朝制品外，其他朝制品均有。（赵小春）

道光
同治
光绪

090 祭蓝釉象首衔环琮式瓶

清乾隆

高 28.9 厘米　口径 8.8 厘米　足径 11.2 厘米

Sacrificial-Blue-Glazed Vase Moulded in the Form of Ancient *Cong* with Elephant-Shaped Ears

Qianlong Period, Qing Dynasty, H: 28.9cm; Diam.(at mouth): 8.8cm; Diam.(at foot): 11.2cm

091 祭蓝釉象首衔环琮式瓶

清嘉庆

高 28.9 厘米　口径 8.8 厘米　足径 11.2 厘米

Sacrificial-Blue-Glazed Vase Moulded in the Form of Ancient *Cong* with Elephant-Shaped Ears

Jiaqing Period, Qing Dynasty, H: 28.9cm; Diam.(at mouth): 8.8cm; Diam.(at foot): 11.2cm

092 祭蓝釉象首衔环琮式瓶

清道光

高 28.9 厘米　口径 8.8 厘米　足径 11.2 厘米

Sacrificial-Blue-Glazed Vase Moulded in the Form of Ancient *Cong* with Elephant-Shaped Ears

Daoguang Period, Qing Dynasty, H: 28.9cm; Diam.(at mouth): 8.8cm; Diam.(at foot): 11.2cm

093 祭蓝釉象首衔环琮式瓶

清同治

高 29.5 厘米　口径 9.0 厘米　足径 12.0 厘米

Sacrificial-Blue-Glazed Vase Moulded in the Form of Ancient *Cong* with Elephant-Shaped Ears

Tongzhi Period, Qing Dynasty, H: 29.5cm; Diam.(at mouth): 9.0cm; Diam.(at foot): 12.0cm

094 祭蓝釉象首衔环琮式瓶

清光绪

高 29.0 厘米　口径 9.0 厘米　足径 11.8 厘米

Sacrificial-Blue-Glazed Vase Moulded in the Form of Ancient *Cong* with Elephant-Shaped Ears

Guangxu Period, Qing Dynasty, H: 29.0cm; Diam.(at mouth): 9.0cm; Diam.(at foot): 11.8cm

庆
咸丰

同治
光绪
宣统

乾隆
嘉庆
道光

同治
光绪
宣统

095 窑变釉杏圆贯耳瓶

清乾隆

高 30.0 厘米　口横 11.2 厘米　口纵 9.0 厘米

足横 11.5 厘米　足纵 8.6 厘米

Jun-Type Square Vase in the Form of Ancient Bronze *Hu* with Two Tubular Handles

Qianlong Period, Qing Dynasty, H: 30.0cm; L(at mouth): 11.2cm; W(at mouth): 9.0cm; L(at foot): 11.5cm; W(at foot): 8.6cm

096 窑变釉杏圆贯耳瓶

清嘉庆

高 30.0 厘米　口横 10.8 厘米　口纵 8.7 厘米

足横 11.8 厘米　足纵 9.0 厘米

***Jun*-Type Square Vase in the Form of Ancient Bronze *Hu* with Two Tubular Handles**

Jiaqing Period, Qing Dynasty, H: 30.0cm; L (at mouth): 10.8cm; W(at mouth): 8.7cm; L(at foot): 11.8cm; W(at foot): 9.0cm

097 窑变釉杏圆贯耳瓶

清道光

高 30.0 厘米　口横 11.0 厘米　口纵 8.7 厘米

足横 12.2 厘米　足纵 9.2 厘米

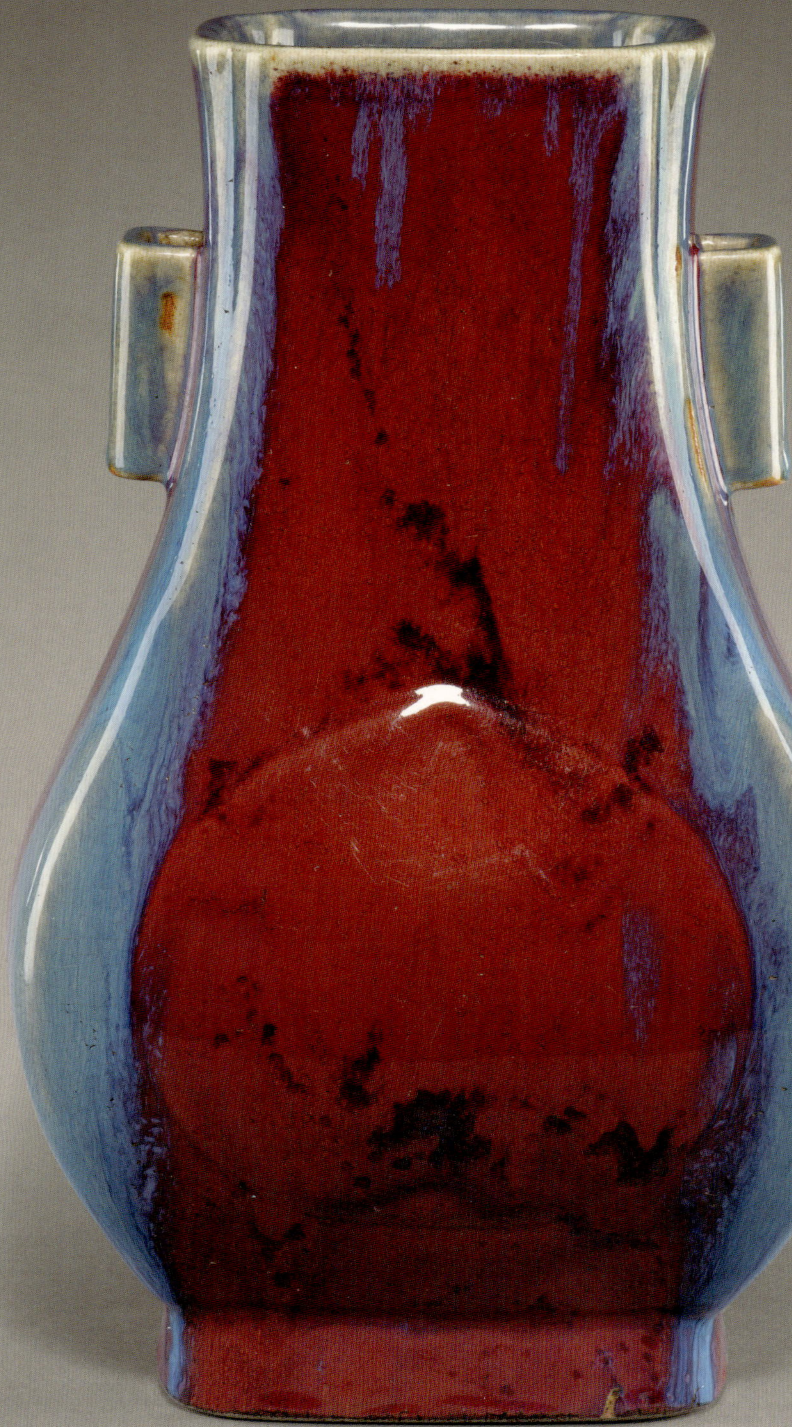

***Jun*-Type Square Vase in the Form of Ancient Bronze *Hu* with Two Tubular Handles**

Daoguang Period, Qing Dynasty, H: 30.0cm; L(at mouth): 11.0cm; W(at mouth): 8.7cm; L(at foot): 12.2cm; W(at foot): 9.2cm

098 窑变釉杏圆贯耳瓶

清咸丰

高 30.0 厘米　口横 11.0 厘米　口纵 8.8 厘米

足横 12.2 厘米　足纵 9.2 厘米

Jun-Type Square Vase in the Form of Ancient Bronze *Hu* with Two Tubular Handles

Xianfeng Period, Qing Dynasty, H: 30.0cm; L(at mouth): 11.0cm; W(at mouth): 8.8cm; L(at foot): 12.2cm; W(at foot): 9.2cm

099 窑变釉杏圆贯耳瓶

清同治

高 30.0 厘米　口横 10.7 厘米　口纵 9.0 厘米

足横 11.8 厘米　足纵 9.0 厘米

***Jun*-Type Square Vase in the Form of Ancient Bronze *Hu* with Two Tubular Handles**

Tongzhi Period, Qing Dynasty, H: 30.0cm; L(at mouth): 10.7cm; W(at mouth): 9.0cm; L(at foot): 11.8cm; W(at foot): 9.0cm

100 窑变釉杏圆贯耳瓶

清光绪

高 30.0 厘米　口横 10.6 厘米　口纵 9.0 厘米

足横 12.0 厘米　足纵 9.2 厘米

***Jun*-Type Square Vase in the Form of Ancient Bronze *Hu* with Two Tubular Handles**

Guangxu Period, Qing Dynasty, H: 30.0cm; L(at mouth): 10.6cm; W(at mouth): 9.0cm; L(at foot): 12.0cm; W(at foot): 9.2cm

101 窑变釉杏圆贯耳瓶

清宣统

高 30.0 厘米　口横 10.0 厘米　口纵 9.0 厘米

足横 12.0 厘米　足纵 9.0 厘米

***Jun*-Type Square Vase in the Form of Ancient Bronze *Hu* with Two Tubular Handles**

Xuantong Period, Qing Dynasty, H: 30.0cm; L(at mouth): 10.0cm; W(at mouth): 9.0cm; L(at foot): 12.0cm; W(at foot): 9.0cm

102 仿哥釉杏圆贯耳瓶

清乾隆

高 30.8 厘米　口横 11.0 厘米　口纵 9.2 厘米

足横 12.0 厘米　足纵 8.6 厘米

***Ge*-Type Square Vase in the Form of Ancient Bronze *Hu* with Two Tubular Handles**

Qianlong Period, Qing Dynasty, H: 30.8cm; L(at mouth): 11.0cm; W(at mouth): 9.2cm; L(at foot): 12.0cm; W(at foot): 8.6cm

103 仿哥釉杏圆贯耳瓶

清嘉庆

高 31.0 厘米　口横 11.2 厘米　口纵 8.3 厘米

足横 11.4 厘米　足纵 8.2 厘米

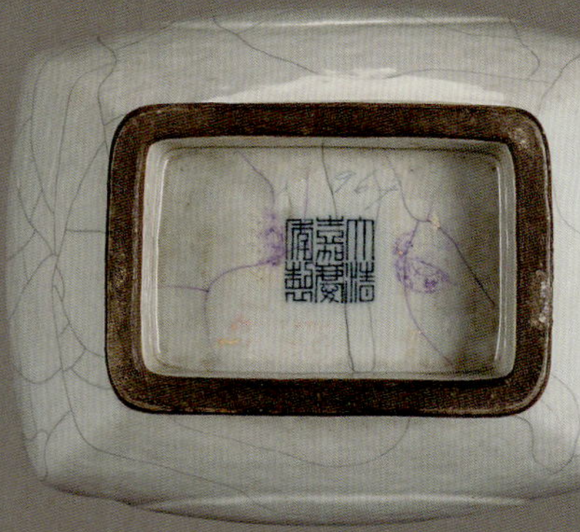

***Ge*-Type Square Vase in the Form of Ancient Bronze *Hu* with Two Tubular Handles**

Jiaqing Period, Qing Dynasty, H: 31.0cm; L(at mouth): 11.2cm; W(at mouth): 8.3cm; L(at foot): 11.4cm; W(at foot): 8.2cm

104 仿哥釉杏圆贯耳瓶

清道光

高 30.1 厘米　口横 11.2 厘米　口纵 9.0 厘米

足横 12.2 厘米　足纵 8.8 厘米

***Ge*-Type Square Vase in the Form of Ancient Bronze *Hu* with Two Tubular Handles**

Daoguang Period, Qing Dynasty, H: 30.1cm; L(at mouth): 11.2cm; W(at mouth): 9.0cm; L(at foot): 12.2cm, W(at foot): 8.8cm

105 仿哥釉杏圆贯耳瓶

清咸丰

高 31.5 厘米　口横 11.5 厘米　口纵 8.6 厘米

足横 11.6 厘米　足纵 8.5 厘米

***Ge*-Type Square Vase in the Form of Ancient Bronze *Hu* with Two Tubular Handles**

Xianfeng Period, Qing Dynasty, H: 31.5cm; L(at mouth): 11.5cm; W(at mouth): 8.6cm; L(at foot): 11.6cm; W(at foot): 8.5cm

106 仿哥釉杏圆贯耳瓶

清同治

高 30.0 厘米　口横 12.0 厘米　口纵 9.0 厘米

足横 12.5 厘米　足纵 9.0 厘米

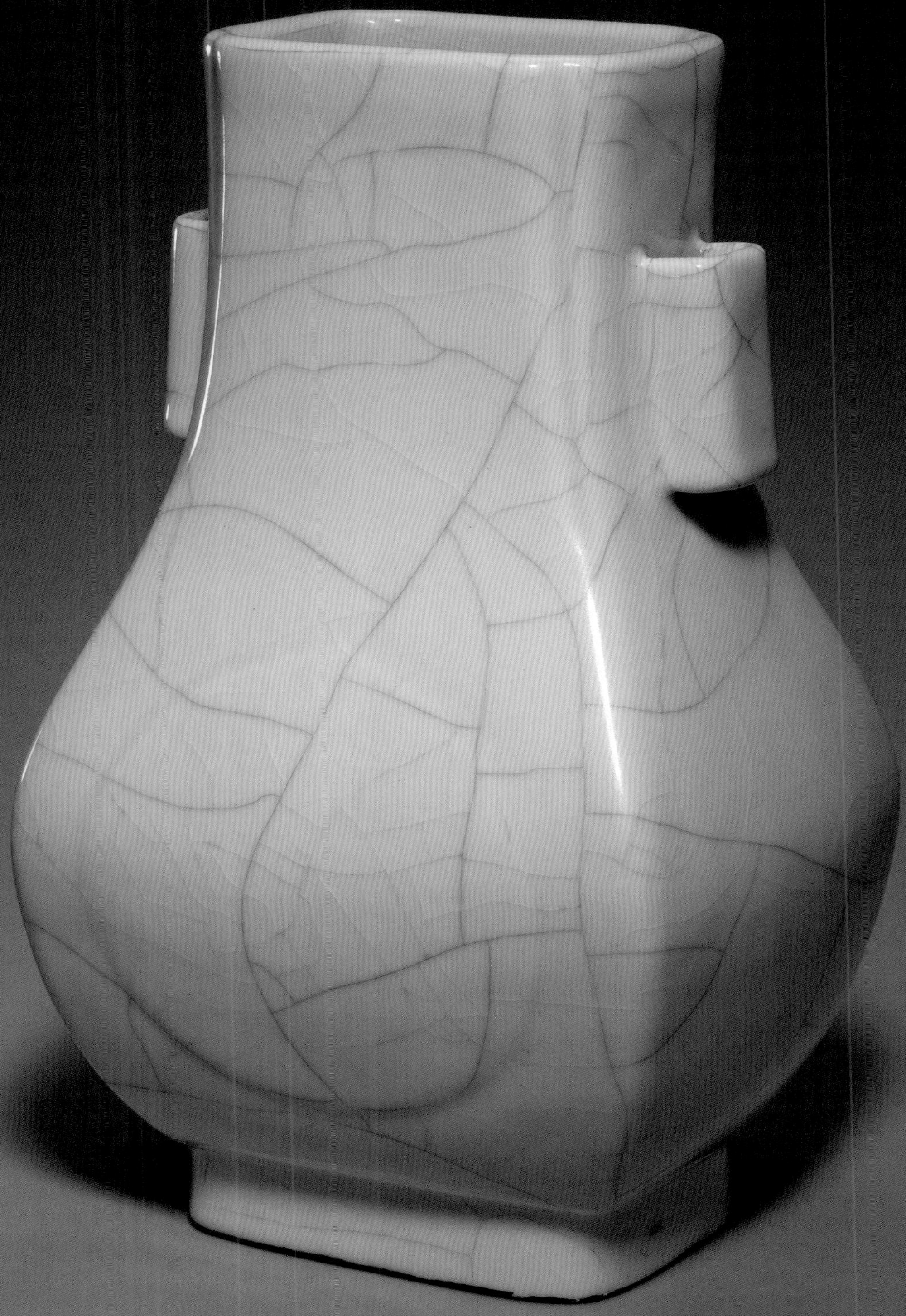

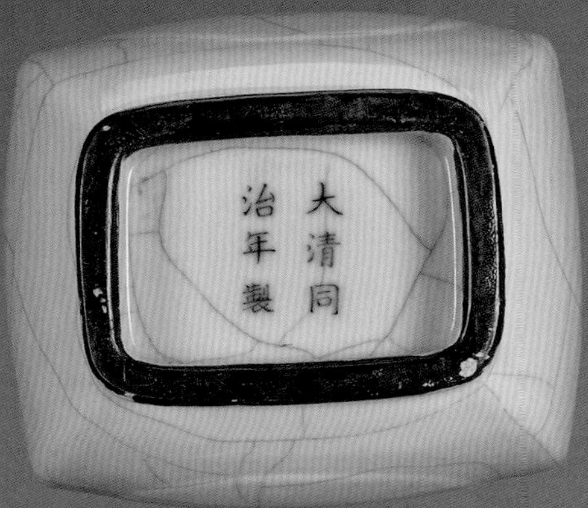

***Ge*-Type Square Vase in the Form of Ancient Bronze *Hu* with Two Tubular Handles**

Tongzhi Period, Qing Dynasty, H: 30.0cm; L(at mouth): 12.0cm; W(at mouth): 9.0cm; L(at foot): 12.5cm; W(at foot): 9.0cm

107 仿哥釉杏圆贯耳瓶

清光绪

高 30.0 厘米　口横 11.5 厘米　口纵 9.0 厘米

足横 12.0 厘米　足纵 9.0 厘米

***Ge*-Type Square Vase in the Form of Ancient Bronze *Hu* with Two Tubular Handles**

Guangxu Period, Qing Dynasty, H: 30.0cm; L(at mouth): 11.5cm; W(at mouth): 9.0cm; L(at foot): 12.0cm; W(at foot): 9.0cm

108 仿哥釉杏圆贯耳瓶

清宣统

高 30.0 厘米　口横 11.0 厘米　口纵 9.0 厘米

足横 12.0 厘米　足纵 9.0 厘米

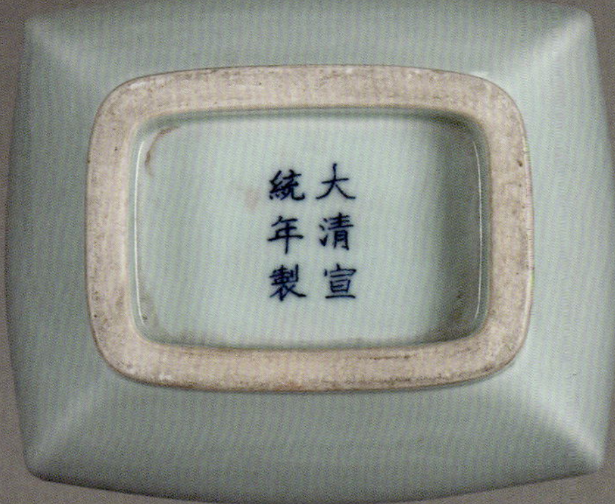

Ge-Type Square Vase in the Form of Ancient Bronze *Hu* with Two Tubular Handles

Xuantong Period, Qing Dynasty, H: 30.0cm; L(at mouth): 11.0cm; W(at mouth): 9.0cm; L(at foot): 12.0cm; W(at foot): 9.0cm

瓶仿新石器时代玉琮造型。均方柱形器身，圆口、短颈、直壁、圈足。器内、外和圈足内均施仿哥釉，釉面开不规则片纹。器身四面均雕刻凸起的八卦纹。外底分别署青花各朝年款。

清代宫廷档案称这种器物为“哥釉四方八卦瓶”。作为清代大运瓷器中的一种，这种瓶从乾隆朝延续至宣统朝。咸丰朝爆发的太平天国运动波及景德镇，对御窑厂造成极大破坏，烧毁御窑厂，窑工四处逃散。同治时重建御窑厂，重新招募窑工，但制瓷技艺大不如前，致使同治、光绪、宣统三朝所烧仿哥釉瓷已很难呈现哥釉的开片效果，虽名曰仿哥釉，但其釉均呈冬青色，且基本无开片。（赵聪月）

乾隆 嘉庆 道光

同治
宣统

109 仿哥釉凸刻八卦纹琮式瓶

清乾隆

高 28.2 厘米　口径 8.2 厘米　足径 10.2 厘米

Ge-Type Vase Moulded in the Form of Ancient Jade *Cong* with Design of the Eight Trigrams

Qianlong Period, Qing Dynasty, H: 28.2cm; Diam.(at mouth): 8.2cm; Diam.(at foot): 10.2cm

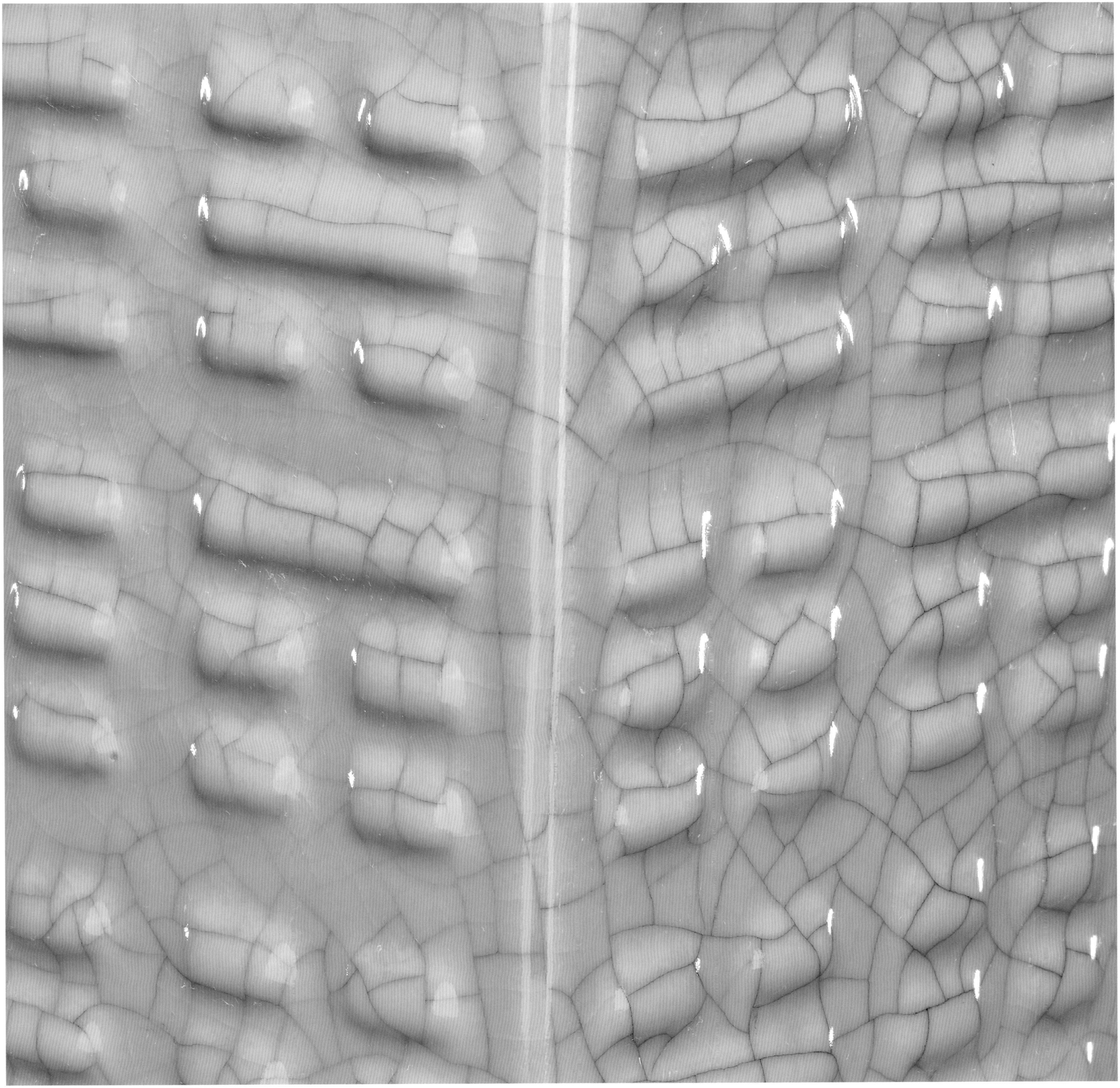

110 仿哥釉凸刻八卦纹琮式瓶

清嘉庆

高 28.2 厘米　口径 8.2 厘米　足径 10.2 厘米

Ge-Type Vase Moulded in the Form of Ancient Jade *Cong* with Design of the Eight Trigrams

Jiaqing Period, Qing Dynasty, H: 28.2cm; Diam.(at mouth): 8.2cm; Diam.(at foot): 10.2cm

111 仿哥釉凸刻八卦纹琮式瓶

清道光

高 28.2 厘米　口径 8.2 厘米　足径 10.2 厘米

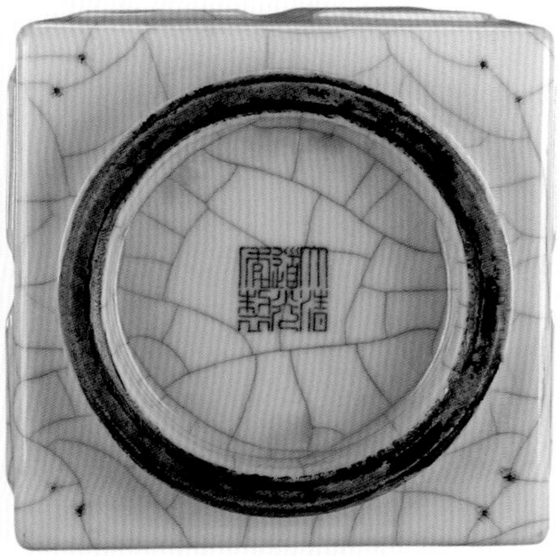

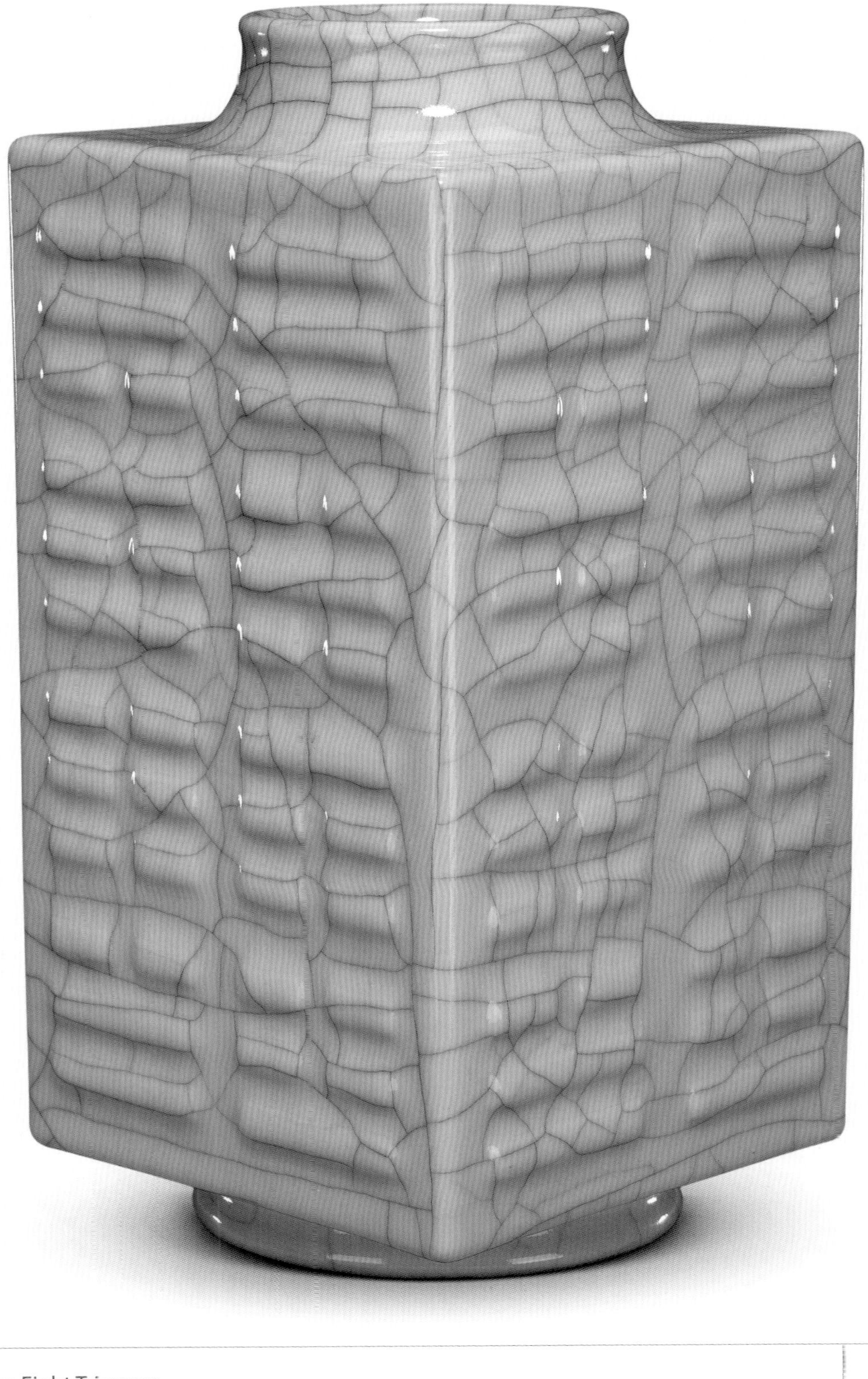

Ge-Type Vase Moulded in the Form of Ancient Jade *Cong* with Design of the Eight Trigrams

Daoguang Period, Qing Dynasty, H: 28.2cm; Diam.(at mouth): 8.2cm; Diam.(at foot): 10.2cm

112 仿哥釉凸刻八卦纹琮式瓶

清咸丰

高 27.8 厘米　口径 8.2 厘米　足径 10.8 厘米

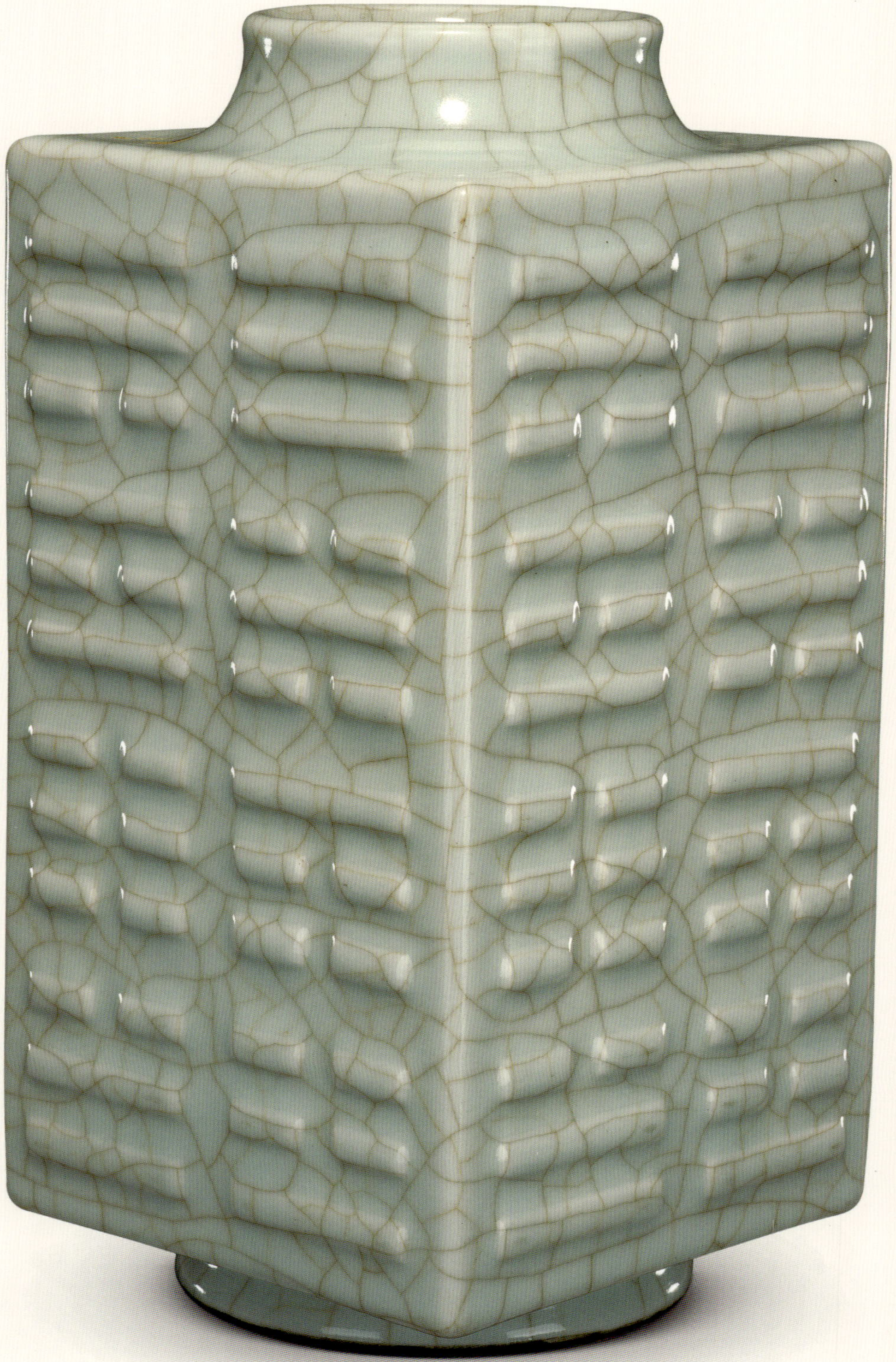

***Ge*-Type Vase Moulded in the Form of Ancient Jade *Cong* with Design of the Eight Trigrams**

Xianfeng Period, Qing Dynasty, H: 27.8cm; Diam.(at mouth): 8.2cm; Diam.(at foot): 10.8cm

113 仿哥釉凸刻八卦纹琮式瓶

清同治

高 28.4 厘米　口径 8.5 厘米　足径 10.0 厘米

Ge-Type Vase Moulded in the Form of Ancient Jade *Cong* with Design of the Eight Trigrams

Tongzhi Period, Qing Dynasty, H: 28.4cm; Diam.(at mouth): 8.5cm; Diam.(at foot): 10.0cm

114 仿哥釉凸刻八卦纹琮式瓶

清光绪

高 27.8 厘米　口径 9.0 厘米　足径 10.8 厘米

***Ge*-Type Vase Moulded in the Form of Ancient Jade *Cong* with Design of the Eight Trigrams**

Guangxu Period, Qing Dynasty, H: 27.8cm; Diam.(at mouth): 9.0cm; Diam.(at foot): 10.8cm

115 仿哥釉凸刻八卦纹琮式瓶

清宣统

高 27.8 厘米　口径 8.8 厘米　足径 10.2 厘米

Ge-Type Vase Moulded in the Form of Ancient Jade *Cong* with Design of the Eight Trigrams

Xuantong Period, Qing Dynasty, H: 27.8cm; Diam.(at mouth): 8.8cm; Diam.(at foot): 10.2cm

厂官釉直颈瓶（一组）

瓶均小口、直颈、扁圆腹、圈足。通体内、外和圈足内均施茶叶末釉，釉质润泽，釉色均匀。外底分别署各朝年款，署款处所施厂官釉被擦拭掉。

厂官釉属于氧化铁和氧化镁的结晶釉，由于烧成工艺的某些差异，厂官釉的色调能呈现多种变化，釉色偏青者俗称“鳝鱼青”，偏黄者俗称“鳝鱼黄”，而釉中分布细密微小黄绿色结晶斑点者俗称“茶叶末”。清代宫廷档案称这种瓶为“厂官釉太极纸槌瓶”。这种瓶从乾隆朝至光绪朝均有烧造，其中以咸丰朝烧造量最少。（吕成龙）

同治
光绪

116 | 厂官釉直颈瓶

清乾隆

高 34.5 厘米　口径 7.2 厘米　足径 15.0 厘米

Tea-Dust Glazed Bottle Vase

Qianlong Period, Qing Dynasty, H: 34.5cm; Diam.(at mouth): 7.2cm; Diam.(at foot): 15.0cm

117 厂官釉直颈瓶

清嘉庆

高 32.5 厘米　口径 7.2 厘米　足径 14.8 厘米

Tea-Dust Glazed Bottle Vase

Jiaqing Period, Qing Dynasty, H: 32.5cm; Diam.(at mouth): 7.2cm; Diam.(at foot): 14.8cm

118 厂官釉直颈瓶

清道光

高 32.5 厘米　口径 7.5 厘米　足径 14.9 厘米

Tea-Dust Glazed Bottle Vase

Daoguang Period, Qing Dynasty, H: 32.5cm; Diam.(at mouth): 7.5cm; Diam.(at foot): 14.9cm

119

厂官釉直颈瓶

清同治

高 33.5 厘米　口径 7.3 厘米　足径 14.8 厘米

Tea-Dust Glazed Bottle Vase

Tongzhi Period, Qing Dynasty, H: 33.5cm; Diam.(at mouth): 7.3cm; Diam.(at foot): 14.8cm

120 厂官釉直颈瓶

清光绪

高 32.5 厘米　口径 7.0 厘米　足径 14.7 厘米

Tea-Dust Glazed Bottle Vase

Guangxu Period, Qing Dynasty, H: 32.5cm; Diam.(at mouth): 7.0cm; Diam.(at foot): 14.7cm

祭红釉玉壶春瓶（一组）

瓶均撇口、束颈、鼓腹、圈足。瓶内和圈足内均施白釉，外壁均施祭红釉。外底分别署青花各朝年款。这种瓶在清代作为传统品种，自康熙朝至宣统朝均有烧造，但康熙朝和雍正朝产品形体略小，真正形成固定大小、样式则始于乾隆朝。虽然据清代宫廷档案记载，得知咸丰朝曾烧造109件祭红釉玉壶春瓶，但故宫博物院藏品中已无清代宫廷遗留物，现所藏两件系1949年后由文联局拨交，其釉色和造型均类似乾隆朝制品，只是釉面略显粗糙。

祭红釉是以氧化铜为着色剂、在高温还原气氛中烧成的单色釉。最早见于唐代的长沙窑，但当时或为偶然出现，不是人为刻意烧成。真正人为创烧的高温铜红釉瓷器始于元代景德镇窑。明代景德镇御窑自洪武朝开始烧造高温铜红釉瓷，直到嘉靖朝，历朝多有烧造，其中以永乐朝、宣德朝产量最大、质量最好，俗称“宝石红釉瓷”。嘉靖朝以后，高温铜红釉瓷的烧造技术逐渐失传，直到清代康熙朝才得以恢复，而且在恢复烧造祭红釉瓷的基础上，又创烧出著名的郎窑红釉、豇豆红釉瓷。（赵聪月）

道光
咸丰
同治
光绪

121 祭红釉玉壶春瓶

清雍正

高 25.0 厘米　口径 7.2 厘米　足径 9.0 厘米

Sacrificial-Red-Glazed *Yu Hu Chun* Bottle Vase

Yongzheng Period, Qing Dynasty, Height: 25.0cm; Diam.(at mouth): 7.2cm; Diam.(at foot): 9.0cm

122 祭红釉玉壶春瓶

清乾隆

高 30.6 厘米　口径 9.0 厘米　足径 11.0 厘米

Sacrificial-Red-Glazed Yu Hu Chun Bottle Vase
Qianlong Period, Qing Dynasty, H: 30.6cm; Diam.(at mouth): 9.0cm; Diam.(at foot): 11.0cm

123 **祭红釉玉壶春瓶**

清嘉庆

高 30.0 厘米　口径 9.3 厘米　足径 11.8 厘米

Sacrificial-Red-Glazed *Yu Hu Chun* Bottle Vase

Jiaqing Period, Qing Dynasty, H: 30.0cm; Diam.(at mouth): 9.3cm; Diam.(at foot): 11.8cm

124 祭红釉玉壶春瓶

清道光

高 29.9 厘米　口径 9.5 厘米　足径 11.8 厘米

Sacrificial-Red-Glazed *Yu Hu Chun* Bottle Vase

Daoguang Period, Qing Dynasty, H: 29.9cm; Diam.(at mouth): 9.5cm; Diam.(at foot): 11.8cm

125 祭红釉玉壶春瓶

清咸丰

高 29.8 厘米　口径 9.4 厘米　足径 11.5 厘米

Sacrificial-Red-Glazed *Yu Hu Chun* Bottle Vase

Xianfeng Period, Qing Dynasty, H: 29.8cm; Diam.(at mouth): 9.4cm; Diam.(at foot): 11.5cm

126 祭红釉玉壶春瓶

清同治

高 29.5 厘米　口径 9.3 厘米　足径 10.8 厘米

Sacrificial-Red-Glazed *Yu Hu Chun* Bottle Vase

Tongzhi Period, Qing Dynasty, H: 29.5cm; Diam.(at mouth): 9.3cm; Diam.(at foot): 10.8cm

127 祭红釉玉壶春瓶

清光绪

高 29.5 厘米　口径 9.5 厘米　足径 11.5 厘米

Sacrificial-Red-Glazed *Yu Hu Chun* Bottle Vase
Guangxu Period, Qing Dynasty, H: 29.5cm; Diam.(at mouth): 9.5cm; Diam.(at foot): 11.5cm

青花缠枝莲纹玉堂春瓶（一组）

瓶均撇口、束颈、鼓腹、外撇圈足。瓶内、外和圈足内均施白釉，外壁青花装饰。口部绘海水纹和下垂如意云头纹，颈下部绘蕉叶纹，近肩处绘回纹。颈、肩相接处和肩部各凸起一道弦纹，肩、腹相接处凸起两道弦纹。肩部凸起弦纹上、下分别绘缠枝花纹和垂如意云头纹。腹部绘缠枝莲纹，近足处和圈足外墙分别绘仰莲瓣纹和卷草纹。外底分别署青花各朝年款。

这种造型的瓶系清代雍正朝景德镇御窑厂新创的一种瓶式，专门用于皇帝赏赐臣属，故俗称“赏瓶”，清代宫廷档案称之为“玉堂春瓶”。清代各朝青花玉堂春瓶均造型端庄、纹饰布局繁而不乱，青花发色纯正。造型虽有定式，但在装饰上可分为有凸弦纹（宫廷档案称之为“起线”）和无凸弦纹两种。各朝所烧造青花赏瓶上的纹饰布局相同，腹部均绘缠枝莲纹，取“青”“莲”谐“清廉”之音，皇帝将这种瓷瓶赏与大臣，有提醒大臣为官需做到“清正廉洁”之意。雍正朝青花赏瓶传世甚少，自乾隆朝至宣统朝历朝均曾大量烧造。同治朝以后，在烧造青花赏瓶的基础上，又新添粉彩、祭蓝釉、祭蓝釉描金等新品种。（吕成龙）

咸丰
同治
光绪
宣统

128 青花缠枝莲纹玉堂春瓶

清乾隆

高 37.5 厘米　口径 9.8 厘米　足径 12.5 厘米

Blue-and-White *Yu Tang Chun* Bottle Vase with Design of Lotus Scrolls

Qianlong Period, Qing Dynasty, H: 37.5cm; Diam.(at mouth): 9.8cm; Diam.(at foot): 12.5cm

129 青花缠枝莲纹玉堂春瓶

清嘉庆

高 36.5 厘米　口径 9.3 厘米　足径 11.8 厘米

Blue-and-White *Yu Tang Chun* Bottle Vase with Design of Lotus Scrolls

Jiaqing Period, Qing Dynasty, H: 36.5cm; Diam.(at mouth): 9.3cm; Diam.(at foot): 11.8cm

130 青花缠枝莲纹玉堂春瓶

清道光

高 36.5 厘米　口径 9.5 厘米　足径 11.8 厘米

Blue-and-White *Yu Tang Chun* Bottle Vase with Design of Lotus Scrolls

Daoguang Period, Qing Dynasty, H: 36.5cm; Diam.(at mouth): 9.5cm; Diam.(at foot): 11.8cm

131 | 青花缠枝莲纹玉堂春瓶

清咸丰

高 36.5 厘米　口径 9.4 厘米　足径 11.8 厘米

Blue-and-White *Yu Tang Chun* Bottle Vase with Design of Lotus Scrolls

Xianfeng Period, Qing Dynasty, H: 36.5cm; Diam.(at mouth): 9.4cm; Diam.(at foot): 11.8cm

132 青花缠枝莲纹玉堂春瓶

清同治

高 39.2 厘米　口径 9.7 厘米　足径 12.7 厘米

Blue-and-White *Yu Tang Chun* Bottle Vase with Design of Lotus Scrolls

Tongzhi Period, Qing Dynasty, H: 39.2cm; Diam.(at mouth): 9.7cm; Diam.(at foot): 12.7cm

133 青花缠枝莲纹玉堂春瓶

清光绪

高 39.0 厘米　口径 9.7 厘米　足径 12.8 厘米

Blue-and-White *Yu Tang Chun* Bottle Vase with Design of Lotus Scrolls

Guangxu Period, Qing Dynasty, H: 39.0cm; Diam.(at mouth): 9.7cm; Diam.(at foot): 12.8cm

134 青花缠枝莲纹玉堂春瓶

清宣统

高 40.0 厘米　口径 10.0 厘米　足径 12.5 厘米

Blue-and-White *Yu Tang Chun* Bottle Vase with Design of Lotus Scrolls

Xuantong Period, Qing Dynasty, H: 40.0cm; Diam.(at mouth): 10.0cm; Diam.(at foot): 12.5cm

青花竹石芭蕉图玉壶春瓶（一组）

瓶均撇口、束颈、垂腹、外撇圈足。瓶内、外和圈足内均施白釉。外壁通体青花装饰。颈部绘 3 层纹饰，自上而下依次为蕉叶纹、卷草纹、如意头纹等。腹部绘修竹、怪石、芭蕉、栏杆、坡地和花草等。近足处绘仰莲瓣纹。圈足外墙绘朵花纹。外底除永乐朝、康熙朝、雍正朝制品外，其他均分别署青花各朝年款。

陶瓷玉壶春瓶之雏形始于隋代，宋代以后流行。青花竹石芭蕉图玉壶春瓶始烧于明代洪武朝景德镇御窑厂，清代自康熙朝至光绪朝均有烧造，纹饰基本相同，但绘画风格和青花发色有所差别。从器形上看，从康熙朝至光绪朝这种玉壶春瓶的颈部逐渐变得粗短，腹部亦逐渐加大，至清代晚期渐失早期玉壶春瓶形体俊秀的风格，显得笨拙。（吕成龙）

道光
咸丰
同治
光绪

135 青花竹石芭蕉图玉壶春瓶

明永乐

高 32.8 厘米　口径 8.2 厘米　足径 13.0 厘米

Blue-and-White *Yu Hu Chun* Bottle Vase with Design of Bamboo, Rock and Palm Tree

Yongle Period, Ming Dynasty, H: 32.8cm; Diam.(at mouth): 8.2cm; Diam.(at foot): 13.0cm

136 青花竹石芭蕉图玉壶春瓶

清康熙

高 34.3 厘米　口径 9.4 厘米　足径 12.7 厘米

Blue-and-White *Yu Hu Chun* Bottle Vase with Design of Bamboo, Rock and Palm Tree

Kangxi Period, Qing Dynasty, H: 34.3cm; Diam.(at mouth): 9.4cm; Diam.(at foot): 12.7cm

137 青花竹石芭蕉图玉壶春瓶

清雍正

高 28.0 厘米　口径 7.0 厘米　足径 9.7 厘米

Blue-and-White *Yu Hu Chun* Bottle Vase with Design of Bamboo, Rock and Palm Tree

Yongzheng Period, Qing Dynasty, H: 28.0cm; Diam.(at mouth): 7.0cm; Diam.(at foot): 9.7cm

138 青花竹石芭蕉图玉壶春瓶

清乾隆

高 29.4 厘米　口径 8.5 厘米　足径 11.6 厘米

Blue-and-White *Yu Hu Chun* Bottle Vase with Design of Bamboo, Rock and Palm Tree

Qianlong Period, Qing Dynasty, H: 29.4cm; Diam.(at mouth): 8.5cm; Diam.(at foot): 11.6cm

139 青花竹石芭蕉图玉壶春瓶

清嘉庆

高 28.6 厘米　口径 8.6 厘米　足径 10.8 厘米

Blue-and-White *Yu Hu Chun* Bottle Vase with Design of Bamboo, Rock and Palm Tree

Jiaqing Period, Qing Dynasty, H: 28.6cm; Diam.(at mouth): 8.6cm; Diam.(at foot): 10.8cm

140 青花竹石芭蕉图玉壶春瓶

清道光

高 28.6 厘米　口径 8.6 厘米　足径 10.8 厘米

Blue-and-White *Yu Hu Chun* Bottle Vase with Design of Bamboo, Rock and Palm Tree

Daoguang Period, Qing Dynasty, H: 28.6cm; Diam.(at mouth): 8.6cm; Diam.(at foot): 10.8cm

141 青花竹石芭蕉图玉壶春瓶

清咸丰

高 28.6 厘米　口径 8.6 厘米　足径 10.8 厘米

Blue-and-White *Yu Hu Chun* Bottle Vase with Design of Bamboo, Rock and Palm Tree

Xianfeng Period, Qing Dynasty, H: 28.6cm; Diam.(at mouth): 8.6cm; Diam.(at foot): 10.8cm

142 青花竹石芭蕉图玉壶春瓶

清同治

高 29.5 厘米　口径 8.7 厘米　足径 11.5 厘米

Blue-and-White *Yu Hu Chun* Bottle Vase with Design of Bamboo, Rock and Palm Tree

Tongzhi Period, Qing Dynasty, H: 29.5cm; Diam.(at mouth): 8.7cm; Diam.(at foot): 11.5cm

143 青花竹石芭蕉图玉壶春瓶

清光绪

高 29.5 厘米　口径 8.5 厘米　足径 11.7 厘米

Blue-and-White *Yu Hu Chun* Bottle Vase with Design of Bamboo, Rock and Palm Tree

Guangxu Period, Qing Dynasty, H: 29.5cm; Diam.(at mouth): 8.5cm; Diam.(at foot): 11.7cm

主题十四

喜庆吉祥
清代晚期大婚成套用瓷

所谓成套用瓷系指同一花色按不同器形烧造的不同尺寸的碗、盘、盒、花盆等生活用瓷。清代成套用瓷主要见于同治、光绪两朝，用于同治大婚和慈禧皇太后万寿。

这里展示的一组瓷器即为同治皇帝大婚用瓷。同治皇帝举行大婚是在同治十一年（1872 年），时年同治皇帝 16 岁。为筹备这次大婚典礼，早在同治六年（1867 年）三月初十日朝廷即命分巡广饶九南道、督理九江关税务、监管窑厂事的景福办理大婚用瓷，共计 14 份并 9 项花色，合计 10072 件。其中，14 份均为成套瓷器，按每种图样烧造海碗、大碗、中碗、汤碗、饭碗、怀碗、九寸盘、七寸盘、五寸盘、四寸碟、三寸碟、二寸五碟、酒盅、羹匙、茶盅、大茶盅、盖碗、茶缸、渣斗、粉盒、胭脂盒、刡头缸、水仙衣、花盆等。

据史料记载，为筹办同治皇帝大婚典礼，共花费 1100 多万两白银，其中为烧造婚礼用瓷，朝廷下令拨款 13 万两白银重建因“太平天国运动”而被毁的御窑厂。即使这样，烧造这批瓷器对于重修后的御窑厂仍困难重重，景福用两年时间才全部监督烧完。同治七年八月二十八日，景福将烧造完成的皇帝大婚用瓷器 7294 件、共装 120 桶造册呈送内务府，但这只是完成传办 14 份中的 10 份及全部 9 项花色活计，剩下的 4 份共计 2778 件完成于同治八年。

这 10072 件瓷器运到皇宫后，被认为“均烧造粗糙，不堪应用”。同治八年十二月二十一日，奏事处总管杨长春传旨“着传知该九江关监督景福照数赔补”。景福于同治九年八月命御窑厂开工重新烧造这批大婚用瓷，直至同治十年十一月照数补造完毕并解送至京城交差。

在此背景下诞生的同治皇帝大婚用瓷，堪称同治朝景德镇御窑厂产品中的代表作之一，也开创中国历史上大规模烧造皇帝大婚用瓷之先河。

Theme 14

For Joyous and Auspicious Moment

Porcelain Sets for Imperial Wedding Ceremony in the Late Qing Dynasty

Porcelain sets, composed of bowls, plates, boxes and flower-pots with same décor but differing in shape and size, were produced for the wedding ceremony of Emperor Tongzhi and the longevity ceremony of Empress Dowager Cixi.

The porcelain listed in this section was produced for Emperor Tongzhi's wedding ceremony held in 1872. The preparations already started as early as five years ago. In 1867, Jing Fu was appointed as imperial supervisor to prepare the porcelain sets: altogether 10,072 pieces of porcelain in 14 sets with 9 designs were to be produced for the wedding. Each set included different-sized bowls and plates, wine cups, tea wares, cosmetic utensils, flower pots, etc. As recorded in historical documents, the preparatory works for the wedding ceremony including the reconstruction of imperial kilns cost 11 million taels of silver. Confronted with numerous difficulties, Jing Fu rolled with the punches and finished the porcelain production within two years. In 1868, 7294 pieces of porcelain in 10 sets were transported to the Imperial Household Department. One year later, the rest of the order, 2778 pieces in 4 sets were completed.

10,072 pieces of porcelain were judged unexpectedly as "inferior products not to be used" after they were transported to the Forbidden City. In 1870, Jing Fu was forced to produce new porcelain sets in the same quantity. It took him another one year to complete the imperial mission. The porcelain sets for Emperor Tongzhi's wedding ceremony were ranked as classic works of Jingdezhen imperial kilns during the Tongzhi period. From then on, it became a custom to produce porcelain sets for imperial wedding ceremony.

这是一组清代同治皇帝大婚用瓷。同治皇帝举行大婚是在同治十一年（1872 年），时年同治皇帝 16 岁。为筹备这次大婚典礼，早在同治六年（1867 年）三月初十日朝廷即命分巡广饶九南道、督理九江关税务、监管窑厂事的景福办理同治皇帝大婚用瓷，共计 14 份又 9 项花色，共计 10072 件。但全部 10072 件瓷器运到皇宫后，被认为“均烧造粗糙，不堪应用”。同治八年十二月二十一日，奏事处总管杨长春传旨“着传知该九江关监督景福照数赔补”。景福于同治九年八月命御窑厂开工重新烧造这批大婚用瓷，直至同治十年十一月照数补造完毕并解送至京城交差。

在此背景下诞生的同治皇帝大婚用瓷，堪称同治朝景德镇御窑厂产品中的代表作之一，也开创中国历史上大规模烧造皇帝大婚用瓷之先河。（吕成龙）

附1 内府色绘黄地粉彩梅鹊图碗纸样

清同治

此图样即同治六年（1867 年）三月初十日朝廷命分巡广饶九南道、督理九江关税务、监管御窑厂事的景福办理同治皇帝大婚用瓷 14 份中的 1 份，档案称“黄地喜雀梅碗样一件”。命照此样烧造海碗、大碗、中碗、汤碗、怀碗、九寸盘、七寸盘、五寸盘、四寸碟、三寸碟、二寸五碟、酒盅各 40 件，羹匙 40 把，饭碗 60 件，茶盅、大茶盅、盖碗、茶缸各 20 件，二寸五见圆渣斗 10 件，二寸见圆粉盒、二寸五见圆㕞头缸、一寸见圆胭脂盒各 4 件，一尺五寸见圆花盆 3 对，长方入角水仙奁一对。共计 686 件把个对。（吕成龙）

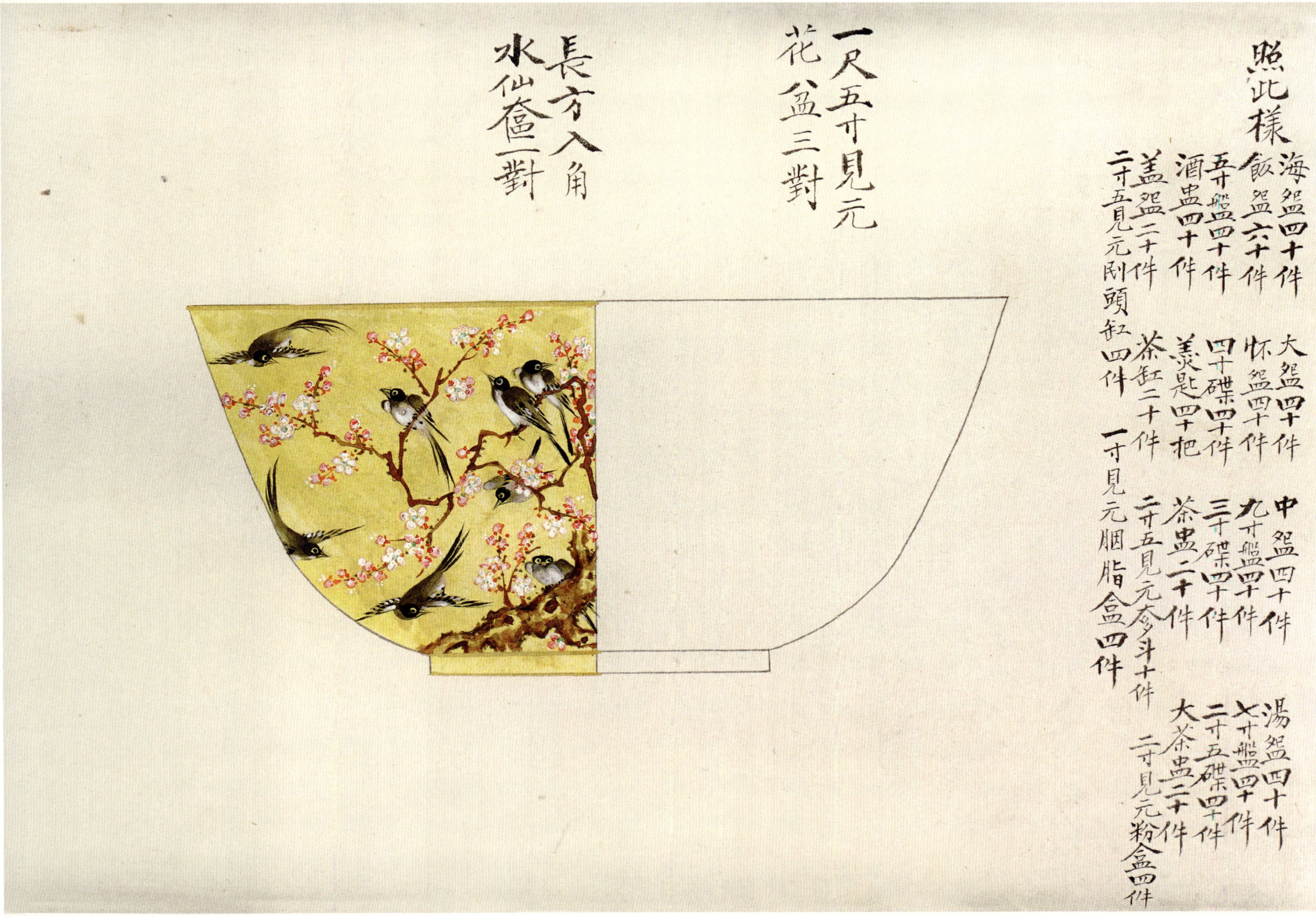

Design Draft of Bowl with Design of Magpies and Prunus Blossoms in *Famille Rose* on Yellow Ground Painted by the Imperial Household Department

Tongzhi Period, Qing Dynasty

均撇口、深弧腹、圈足。碗内和圈足内均施白釉，外壁黄地粉彩梅鹊图装饰。口沿、足端和足跟均涂金彩。外底署矾红彩楷体“同治年制”四字双行款。

据清代宫廷档案记载，当时照画样烧造的碗、盅类共有11种，即海碗（口径20.5厘米左右）、大碗（口径17.5厘米左右）、中碗（口径14.5厘米左右）、汤碗（口径12.5厘米左右）、饭碗（口径10.5厘米）及怀碗（口径8.5厘米左右）、盖碗 （口径10.5厘米左右）、大茶盅（口径10.4厘米左右）、茶盅（口径8.5厘米左右）、茶缸（口径8.5厘米左右）、酒盅等。（唐雪梅）

144 黄地粉彩梅鹊图碗

清同治

高 9.5 厘米　口径 20.5 厘米　足径 8.0 厘米

此尺寸碗即宫廷档案中所曰“海碗”。（唐雪梅）

Bowl with Design of Magpies and Prunus Blossoms in *Famille Rose* on Yellow Ground

Tongzhi Period, Qing Dynasty, H: 9.5cm; Diam.(at mouth): 20.5cm; Diam.(at foot): 8.0cm

145 黄地粉彩梅鹊图碗

清同治

高 9.0 厘米　口径 17.9 厘米　足径 7.8 厘米

此尺寸碗即宫廷档案中所曰“大碗”。（唐雪梅）

Bowl with Design of Magpies and Prunus Blossoms in *Famille Rose* on Yellow Ground

Tongzhi Period, Qing Dynasty, H: 9.0cm; Diam.(at mouth): 17.9cm; Diam.(at foot): 7.8cm

146 黄地粉彩梅鹊图碗

清同治

高 6.8 厘米　口径 14.3 厘米　足径 6.3 厘米

此尺寸碗即宫廷档案中所曰“中碗”。（唐雪梅）

Bowl with Design of Magpies and Prunus Blossoms in *Famille Rose* on Yellow Ground

Tongzhi Period, Qing Dynasty, H: 6.8cm; Diam.(at mouth): 14.3cm; Diam.(at foot): 6.3cm

147 黄地粉彩梅鹊图碗

清同治

高 5.8 厘米 口径 12.4 厘米 足径 5.0 厘米

此尺寸碗即宫廷档案中所曰“汤碗”。（唐雪梅）

Soup Bowl with Design of Magpies and Prunus Blossoms in *Famille Rose* on Yellow Ground

Tongzhi Period, Qing Dynasty, H: 5.8cm; Diam.(at mouth): 12.4cm; Diam.(at foot): 5.0cm

148 黄地粉彩梅鹊图碗

清同治

高 5.6 厘米　口径 10.5 厘米　足径 4.4 厘米

此尺寸碗即宫廷档案中所曰“饭碗”。（唐雪梅）

Rice Bowl with Design of Magpies and Prunus Blossoms in *Famille Rose* on Yellow Ground
Tongzhi Period, Qing Dynasty, H: 5.6cm; Diam.(at mouth): 10.5cm; Diam.(at foot): 4.4cm

149 黄地粉彩梅鹊图碗

清同治

高 6.2 厘米　口径 10.4 厘米　足径 4.5 厘米

此种尺寸的碗即宫廷档案中所曰“大茶盅”。（唐雪梅）

Tea Bowl with Design of Magpies and Prunus Blossoms in *Famille Rose* on Yellow Ground

Tongzhi Period, Qing Dynasty, H: 6.2cm; Diam.(at mouth): 10.4cm; Diam.(at foot): 4.5cm

150 黄地粉彩梅鹊图杯

清同治

高 5.9 厘米　口径 8.8 厘米　足径 4.0 厘米

此种尺寸的杯即宫廷档案所曰“茶盅”。（唐雪梅）

Tea Bowl with Design of Magpies and Prunus Blossoms in *Famille Rose* on Yellow Ground

Tongzhi Period, Qing Dynasty, H: 5.9cm; Diam.(at mouth): 8.8cm; Diam.(at foot): 4.0cm

151 黄地粉彩梅鹊图杯

清同治

高 6.2 厘米　口径 8.0 厘米　足径 3.9 厘米

此种尺寸的杯即宫廷档案所曰‘茶缸”。（唐雪梅）

Tea Bowl with Design of Magpies and Prunus Blossoms in *Famille Rose* on Yellow Ground

Tongzhi Period, Qing Dynasty, H: 6.2cm; Diam.(at mouth): 8.0cm; Diam.(at foot): 3.9cm

盘、碟类

均敞口、浅弧腹、圈足。盘外壁和圈足内均施白釉。盘内淡黄地粉彩梅鹊图装饰，外壁绘 3 组粉彩折枝牡丹纹。外底均署矾红彩楷体“同治年制”四字双行款。

据清代宫廷档案记载，当时照画样烧造的盘、碟类共有 6 种，即九寸盘（口径 27 厘米左右）、七寸盘（口径 21 厘米左右）、五寸盘（口径 15 厘米左右）、四寸碟（口径 12 厘米左右）、三寸碟（口径 10 厘米左右）、二寸五碟（口径 7 厘米左右）等。（唐雪梅）

152 黄地粉彩梅鹊图盘

清同治

高 5.4 厘米　口径 27.5 厘米　足径 17.0 厘米

此尺寸盘即宫廷档案中所曰“九寸盘”。（唐雪梅）

Plate with Design of Magpies and Prunus Blossoms in *Famille Rose* on Yellow Ground

Tongzhi Period, Qing Dynasty, H: 5.4cm; Diam.(at mouth): 27.5cm; Diam.(at foot): 17.0cm

153 黄地粉彩梅鹊图盘

清同治

高 5.1 厘米　口径 22.0 厘米　足径 13.1 厘米

此尺寸盘即宫廷档案中所曰“七寸盘”。（唐雪梅）

Plate with Design of Magpies and Prunus Blossoms in *Famille Rose* on Yellow Ground

Tongzhi Period, Qing Dynasty, H: 5.1cm; Diam.(at mouth): 22.0cm; Diam.(at foot): 13.1cm

154 黄地粉彩梅鹊图盘

清同治

高 2.4 厘米　口径 10.1 厘米　足径 6.6 厘米

此尺寸碟即宫廷档案中所曰“三寸碟”。（唐雪梅）

Saucer with Design of Magpies and Prunus Blossoms in *Famille Rose* on Yellow Ground

Tongzhi Period, Qing Dynasty, H: 2.4cm; Diam.(at mouth): 10.1cm; Diam.(at foot): 6.6cm

155 黄地粉彩梅鹊图碟

清同治

高 2.8 厘米　口径 7.6 厘米　足径 4.2 厘米

此尺寸碟即宫廷档案中所曰“二寸五碟”。（唐雪梅）

Saucer with Design of Magpies and Prunus Blossoms in *Famille Rose* on Yellow Ground

Tongzhi Period, Qing Dynasty, H: 2.8cm; Diam.(at mouth): 7.6cm; Diam.(at foot): 4.2cm

156 黄地粉彩梅鹊图羹匙

清同治

长 17.2 厘米　宽 5.5 厘米

羹匙长柄、平底。匙内淡黄地粉彩梅鹊图装饰，外壁白釉地上绘 3 组粉彩折枝花纹。外底署矾红彩楷体“同治年制”四字双行款。故宫博物院现藏绘这种图案的同治皇帝大婚用羹匙计有 32 件。（唐雪梅）

Soup Spoon with Design of Magpies and Prunus Blossoms in *Famille Rose* on Yellow Ground

Tongzhi Period, Qing Dynasty, L: 17.2cm; W: 5.5cm

157 黄地粉彩梅鹊图渣斗

清同治

高 8.8 厘米　口径 8.2 厘米　足径 5.2 厘米

渣斗均撇口、阔颈、圆腹、圈足。渣斗内和圈足内均施白釉。渣斗内光素，外壁以淡黄地粉彩梅鹊图装饰。外底署矾红彩楷体“同治年制”四字双行款。故宫博物院现藏绘这种图案的同治皇帝大婚用渣斗计有 12 件。这种渣斗即宫廷档案所曰“奓斗”。（唐雪梅）

Zhadou Spitton with Design of Magpies and Prunus Blossoms in *Famille Rose* on Yellow Ground

Tongzhi Period, Qing Dynasty, H: 8.8m; Diam.(at mouth): 8.2cm; Diam.(at foot): 5.2cm

158 黄地粉彩梅鹊图盒

清同治

通高 4.0 厘米　口径 7.3 厘米　足径 5.2 厘米

盒呈馒头形。均敞口、浅弧腹、圈足。盒内和圈足内均施白釉。上、下子、母口扣合。盒外通体以淡黄地粉彩梅鹊图装饰。外底署矾红彩楷体“同治年制”四字双行款。这种盒即当时烧造清单中所曰“粉盒”。（唐雪梅）

Round Box and Cover with Design of Magpies and Prunus Blossoms in *Famille Rose* on Yellow Ground

Tongzhi Period, Qing Dynasty, H(with cover): 4.0cm; Diam.(at mouth): 7.3cm; Diam.(at foot): 5.2cm

主题十五

富丽华贵

清代晚期万寿成套用瓷

由于历史原因，同治、光绪两朝中国的朝政大权掌握在慈禧皇太后手中，她在这两朝经历了四十、五十、六十、七十岁大寿，景德镇御窑专门为其寿诞烧造瓷器。在同时期御窑瓷器中，皇太后万寿用瓷不仅数量较大，而且做工精美。

慈禧皇太后使用的瓷器常署有其居住的宫殿名称，最著名的当为署有“大雅斋”“天地一家春”款识的所谓“大雅斋瓷器”，包含鱼缸、碗、盘、碟、羹匙、渣斗、茶碗、圆盒等多种造型。这批瓷器始烧于同治十三年（1874 年），烧成于光绪元年（1875 年）、二年。据清代宫廷档案记载，同治十三年三月三十日，内务府将大雅斋瓷器画样交与景德镇御窑厂，并传旨“统限于本年九月内呈进”，为的是赶上当年十月十日慈禧皇太后四十岁大寿。但由于时间太紧，这批瓷器未能赶在慈禧皇太后寿诞之前烧造完成并运至京城。

Theme 15

Luxurious Splendor

Longevity Porcelain Sets for Celebrating Imperial Birthdays in the Late Qing Dynasty

The virtural ruler of Tongzhi and Guangxu periods was Empress Dowager Cixi, who experienced her 40th, 50th, 60th and 70th birthday during that period. Large amounts of exquisite porcelain were produced at Jingdezhen imperial kilns for celebrating her birthday.

Those pieces of porcelain, including fish tanks, bowls, plates, dishes, tea wares, etc., are usually inscribed with the name of the palace which Cixi lived in, the most prominent one among which is the mark of Da Ya Zhai. In 1874, Jingdezhen imperial kilns received manuscripts together with time limits for production from the Imperial Household Department for the celebration of Cizi's 40th birthday in the same year. However, the imperial kilns were not able to complete the porcelain production in time due to the short of time.

大雅斋瓷器均依宫廷发出的纸样烧造，同一纹样绘在不同器形上。本组瓷器即为依照同一纸样烧造而成。纸质画样黄签记载："照此样，翡翠地水墨葵花鱼缸二尺六寸见圆二对、一尺见圆四对、九寸见圆二对……海碗二十件、大碗三十件、中碗四十件、怀碗六十件，九寸盘子二十件、七寸盘子三十件，五寸碟四十件、三寸碟四十件，长把羹匙四十件，奓斗四十件，茶碗四十件，盖碗四十件，一尺见圆盒四对，五寸见圆盒子四对。"（唐雪梅）

附2 内府色绘绿地黑彩花鸟图缸纸样

清光绪

Design Draft of Jar with Flower and Bird in Black Enamel on Green Ground Painted by the Imperial Household Department

Guangxu Period, Qing Dynasty

159 **松石绿地粉彩花鸟图鱼缸**

清光绪

高 45.0 厘米　口径 42.0 厘米　足径 39.0 厘米

缸呈钵形，故亦称钵缸。敛口、鼓腹、腹下渐收敛、圈足。缸内和圈足内均施白釉，外壁松石绿地粉彩花鸟图装饰。以浓淡不同的黑彩描绘数种盛开的花卉，花枝摇曳，空中伴有飞雁。口沿下画面空白处自右向左署楷体“大雅斋”款，右侧钤矾红彩篆体“天地一家春”闲章。

此缸形体硕大饱满，用于养鱼。图案以秋菊、秋葵、秋雁等组合而成，寓意“三秋献瑞”。（郭玉昆）

Fish Bowl with Design of Flowers and Birds in Black Colour on Turquoise Green Ground

Guangxu Period, Qing Dynasty, H: 45.0cm; Diam.(at mouth): 42.0cm; Diam.(at foot): 39.0cm

160 松石绿地粉彩花鸟图渣斗

清光绪

高 9.0 厘米　口径 9.6 厘米　足径 6.0 厘米

渣斗撇口、阔颈、鼓腹、圈足。足内施白釉，渣斗内、外均施松石绿釉，内壁光素无纹饰。口沿涂金彩。外壁以粉彩描绘两组花鸟图，两组图案之间空白处署矾红彩楷体“大雅斋”款，右侧钤矾红彩篆体“天地一家春”闲章。外底署矾红彩楷体“永庆长春”四字双行款。菊花、秋葵和秋雁组合，在清代档案中被称作“三秋图”。（赵聪月）

Zhadou Spitton with Design of Flowers and Birds in Black Colour on Turquoise Green Ground

Guangxu Period, Qing Dynasty, H: 9.0cm; Diam.(at mouth): 9.6cm; Diam.(at foot): 6.0cm

大雅齋

161 松石绿地粉彩花鸟图圆盒

清光绪

通高 11.5 厘米 口径 15.0 厘米 足径 10.5 厘米

盒呈馒头形，上下子、母口扣合，圈足。盒内和圈足内均施白釉。外壁松石绿地粉彩花鸟图装饰。盒盖画面空白处署矾红彩楷体“大雅斋”款，右侧钤矾红彩篆体“天地一家春”闲章。外底署矾红彩楷体“永庆长春”四字双行款。（赵小春）

Round Box and Cover with Design of Flowers and Birds in Black Colour on Turquoise Green Ground

Guangxu Period, Qing Dynasty, H(with cover): 11.5cm; Diam.(at mouth): 15.0cm; Diam.(at foot): 10.5cm

大雅齋

162 松石绿地粉彩花鸟图碗

清光绪

高 5.3 厘米　口径 10.5 厘米　足径 4.3 厘米

碗撇口、深弧腹、圈足。碗内和圈足内均施白釉。外壁松石绿地上饰粉彩菊花、秋葵和飞雁图。口沿涂金彩，近口沿画面空白处自右向左署矾红彩“大雅斋”款，右侧钤矾红彩篆体“天地一家春”闲章。外底署矾红彩楷体“永庆长春”四字双行款。（赵小春）

Bowl with Design of Flowers and Birds in Black Colour on Turquoise Green Ground

Guangxu Period, Qing Dynasty, H: 5.3cm; Diam.(at mouth): 10.5cm; Diam.(at foot): 4.3cm

163 松石绿地粉彩花鸟图碗

清光绪

高 6.1 厘米　口径 10.4 厘米　足径 4.3 厘米

碗撇口、深弧腹、圈足。碗内和圈足内均施白釉，外壁松石绿地上装饰粉彩菊花、秋葵和秋雁图。口沿涂金彩，近口沿画面空白处自右向左署矾红彩楷体“大雅斋”款，右侧钤矾红彩篆体“天地一家春”闲章。外底署矾红彩楷体“永庆长春”四字双行款。

依此碗造型和尺寸判断应属于盖碗的主体，惜盖已佚。（唐雪梅）

Bowl with Design of Flowers and Birds in Black Colour on Turquoise Green Ground

Guangxu Period, Qing Dynasty, H: 6.1cm; Diam.(at mouth): 10.4cm; Diam.(at foot): 4.3cm

164 松石绿地粉彩花鸟图高足碗

清光绪

高 8.7 厘米　口径 11.0 厘米　足径 5.9 厘米

碗撇口、深弧腹、瘦底，下承以中空外撇高足。碗内和足内均施白釉。外壁松石绿地粉彩花鸟图装饰。口沿和高足上部凸起弦纹处涂抹金彩，近足处绘粉彩海水江崖纹。近口沿画面空白处自右向左署矾红彩楷体“大雅斋”款，右侧钤矾红彩篆体“天地一家春”闲章。（高晓然）

Stem Bowl with Design of Flowers and Birds in Black Colour on Turquoise Green Ground

Guangxu Period, Qing Dynasty, H: 8.7cm; Diam.(at mouth): 11.0cm; Diam.(at foot): 5.9cm

165 外白地粉彩折枝牡丹内松石绿地粉彩花鸟图盘

清光绪

高 5.2 厘米　口径 28.0 厘米　足径 17.0 厘米

盘敞口、浅弧腹、圈足。盘内松石绿地粉彩花鸟图装饰，口沿涂金彩，下方画面空白处自右向左署矾红彩楷体“大雅斋”款，右侧钤矾红彩篆体“天地一家春”闲章。外壁白釉地上绘 3 组粉彩折枝花纹。外底署矾红彩楷体“永庆长春”四字双行款。（董建丽）

Plate with Design of Flowers and Birds in Black Colour on Turquoise Green Ground Inside and Peony Sprays in *Famille Rose* Outside

Guangxu Period, Qing Dynasty, H: 5.2cm; Diam.(at mouth): 28.0cm; Diam.(at foot): 17.0cm

166 外白地粉彩折枝牡丹内松石绿地粉彩花鸟图高足盘

清光绪

高 11.3 厘米　口径 24.8 厘米　足径 9.7 厘米

盘敞口、浅弧腹、瘦底，下承以外撇中空高足。盘内松石绿地粉彩花鸟图装饰，口沿涂金彩，下方画面空白处自右向左署矾红彩楷体“大雅斋”款，右侧钤矾红彩篆体“天地一家春”闲章。外壁白釉地上绘 3 组粉彩折枝花纹。高足上部凸起的弦纹涂金彩，弦纹下绘粉彩海水江崖纹。（高晓然）

Stem Plate with Design of Flowers and Birds in Black Colour on Turquoise Green Ground Inside and Peony Sprays in *Famille Rose* Outside

Guangxu Period, Qing Dynasty, H: 11.3cm; Diam.(at mouth): 24.8cm; Diam.(at foot): 9.7cm

大雅齋

主题十六

敬天法祖
清代宫廷祭祀用瓷

明代祭祀制度已较完备，《大明会典》卷二百一织造之“器用”条载：“凡祭祀器皿，洪武元年令：太庙器皿易以金造；乘舆服御诸物，应用金者，以铜代之。二年定，祭器皆用瓷。”该书又载，嘉靖九年，朝廷规定“四郊各陵瓷器：圜丘青色，方丘黄色，日坛赤色，月坛白色。行江西饶州府如式烧解”。由此确定了明代宫廷“祭器皆用瓷”的基本制度。

文献记载和传世实物表明，清代初期的坛庙祭祀制度皆沿袭明代旧制，以瓷器作祭器。但由于传统祭祀用器中的登、铏、簠、簋、笾、豆等成型和烧成难度均很大，因此，不得不以瓷质碗、盘等替代。直至乾隆十三年（1748 年）重新改制以后，才依传统器形烧造各色瓷质祭礼用器。《清实录》卷三〇六载：“（乾隆十三年）戊辰春正月丁亥，定祀典祭器。谕：国家敬天尊祖，礼备乐和，品物具陈，告丰告洁，所以将诚敬昭典则也。考之前古，笾豆簠簋诸祭器，或用金玉，以示贵重，或用陶匏，以崇质素，各有精义存乎其间，历代相仍，去古寖远，至明洪武时，更定旧章，祭品祭器悉遵古，而祭器则惟存其名，以瓷代之。我朝坛庙，陈设祭品，器亦用瓷，盖沿前明之旧……凡陶必辨色，圜丘、祈谷、常雩青，方泽黄，日坛赤，月坛白，社稷、先农黄。”由此可知，圜丘坛（天坛）、祈谷坛、常雩坛等祭祀用祭蓝（青）釉瓷器，方泽坛（地坛）、社稷坛、先农坛等祭祀用黄釉瓷器，日坛祭祀用红釉瓷器，月坛祭祀用白釉瓷器。这种规定符合自然法则，反映了古人顺乎自然、与自然和谐相处的理念。因为天呈蓝色、土呈黄色、刚升起的太阳呈红色、月亮呈白色，所以要用与之颜色相同的瓷器作祭器。另外，清代皇帝前往不同的祭祀场所行祭礼时，还要穿不同颜色的朝服、佩戴不同颜色的朝珠。即分别穿蓝色、黄色、大红色、月白色朝袍，分别佩戴青金石、金珀、珊瑚、绿松石朝珠，于冬至时节祭祀天坛、夏至时节祭祀地坛、春分时节祭祀日坛、秋分时节祭祀月坛。这样做，都是上述理念的反映。

Theme 16

In Reverence of Heaven and Worship of Ancestors

Imperial Porcelain for Sacrifice in the Qing Dynasty

The ritual of court sacrifice in the Ming Dynasty, whose completeness and maturity could be proved by the *Da Ming Hui Dian* (Volume 201 Term *Qi Yong* in the *Zhi Zao* section). It was recorded that the regulation on the materials used for different sacrificial offerings or utensils could be traced back to the 1st year of the Hongwu (the founding emperor of the Ming Dynasty) period. One year later, a revision stated that sacrificial utensils should be porcelain. In the 9th year of the Jiajing period, further revision was made on the use of porcelain in different colours for different altars The basic principle of using porcelain utensils for sacrifice in the Ming Dynasty was thus developed.

Documents and heritage items proved that the Qing Dynasty followed the rituals of sacrifice in temples from the previous dynasty, Ming. However, since it was very challenging to mould and fire traditional sacrificial vessels, they had to be replaced with porcelain bowls or plates. It was not till the 13th year of Qianlong period that sacrificial vessels with various colours of glaze were able to be manufactured in traditional modelling. Further regulation since then suggests that weather-related rituals should use blue-glazed or celadon porcelains, land- or agriculture-related rituals use yellow-glazed ones, rituals to the sun use red-glazed ones, and rituals to the moon use white-glazed ones. Such provisions conformed to the laws of nature and reflected the philosophy of living in harmony with nature in ancient China: the sky appears blue and the earth yellow while red is for the rising sun and white for the moon—the colours of sacrificial porcelain must be in accordance with them. In addition, the emperors of the Qing Dynasty wore court dresses in different colours and dressed up with different court beads accordingly to show their respect to the philosophy. More specifically, the emperors, wearing blue court dress and court beads of lapis lazuli, offered weather-related sacrifice in the Temple of Heaven on the day of the winter solstice. On the occasion of agriculture-related rituals in the Temple of Earth on the summer solstice, they wore yellow court dress with court beads of yellow amber. Red court dress with court beads of coral was for rituals to the sun in the Temple of the Sun on the spring equinox while court dress in moon-white with court beads of turquoise for rituals to the moon in the Temple of the Moon on the autumn equinox.

167 浇黄釉仿古铜纹豆

清乾隆

通高 26.8 厘米　口径 16.1 厘米

豆造型、纹饰与《皇朝礼器图式》记载相符。通体施黄釉，外壁刻水波纹、云纹、回纹、黻纹等，盖内顶和豆外底均阴刻篆体“大清乾隆年制”六字三行款。

豆是商、周时期的食器，后发展成为重要的祭器，用于盛放韭菹、青菹、芹菹、笋菹、鱼醢、鹿醢、兔醢、醓醢、脾析、豚拍等。《乡射记》注：“豆宜濡物，盛齑（细切的肉）醓（肉酱）菹（腌菜）臡（带骨的肉酱）之属。”清代祭器可根据不同材质、颜色区别其在祭祀中的不同功用和使用场合。据《皇朝礼器图式》记载，豆为乾隆十三年（1748 年）钦定的祭器，腹为垂云纹、回纹，校围波纹、金钣纹，足为黻纹，盖为波纹、回纹，顶为绹钮。黄色瓷豆用于地坛正位、配位、从位，社稷坛正位、配位，以及先农坛、先蚕坛的祭祀活动。（鲍楠）

Covered Vessel Moulded in the Form of Ancient Bronze *Dou* with Incised Archaistic Bronze Motifs in Bright-Yellow Glaze

Qianlong Period, Qing Dynasty, H(with cover): 26.8cm; Diam.(at mouth): 16.1cm

168 浇黄釉仿古铜纹簠

清乾隆

通高 23.6 厘米　口横 25.5 厘米　口纵 20.8 厘米

簠呈方斗形，腹壁斜收，盖顶出波浪形冠状边，属于仿古代青铜器造型。通体施黄釉。底足四边中间均有莲瓣形镂空，腹部均置半环龙耳，外壁刻有夔龙纹、回纹、云纹等。造型庄重，形制规范，做工精细，与《皇朝礼器图式》记载相符。盖内顶部和外底均阴刻篆体“大清乾隆年制”六字三行款。

簠最早是中国古代宴飨时盛放稻、粱的器具，后被用于祭祀，成为礼器。《周礼·地官·舍人》注曰：“方曰簠，盛稻粱器。”《礼记·乐记》载：“簠簋俎豆，制度文章，礼之器也。”《周礼·舍人》曰：“凡祭祀共簠簋。”祭祀时，簠簋总是同时出现。清代祭器可根据不同材质、颜色区别其在祭祀中的不同功用和使用场合。据《皇朝礼器图式》记载，簠为乾隆十三年（1748 年）钦定祭器，面为夔龙纹，束为回纹，足为云纹，两耳附以夔龙。盖上有棱，亦附以坛龙耳。黄色瓷簠用于地坛正位、配位、从位，社稷坛正位、配位，先农坛、先蚕坛的祭祀活动。（鲍楠）

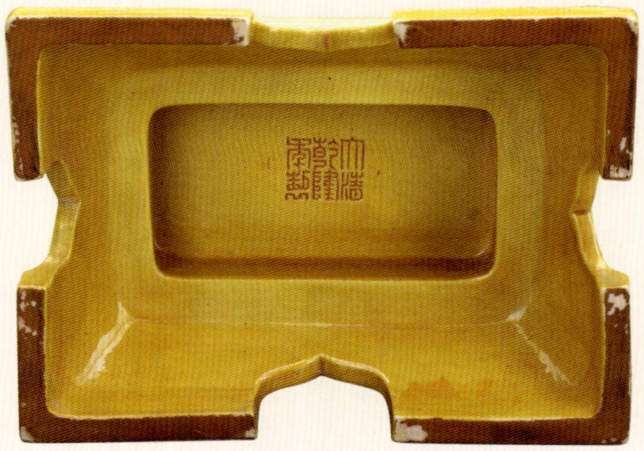

Bright-Yellow-Glazed Covered Square Vessel Moulded in the Form of Ancient Bronze *Fu* with Incised Design of Archaistic Bronze Motifs

Qianlong Period, Qing Dynasty, H(with cover): 23.6cm; L(at mouth): 25.5cm; W(at mouth): 20.8cm

169 浇黄釉仿古铜纹簋

清道光

通高 20.2 厘米　口横 19.6 厘米　口纵 15.3 厘米

仿古铜簋造型。簋身呈椭圆形，腹部两侧对称置夔凤耳。通体施黄釉，盖顶置四棱，盖边刻云纹、回纹。腹部至足部刻回纹、云纹、黻纹等。造型规整，做工精细，与《皇朝礼器图式》记载相符。盖内顶和簋外底均阴刻“大清道光年制”六字三行款。

簋最早是中国古代宴飨时盛放黍、稷的器具，后被用于祭祀，成为礼器。《周礼 · 地官 · 舍人》注曰：“圆曰簋，盛黍稷器。”清代祭器可根据不同材质、颜色区别其在祭祀中的不同功用和使用场合。据《皇朝礼器图式》载，簋为乾隆十三年（1748 年）钦定祭器，制圆而椭，口为回纹，腹为云纹，束为黻纹，足为星云纹，两耳附以夔凤。盖面为云纹，口为回纹，上有棱四出。黄色瓷簋主要用于地坛正位、配位、从位，社稷坛正位、配位，先农坛、先蚕坛的祭祀活动。（鲍楠）

Bright-Yellow-Glazed Covered Round Vessel Moulded in the Form of Ancient Bronze *Gui* with Incised Design of Archaistic Bronze Motifs

Daoguang Period, Qing Dynasty, H(with cover): 20.2cm; L(at mouth): 19.6cm; W(at mouth): 15.3cm

170 浇黄釉涂金彩爵

清乾隆

高 16.3 厘米　流长 17.7 厘米

爵无柄、圆柱形足。口沿、两柱、三足施黄釉，爵身涂金，一侧饰有环纹。造型与史料记载的“有柄，足修而锐，形若戈”有出入，装饰与《皇朝礼器图式》记载的“腹为雷纹，饕餮形”亦不同。说明不同时期爵杯的造型、纹饰等细节会有所变化。外底阴刻篆体“乾隆年制”四字双行款。

爵为商、周时期的酒器，也是重要的祭器。《说文》云：“爵，礼器，象雀之形。”陆佃《礼象》云：“古铜爵，有首，有尾，有柱，有足，有柄。”《宣和博古图》谓：“前若喝，后若尾，足修而锐，形若戈然，两柱为耳。”清代祭器可根据不同材质、颜色区别其在祭祀中的不同功用和使用场合。据《皇朝礼器图式》记载，爵为乾隆十三年（1748 年）钦定祭器，腹为雷纹，饕餮形。黄色瓷爵用于地坛从位、社稷坛配位，以及先农坛、先蚕坛的祭祀活动。（鲍楠）

Gilt-Decorated Bright-Yellow-Glazed Vessel Moulded in the Form of Ancient Bronze *Jue*

Qianlong Period, Qing Dynasty, H: 16.3cm; L of Spout: 17.7cm

171 浇黄釉犕耳尊

清道光

高 27.5 厘米　口径 15.5 厘米　足径 13.8 厘米

尊撇口、短束颈、溜肩、鼓腹、腹下内收、圈足。肩部对称置犕首耳。内、外和圈足内均施黄釉，足底无釉。外底黄釉下阴刻篆体“大清道光年制”六字三行款。

此种祭祀用瓷尊见于清代《皇朝礼器图式》等多部文献记载，为清代乾隆十三年（1748 年）以来钦定八种祭器之一。除浇黄釉品种外，记载还有白、赤、青和月白等釉色。（唐雪梅）

Bright-Yellow-Glazed Vessel Moulded in the Form of Ancient Bronze *Zun* with Rhino-Shaped Ears

Daoguang Period, Qing Dynasty, H: 27.5cm; Diam.(at mouth): 15.5cm; Diam.(at foot): 13.8cm

172 浇黄釉盖罐（一对）

清宣统

通高 28.0 厘米　口径 9.5 厘米　足径 11.5 厘米

罐撇口、短束颈、鼓腹、腹下渐收敛、圈足。附伞形盖，盖顶置圆珠钮。内、外和圈足内均施黄釉。颈部自右向左横书青花楷体“坤宁宫祭器”。外底署青花楷体“大清宣统年制”六字双行款。

此盖罐为清代内廷祭祀用品。与国家祭祀用器有别，依清朝旧俗制作使用。依文献记载，内廷祭祀中使用瓷器者仅见于坤宁宫，此器当为在坤宁宫举行萨满教祭祀时所用。（唐雪梅）

Pair of Bright-Yellow-Glazed Jars and Covers

Xuantong Period, Qing Dynasty, H(with cover): 28.0cm; Diam.(at mouth): 9.5cm; Diam.(at foot): 11.5cm

坤寧宮祭器

坤寧宮祭器

173 白釉仿古铜纹登

清乾隆

通高 27.3 厘米　口径 16.1 厘米

登上部呈碗形，下接圆柱形足，足下有覆钵形底。通体内、外施青白色釉。附伞形盖，盖顶置圆珠钮。盖面刻回纹、云纹，盖口和登口部均刻回纹，腹部刻雷纹，足部刻云纹。造型规整，做工精细，与《皇朝礼器图式》记载相符。盖内顶和登外底均阴刻篆体“大清乾隆年制”六字三行款。

登原是中国古代贵族宴享时盛放食物的青铜器皿，后发展为祭祀用礼器，并出现瓷质登。用于盛放太羹（又称大羹，指不加任何调味品的肉汤）。其外形与豆相似，最直观的区分方法是观察盖钮，豆为绹钮（即绳钮），登为圆钮。聂崇义《三礼图》曰：“以其盛湆，故有盖。”清代祭器可根据不同材质、颜色区别其在祭祀中的不同功用和使用场合。据《皇朝礼器图式》记载，瓷登是乾隆十三年（1748 年）钦定祭器，器身口为回纹，中为雷纹，柱为饕餮，足为垂云纹。盖上为星纹，中为垂云纹，口亦为回纹。白釉瓷登用于先农坛、太岁坛正位和配位的祭祀活动。（鲍楠）

White-Glazed Covered Vessel Moulded in the Form of Ancient Bronze *Deng* with Incised Design of Archaistic Bronze Motifs

Qianlong Period, Qing Dynasty, H(with cover): 27.3cm; Diam.(at mouth): 16.1cm

174 **白釉仿古铜纹簠**

清乾隆

通高 23.5 厘米　口横 25.5 厘米　口纵 20.6 厘米

簠呈方斗形，仿古铜造型。腹壁斜收，盖顶置波浪形冠状棱。底足四边中间均有莲瓣状镂空，盖和腹部均置半环龙耳。通体施青白色釉。外壁刻夔龙纹、回纹、云纹等。造型规整，做工精细，与《皇朝礼器图式》记载相符。盖内顶和簠外底均阴刻篆体“大清乾隆年制”六字三行款。

白釉瓷簠用于先农坛、太岁坛正位和配位的祭祀活动。（鲍楠）

White-Glazed Covered Square Vessel in the Form of Ancient Bronze *Fu* with Incised Design of Archaistic Bronze Motifs

Qianlong Period, Qing Dynasty, H(with cover): 23.5cm; L(at mouth): 25.5cm; W(at mouth): 20.6cm

175 白釉仿古铜纹簋

清乾隆

通高 24.0 厘米　口横 23.5 厘米　口纵 18.7 厘米

簋呈椭圆体形，仿青铜器造型。腹部两侧对称置夔凤耳。通体施青白色釉。盖上置四棱，盖边刻云纹、回纹。簋外壁刻回纹、云纹、黻纹等。造型规整，做工精细，与《皇朝礼器图式》记载相符。盖内顶和簋外底均阴刻篆体“大清乾隆年制”六字三行款。

白色瓷簋用于先农坛、太岁坛正位和配位祭祀活动。（鲍楠）

White-Glazed Covered Round Vessel in the Form of Ancient Bronze *Gui* with Incised Design of Archaistic Bronze Motifs

Qianlong Period, Qing Dynasty, H(with cover): 24.0cm; L(at mouth): 23.5cm; W(at mouth): 18.7cm

176 白釉仿古铜纹铏

清乾隆

通高 26.7 厘米　口径 16.7 厘米

铏仿古铜铏造型。椭圆体形，盖上置三棱，腹部两侧对称置牺耳。通体施白釉。通体刻划藻纹、回纹、贝纹、云纹等。造型规整，做工精细，与《皇朝礼器图式》记载相符。盖内顶和铏外底均阴刻篆体“大清乾隆年制”六字三行款。

铏是古代盛羹的器皿，后被用于祭祀，成为礼器，用于盛放和羹（指配以各种调味品做成的肉汤）。《周礼·亨人》载：“祭祀，共铏羹。”注曰：“谓羹加五味，盛以铏器也。”清代祭器可根据不同材质、颜色区别其在祭祀中的不同功用和使用场合。据《皇朝礼器图式》记载，瓷铏为乾隆十三年（1748 年）钦定祭器，两耳为牺形，外壁自上而下依次绘藻纹、回纹、龟背锦纹等。盖外壁刻藻纹、回纹、雷纹，卍字锦纹等，上有三峰，饰以云纹，足纹同。白色瓷铏用于先农坛、太岁坛正位和配位的祭祀活动。（鲍楠）

White-Glazed Covered Vessel Moulded in the Form of Ancient Bronze *Xing* with Incised Design of Archaistic Bronze Motifs

Qianlong Period, Qing Dynasty, H(with cover): 26.7cm; Diam.(at mouth): 16.7cm

177 白釉仿古铜纹爵

清乾隆

高 18.0 厘米　流长 18.0 厘米

爵三戈足，腹部饰饕餮纹。通体施白釉，其纹饰与《皇朝礼器图式》记载的“腹为雷纹，饕餮形”基本相符。底部阴刻篆书“大清乾隆年制”六字三行款。

月白色瓷爵用于先农坛、太岁坛正位、配位的祭祀活动。（鲍楠）

White-Glazed Vessel in the Form of Ancient Bronze *Jue* with Incised Design of Archaistic Bronze Motifs

Qianlong Period, Qing Dynasty, H: 18.0cm; L of spout: 18.0cm

178 茄皮紫釉爵

清乾隆

高 10.8 厘米　流长 12.2 厘米

爵造型仿古铜爵。短流、有柄、三柱足。通体施茄皮紫釉，素面无纹饰。尺寸较祭祀常用爵小。外底阴刻篆体“乾隆年制”四字双行款，为乾隆时期的仿古产品。

蓝（青）色瓷爵用于天坛从位的祭祀活动。（鲍楠）

Aubergine-Glazed Vessel Moulded in the Form of Ancient Bronze *Jue*

Qianlong Period, Qing Dynasty, H: 10.8cm; L of Spout: 12.2cm

179 祭蓝釉仿古铜纹豆

清嘉庆

通高 26.0 厘米　口径 16.1 厘米

豆造型模仿古铜豆。钮为绳状。通体施祭蓝釉。外壁刻水波纹、云纹、回纹、黻纹等。盖内顶和豆外底均阴刻篆体“大清嘉庆年制”六字三行款。造型、纹饰与《皇朝礼器图式》记载大致相符，但与乾隆朝瓷豆相比，纹饰细节有差异。

祭蓝（青）色瓷豆用于天坛正位、配位、从位，祈谷坛正位、配位的祭祀活动。（鲍楠）

Sacrificial-Blue-Glazed Covered Vessel Moulded in the Form of Ancient Bronze *Dou* with Incised Design of Archaistic Bronze Motifs

Jiaqing Period, Qing Dynasty, H(with cover): 26.0cm; Diam.(at mouth): 16.1cm

180 # 祭蓝釉仿古铜纹簠

清嘉庆

通高 23.5 厘米　口横 25.1 厘米　口纵 19.5 厘米

簠造型、纹饰均模仿古铜簠。方斗形，腹壁斜收，顶置波浪形冠状棱。底足四边中部均有莲瓣形镂空，盖和器身均置半环龙耳。通体施祭蓝釉，外壁刻有夔龙纹、回纹、云纹等。造型规整，做工精细，与《皇朝礼器图式》记载相符。盖内顶和簠外底均阴刻篆体“大清嘉庆年制”六字三行款。

祭蓝（青）色瓷簠用于天坛正位、配位、从位以及祈谷坛正位、配位的祭祀活动。（鲍楠）

Sacrificial-Blue-Glazed Covered Square Vessel Moulded in the Form of Ancient Bronze *Fu* with Incised Design of Archaistic Bronze Motifs

Jiaqing Period, Qing Dynasty, H(with cover): 23.5cm; L(at mouth): 25.1cm; W(at mouth): 19.5cm

181 祭蓝釉仿古铜纹簋

清嘉庆

通高 23.0 厘米　口横 21.4 厘米　口纵 16.6 厘米

簋造型仿古铜簋。椭圆形，器身两侧置夔凤耳。通体施祭蓝釉，仿古造型。盖上置四棱，盖面刻云纹、回纹。簋体外壁刻回纹、云纹、黻纹等。造型规整，做工精细，与《皇朝礼器图式》记载相符。盖内顶和簋外底均阴刻篆体“大清嘉庆年制”六字三行款。

祭蓝（青）色瓷簋用于天坛正位、配位、从位，祈谷坛正位、配位的祭祀活动。（鲍楠）

Sacrificial-Blue-Glazed Covered Round Vessel Moulded in the Form of Ancient Bronze *Gui* with Incised Design of Archaistic Bronze Motifs

Jiaqing Period, Qing Dynasty, H(with cover): 23.0cm; L(at mouth): 21.4cm; W(at mouth): 16.6cm

182 祭蓝釉高足碗

清雍正

高 10.5 厘米　口径 18.3 厘米　足径 7.5 厘米

碗敞口、深弧腹、瘦底，底下承以外撇高足。碗内和高足内均施白釉，外施祭蓝釉。外底署青花篆体“大清雍正年制”六字三行款。（唐雪梅）

Sacrificial-Blue-Glazed Stem Bowl

Yongzheng Period, Qing Dynasty, H: 10.5cm; Diam.(at mouth): 18.3cm; Diam.(at foot): 7.5cm

183 祭红釉盅

清雍正

高 5.0 厘米　口径 5.7 厘米　足径 2.5 厘米

盅敞口、深弧腹、圈足。外壁施祭红釉，盅内和圈足内均施白釉。外底署青花楷体“大清雍正年制”六字双行外围双方框款。（唐雪梅）

Sacrificial-Red-Glazed Cup

Yongzheng Period, Qing Dynasty, H: 5.0cm; Diam.(at mouth): 5.7cm; Diam.(at foot): 2.5cm

184 祭红釉墩式碗

清雍正

高 6.0 厘米　口径 15.0 厘米　足径 6.5 厘米

碗敞口、深弧腹、圈足。外壁施祭红釉，碗内和圈足内均施白釉。外底署青花楷体“大清雍正年制”六字双行外围双圈款。（唐雪梅）

Sacrificial-Red-Glazed Deep Bowl

Yongzheng Period, Qing Dynasty, H: 6.0cm; Diam.(at mouth): 15.0cm; Diam.(at foot): 6.5cm

185 **祭红釉碗**

清雍正

高 6.0 厘米　口径 15.5 厘米　足径 5.2 厘米

碗敞口、深弧腹、圈足。外壁施祭红釉，碗内和圈足内均施白釉。外底署青花楷体“大清雍正年制”六字双行外围双圈款。（唐雪梅）

Sacrificial-Red-Glazed Bowl

Yongzheng Period, Qing Dynasty, H: 6.0cm; Diam.(at mouth): 15.5cm; Diam.(at foot): 5.2cm

186 祭红釉高足碗

清雍正

高 12.5 厘米　口径 18.0 厘米　足径 6.7 厘米

碗敞口、深弧腹、瘦底，下承以中空外撇高足。外壁施祭红釉，碗内和高足内均施白釉。高足内壁自右向左署青花楷体“大清雍正年制”款。（唐雪梅）

Sacrificial-Red-Glazed Stem Bowl

Yongzheng Period, Qing Dynasty, H: 12.5cm; Diam.(at mouth): 18.0cm; Diam.(at foot): 6.7cm

187 祭红釉盘

清雍正

高 3.5 厘米　口径 16.0 厘米　足径 10.0 厘米

盘撇口、浅弧腹、圈足。外壁施祭红釉，盘内和圈足内均施白釉。外底署青花楷体“大清雍正年制”六字双行外围双圈款。（唐雪梅）

Sacrificial-Red-Glazed Plate

Yongzheng Period, Qing Dynasty, H: 3.5cm; Diam.(at mouth): 16.0cm; Diam.(at foot): 10.0cm

188 祭红釉高足盘

清雍正

高 8.5 厘米　口径 20.5 厘米　足径 8.0 厘米

盘敞口、浅弧腹、瘦底，下承以中空外撇高足。高足自下而上三分之二处凸起一道弦纹。外壁施祭红釉，盘内和高足内均施白釉。外底署青花楷体“大清雍正年制”六字三行款。（唐雪梅）

Sacrificial-Red-Glazed Stem Plate

Yongzheng Period, Qing Dynasty, H: 8.5cm; Diam.(at mouth): 20.5cm; Diam.(at foot): 8.0cm

主题十七

庄严法相

清代宫廷宗教用瓷

清代历朝帝王均十分重视宗教，逐渐形成比以往朝代更具特色的宗教文化。紫禁城里与宗教相关的神殿佛堂，不仅数量多，而且种类全，可谓“儒、释、道”三教并存，圣人、佛相、天尊同在。此外，一些民间俗神和清代满族人所崇信的萨满祭祀，也各占有一席之地。

清代紫禁城内最重要的宗教形式是藏传佛教。故宫博物院收藏的瓷器中有不少清代宫廷遗留的藏传佛教用品，以乾隆朝景德镇御窑产品最为多见。如五供、佛塔、七珍、八宝、观音像、无量寿佛像、释迦牟尼佛像等。此类瓷器结构复杂，致使烧成难度极大。清宫档案记载乾隆十三年（1748 年）督陶官唐英奉旨烧造观音像，久造未成，乾隆帝严厉斥责唐英“烧造的观音如何还不得”，“想是唐英不至诚，着他至至诚诚烧造”，可印证这类瓷器烧造之不易。

Theme 17

Solemn Appearance

Imperial Porcelain for Religious Purpose in the Qing Dynasty

The emperors of the Qing Dynasty attached considerable importance to religion so that a religious view more distinctive than those of the previous dynasties was gradually developed. There are numerous religious shrines and holy temples in the Forbidden City, covering Confucianism, Buddhism and Taoism, where saint, Buddha and supernatural being co-existed. Likewise, some supernatural beings in folk tales and Manchu Shamanism managed to find their positions in it.

The most important religion in the Forbidden City at that time, however, was Tibetan Buddhism. Not a few of porcelains among the Palace Museum's collection are objects for Tibetan Buddhism used by the Imperial Court of the Qing Dynasty, such as altar set, Buddhist Pagoda, the Seven Buddhist Treasure, the Eight Buddist Auspicious Emblems, Figure of Bodhisattva *Guanyin*, Figure of Amitayus Buddha, Figure of Sakyamuni Buddha, etc. Most of them were fired by imperial kilns during the reign of the Qianlong Emperor. It was extremely challenging to fire these pieces of porcelains since their structures were highly complex. According to archive recorded for an occurrence in the 13th year of the Qianlong period, *TANG Ying*, the supervisor of the Imperial Porcelain Manufactory, failed to deliver a *Guanyin* figure for the court after repeated attempts for a long time. Qianlong Emperor blamed him severely for not being able to fire it with his deepest sincerity. This record is sufficient to prove how difficult it was to fire those porcelains.

松石绿地粉彩勾莲八吉祥纹五供（一组）

这套五供皆以松石绿色釉为地，绘八吉祥纹，周围辅以缠枝纹，炉口沿处、觚颈处均自右向左署金彩篆体“大清乾隆年制”六字一排款。此套五供造型规整、釉色均匀，所绘纹饰线条流畅，是乾隆朝景德镇御窑厂专门为宫廷佛堂烧造的供器。

五供，又称五具足、五献，为佛前庄严之物，由香炉、二烛台、二花瓶组成。在佛界，五供之香炉、烛台、花瓶具有不同含义。佛教认为炉燃香既可驱除恶臭断烦恼，又可提神醒脑增益；另以香比喻佛法之功德，上可达三境十天，下彻于九幽五道，传播佛法使众生受益。烛台的使用源于印度佛前献灯明之举，喻义在佛塔、佛像、经卷前燃灯能护大功德；另一方面也把灯明比喻成佛法和智慧，喻以智慧照破愚痴。花供养同样源于印度佛教仪式，由原先的散花盛于盘中，逐步演变为剪枝供佛，也有用纸、木做成莲花、荷叶等形象，染色涂金供于佛前，被称为常花。佛前供花既可装饰环境，又可使供养者获无量功德。（安静）

189 松石绿地粉彩勾莲八吉祥纹五供之——烛台（一对）

清乾隆

高 28.0 厘米　足径 12.9 厘米

Pair of Candle Stands with Design of the Eight Buddhist Auspicious Emblems and Delineated Lotus in *Famille Rose* on Turquoise Green Ground

Qianlong Period, Qing Dynasty, H: 28.0cm; Diam.(at foot): 12.9cm

190 松石绿地粉彩勾莲八吉祥纹五供之——花觚（一对）

清乾隆

高 28.0 厘米　口径 15.2 厘米

Pair of Beaker-Shaped Vases with Design of the Eight Buddhist Auspicious Emblems and Delineated Lotus in *Famille Rose* on Turquoise Green Ground

Qianlong Period, Qing Dynasty, H: 28.0cm; Diam.(at mouth): 15.2cm

191 松石绿地粉彩勾莲八吉祥纹五供之——香炉

清乾隆

高 28.5 厘米　口径 16.7 厘米　宽 29.3 厘米

Incense Burner with Design of the Eight Buddhist Auspicious Emblems and Delineated Lotus in *Famille Rose* on Turquoise Green Ground

Qianlong Period, Qing Dynasty, H: 28.5cm; Diam.(at mouth): 16.7cm; W: 29.3cm

192 黄绿地粉彩勾莲纹佛塔（一对）

清乾隆

高 31.0 厘米　底径 16.1 厘米

此塔为藏式塔。顶置如意宝瓶；下接宝盖，盖面饰淡黄地粉彩折枝宝相花纹，盖边饰淡粉红地胭脂红彩璎珞纹；颈部饰象征十三天的黄绿地粉彩折枝宝相花纹十三相轮；腹部饰黄绿地粉彩勾莲、兽面、璎珞纹等。腹部内空，开一欢门，内可放置佛像。最下是须弥方座，以粉红地缠枝、莲瓣纹等装饰。此塔属于供养塔，一般置于佛前供案上，以示观想。该塔系分段成型并烧成后，再黏合而成。做工精细，设色华丽，当为乾隆朝景德镇御窑厂专门为宫中佛堂烧造的供器。

塔最常见的是佛塔，意为坟、庙、高显处等，起源于印度。建塔原义有三种，即表人胜、为起信、为报恩。后为佛教所沿用，存放诸佛菩萨、祖师、高僧之遗骨舍利或佛经，以彰表其功德，并作供养礼拜用。久而演化为佛教的典型象征，并演变出多种形式。（安静）

Pair of Buddhist Pagodas with Design of Delineated Lotus in *Famille Rose* on Yellow and Green Ground

Qianlong Period, Qing Dynasty, H: 31.0cm; Diam.(at bottom): 16.1cm

193 祭蓝地粉彩勾莲纹佛塔

清乾隆

高 43.4 厘米　底径 18.3 厘米

此塔为藏式塔。中空，顶置如意宝瓶，下为粉色地宝盖。宝盖下是十三相轮，象征十三天。十三相轮、腹部均施祭蓝釉，釉上以金彩描绘勾莲、兽面、璎珞纹等。腹部正面开有欢门，内可置佛像。下承以白釉须弥方座，釉上以矾红彩描绘缠枝莲、莲瓣等图案。塔座中空，内可放置佛经。

此塔属于供养塔，一般置于佛前供案上。根据其制作工艺、瓷质、釉色、纹饰等判断，应是乾隆朝景德镇御窑厂专门为宫廷佛堂烧造的礼佛用器。（郑宏）

Buddhist Pagoda with Design of Delineated Lotus in *Famille Rose* on Sacrificial-Blue Ground

Qianlong Period, Qing Dynasty, H: 43.4cm; Diam.(at bottom): 18.3cm

194 粉彩三大士——狮犼观音菩萨

清乾隆

通高 92.0 厘米

底座高 22.0 厘米　长 56.0 厘米　宽 35.5 厘米

这尊狮犼观音菩萨雕像为分段烧制，上部为观音菩萨像，头戴五叶菩萨冠，冠带飘于耳的两侧，面相祥和，裸上身，胸佩璎珞，臂挽袈裟，左手拈莲茎于胸前；右手拈莲茎置于右膝。莲花沿双臂缠绕于左右肩头。下身着杏红地金色花纹裙，以右舒式坐于单层莲台上，赤双足，右脚踏小莲花。莲座下为观音菩萨的坐骑“犼”。“犼”外形如狮，通体施淡黄釉，头朝前向，身直立，四足抓地，瞪眼，张口作“吼”状。“犼”的头、颈与尾部饰金色鬃毛，颈系瑞音铃，身披璎珞，且其背部披蓝边黄地龙纹搭理，搭理两侧垂穗。观音菩萨及莲座侧置于“犼”的背上。观音像、莲座与“犼”间有暗榫相连接。“犼”的四足亦各踏一朵小莲花。在最下面，为长方形束腰紫檀木座，座面剔有四小莲花凹槽，紫檀木座四边刻有缠枝莲纹。

从这件狮犼观音像制作工艺看，佛像与坐骑均以塑、雕相结合手法制作而成，且施各色釉。从瓷佛像复杂的制作工艺、细密的瓷质、艳丽的釉色，可以确定，这是景德镇御窑厂专为清宫佛堂所烧造。

狮犼观音，亦称“阿摩提观音”，为三十三观音菩萨应身之一。以“吼”代表佛法宏大、威猛，可驱除恶魔，消除恐惧与疾苦。然“狮犼观音”在流传中，“吼”与“犼”字曾出现混淆。有学者认为，“犼”在东汉《说文解字》中并无此字。至宋《集韵 · 上厚》中，才以一种神兽出现。因“犼”的塑形又与“狮”十分相似，为有别文殊菩萨坐骑的“狮子吼”，改称观音菩萨之坐骑为“犼”。据明代《帝京景物略 · 西域双林寺》称：“寺殿所供，折法中三大士，西番变相也。像皆裸而跣，有冠，有裳，有金璎珞。犼、象、狮各出其座下。”狮犼观音曾盛行于明清时期，在汉、藏多地均有供奉。（李中路）

Famille Rose Figure of Bodhisattva Guanyin Riding a Lion

Qianlong Period, Qing Dynasty, H(with lion): 92.0cm; H(base):22.0cm; L(base): 56.0cm; W(base): 35.5cm

195 粉彩七珍——
金轮宝、摩尼宝、大臣宝、玉女宝、
白象宝、胜马宝、将军宝

清乾隆

通高 25.5 厘米　足径 10.4 厘米

这组七珍皆由七政宝插件和底座构成。通体粉彩装饰，彩料纯正，设色华丽。上插七政宝，形象生动，比例匀称。座外底均署矾红彩篆体“大清乾隆年制”六字三行款。堪称典型的乾隆朝景德镇御窑厂专门为宫廷佛堂烧造的佛前供器。

七珍亦称“七政宝”，由金轮宝、摩尼宝、大臣宝、玉女宝、白象宝、胜马宝、将军宝等组成。据佛经讲，七珍原为古印度神话中的转轮王以福力所生的 7 件宝物，既是转轮王的治国之宝，也是转轮王所拥有的权力象征。七珍还受到转轮王法力的保护。这 7 件宝物后来皆被佛教所沿袭，成为佛前供器。（安静）

金轮宝

摩尼宝

大臣宝

Famille Rose Statue *Gold Wheel, Mani Pearls, Able Ministers, Jewels, White Elephants, Dark Swift Horse, Loyal Generals* of the Seven Buddhist Treasures

Qianlong Period, Qing Dynasty, H(with base): 25.5cm; Diam.(at foot): 10.4cm

玉女宝

白象宝

胜马宝

将军宝

196 粉彩八宝
——法轮、胜幢、吉祥结、右旋海螺、妙莲、宝瓶、金鱼、宝伞

清乾隆

通高 23.2 厘米　足径 8.6 厘米

八宝均下承覆莲座，中间有云纹柱支撑。均通体以粉彩装饰，适当描绘金彩。造型别致，工艺精湛，装饰繁缛，设色富丽，具有典型的乾隆朝御窑瓷器特征。外底均署矾红彩篆体“大清乾隆年制”六字三行款。

八宝亦称“八吉祥”，属于佛前供器。通常与七珍（七政宝）合供于佛前。八宝由法轮、胜幢、吉祥结、右旋海螺、妙莲、宝瓶、金鱼、宝伞等 8 件宝物组成。在佛教文化中，它们分别象征佛教的 8 种吉祥寓意。即：法轮代表佛说大法圆转万劫不息；胜幢代表遍覆三千净一切乐；吉祥结代表徘徊贯彻，一切通明；右旋海螺代表菩萨果妙音吉祥；妙莲代表出五浊（劫浊、众生浊、命浊、烦恼浊、见浊等）世无所染；宝瓶代表福智圆满，具完无漏；金鱼代表坚固活泼，能解坏劫；宝伞代表张弛自如，曲覆众生。（安静）

法轮　胜幢　吉祥结　右旋海螺

Set of *Famille Rose* Eight Buddhist Auspicious Emblems – Wheel of Dharma, Canopy , Knotted Cord, White Conch Shell, Lotus Flower, Water Bottle, Two Golden Fishes, Precious Parasol

Qianlong Period, Qing Dynasty, H(with base): 23.2cm; Diam.(at foot): 8.6cm

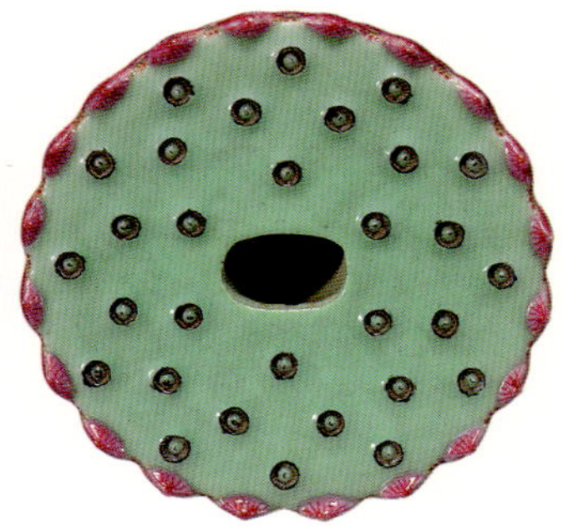

妙莲

宝瓶

金鱼

宝伞

197 粉彩加金无量寿佛坐像

清乾隆

通高 35.0 厘米　长 24.0 厘米　宽 20.0 厘米

此坐像属于藏传佛教造像。由像身、瓷座、木座三部分组成。无量寿佛头戴五叶冠，额束缯带，缯带至肩后上翘，绀发，发辫分绺，垂于肩部。双耳饰珰。身披披帛，披帛绕臂后下垂至座前。上身袒露，胸饰璎珞，臂腕饰钏，下穿饰有团花等图案的黄色长裙，长裙外穿饰有菊花等图案的暗红色短裙。双手托宝瓶，宝瓶上有莲花与摩尼宝。结跏趺坐。脚腕与足边饰联珠纹。面部与上身袒露处施金彩。座为施红彩近似倒三角形莲花台座。下承以木座。有黄条一，条上仅存“圣母皇太……赐”等字。此像原有方形佛龛，存放在紫禁城毓庆宫内。

毓庆宫原是康熙朝太子胤礽的住所，室内陈设在乾隆、嘉庆及光绪等朝曾有变动。据《故宫物品点查报告》记载，毓庆宫曾有佛教尊像、法器等陈设。依据佛像风格及黄条内容推测，此像可能在光绪朝被放置此处。（冯贺军）

Gilt-Decorated *Famille Rose* Figure of Seated Amitayus Buddha

Qianlong Period, Qing Dynasty, H(with base): 35.0cm; L: 24.0cm; W: 20.0cm

198　粉彩无量寿佛坐像

清乾隆

通高 29.3 厘米　底宽 21.2 厘米

此尊无量寿佛分佛身和底座两部分，系分别烧成后再组装而成。上部无量寿佛，全跏趺式坐于莲花座上。头戴五叶冠，蓝色发髻披于两肩，相貌端庄，鼻如悬胆，小口，大耳绝伦，佩以耳饰。上身披豆绿色袈裟，袈裟绘缠枝莲纹；下身穿松石绿地红色锦边粉彩花卉纹裙，胸佩粉彩嵌石璎珞，臂戴钏，挽豆绿色飘带；双手施禅定印，托淡红色摩尼宝瓶。在五叶冠、璎珞、臂钏、手环、脚环上，施以多色釉彩，代表镶嵌的红宝石、蓝宝石、绿松石、青金石等配饰。佛像体内中空，在身体下方开有一圆形孔洞，用于装藏。莲花座面正中也开有孔洞，孔洞四周立边设有榫件，可与佛像连为一体。莲座束腰，以“立粉”技法上、下对称勾勒仰、俯莲瓣轮廓。莲座两端垂有飘带。莲座底部内空，施以松石绿釉。

无量寿佛即阿弥陀佛，亦称“无量光佛”“接引佛”。系“西方极乐世界”的教主，它与观音菩萨、大势至菩萨并称“西方三圣”。

关于阿弥陀佛名号之由来，据梵本《阿弥陀经》和《称赞净土佛摄受经》载，此佛寿命无数、妙光无边，故后人又称之为无量寿佛、无量光佛。

由于无量寿佛被视为长寿象征，故清代宫廷常将其作为“吉祥之品”，供奉在清宫佛堂。每逢帝后寿诞吉庆日，文武百官竞将无量寿佛作祝寿寿礼进献到宫中，以祝福帝后万寿无疆。据乾隆《万寿庆典成案》载，仅乾隆四十五年（1780 年），百官进献的无量寿佛即多达 19934 尊。而清宫造办处也根据圣意制造过大量无量寿佛。因此，清宫里的无量寿佛不仅数量多、供奉广泛，而且材质也非常丰富，除瓷质外，还见有玉、珐琅、银、金质等，其中以铜镀金无量寿佛数量最多。无量寿佛虽“千佛一面”，但却给人们带来了无限美好遐想和祝福。

从这件无量寿佛胎质坚致、釉彩华丽之风格看，当为乾隆朝景德镇御窑厂专门为当时宫中佛堂所烧造。（李中路）

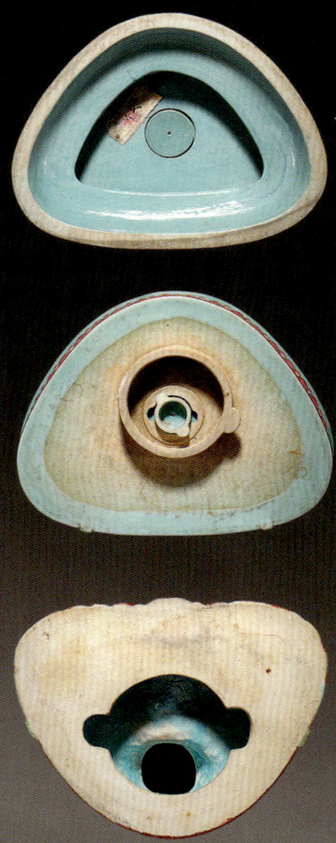

Famille Rose Figure of Seated Amitayus Buddha

Qianlong Period, Qing Dynasty, H(with base): 29.3cm; W(at base): 21.2cm

199 粉彩无量寿佛坐像

清乾隆

通高 29.3 厘米　底宽 21.2 厘米

这尊无量寿佛雕像分佛身和底座两部分，系分别烧成后再组装而成。其上部无量寿佛，相貌端庄，大耳绝伦。头戴五叶冠，上身披豆绿色袈裟，袈裟饰浅黄色斑点；下身穿明黄地金色团花纹裙，胸佩金彩嵌石璎珞，臂挽绿色飘带，全跏趺式坐于莲花座上。双手施禅定印，且手托淡红色摩尼宝瓶。在其五叶冠、璎珞、臂钏、手环、脚环上，施以多色釉彩，代表镶嵌的红宝石、蓝宝石、绿松石、青金石等配饰。佛像体内中空，在身体下方开有一圆形孔洞，用于装藏。佛像坐在椭圆形莲花座上，座面正中也开有孔洞，孔洞四周立边并设有榫件，可与佛像连为一体。莲座束腰，以"立粉"技法上、下对称勾勒红色仰、俯莲瓣。莲坐两端垂有飘带。莲座底部内空，施以松石绿釉。

从这件无量寿佛胎质坚致、釉彩华丽之风格看，当为乾隆朝景德镇御窑厂专门为当时宫中佛堂所烧造。(李中路)

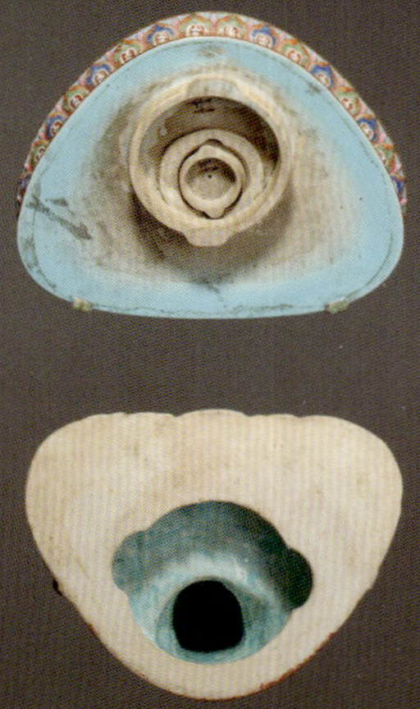

Famille Rose Figure of Seated Amitayus Buddha

Qianlong Period, Qing Dynasty, H(with base): 29.3cm; W(at base): 21.2cm

200 粉彩阿弥陀佛坐像

清乾隆

通高 45.5 厘米　底宽 28.7 厘米

此尊粉彩佛像面容祥和，螺发，圆脸宽额，双目低垂，耳大绝伦，发中带有肉髻。其面部、手和胸部均施金彩，使佛像更显神圣庄严。佛像上身穿红色锦边暗花袈裟，下身着橘红色锦边暗花裙。佛像身体中空，在其背部开有一圆形小孔，用于装藏，并扣有圆盖。佛像双手施禅定印，以全跏趺式坐于莲花座上。座束腰，上、下对称刻仰、俯莲瓣纹，莲瓣均以藕荷色彩描绘。莲座底部内空，施以松石绿釉。

此佛像造型规整、胎质坚致、色彩华丽，当为乾隆朝景德镇御窑厂专门为宫中佛堂所烧造。（李中路）

Famille Rose Figure of Seated Amitabha

Qianlong Period, Qing Dynasty, H(with base): 45.5cm; W(at base): 28.7cm

201 粉彩阿弥陀佛坐像

清乾隆

通高 45.5 厘米　底宽 28.7 厘米

此尊粉彩佛像面容祥和，螺发，圆脸宽额，双目低垂，耳大绝伦，发中带有肉髻。其面部、手和胸部均施金彩，使佛像更显神圣庄严。佛像上身穿红色锦边暗花袈裟，下身着橘红色锦边暗花裙。佛像身体中空，在其背部开有一圆形小孔，用于装藏，并扣有圆盖。佛像双手施禅定印（左手拇指旧伤缺），以全跏趺式坐于莲花座上。座束腰，上、下对称仰、俯莲瓣纹，莲瓣均以藕荷色彩描绘。莲座底部内空，施以松石绿釉。

此佛像造型规整、胎质坚致、色彩华丽，当为乾隆朝景德镇御窑厂专门为宫中佛堂所烧造。（李中路）

Famille Rose Figure of Seated Amitabha

Qianlong Period, Qing Dynasty, H(with base): 45.5cm; W(at base): 28.7cm

202 粉彩释迦牟尼佛坐像

清乾隆

通高 45.5 厘米　底宽 28.7 厘米

此尊粉彩佛像面容祥和，螺发，圆脸宽额，双目低垂，耳大绝伦，发中带有肉髻。其面部、手和胸部均施金彩，使佛像更显神圣庄严。佛像上身穿红色锦边暗花袈裟，下身着橘红色锦边暗花裙。佛像身体中空，在其背部开有一圆形小孔，用于装藏，并扣有圆盖。佛像左手托钵（缺失），施禅定印，右手于胸前施说法印，以全跏趺式坐于莲花座上。座束腰，上、下对称绘仰、俯莲瓣纹，莲瓣均以藕荷色彩描绘。莲座底部内空，施以松石绿釉。

此佛像造型规整、胎质坚致、色彩华丽，当为乾隆朝景德镇御窑厂专门为宫中佛堂所烧造。（李中路）

Famille Rose Figure of Seated Shakyamuni Buddha
Qianlong Period, Qing Dynasty, H(with base): 45.5cm; W(at base): 28.7cm

203 粉彩观音菩萨坐像

清乾隆

通高 29.8 厘米　座长 20.9 厘米　座宽 16.9 厘米

汉传佛教造像。像之身体、台座分体制作，组合而成。观音束高发髻，发丝细密卷曲，插如意头簪子。头戴浅蓝色观音兜，颈饰项圈，项圈上垂坠串珠璎珞。身穿白色天衣，天衣上刻划繁密的花卉图案。双手合十，下穿浅绿色长裙，结跏趺坐于施浅红彩近似倒三角形的莲花台座上。像背开有榫口的孔，供装藏用。（冯贺军）

Famille Rose Figure of Seated Bodhisattva Guanyin

Qianlong Period, Qing Dynasty, H(with base): 29.8cm; L(at base): 20.9cm; W(at base): 16.9cm

204 粉彩阿弥陀佛坐像

清乾隆

通高 33.6 厘米

此尊佛像头戴五叶冠，发髻高挽，面容清秀，略带微笑，双目低垂，耳大绝伦，颇显祥和。其面、手和胸部皆施肉粉色釉。上身穿浅蓝地云纹红色锦边袈裟，下身着黄地金色团花裙。胸佩璎珞。佛像身体中空，双手施禅定印，以全跏趺式坐于莲花座上。背部开有一圆形小孔，用于装藏，并扣有圆形小盖。座面绘莲子图案。莲座中间束腰，以上下对称的雕瓷方法，雕刻多层仰、俯莲瓣。莲座底部内空，并施以松石绿釉。

此尊造像具有浓重的汉像风格。其造型规整、胎质坚致、色彩华丽，当为乾隆朝景德镇御窑厂专门为宫中佛堂所烧造。（李中路）

Famille Rose Figure of Seated Amitabha

Qianlong Period, Qing Dynasty, H(with base): 33.6cm

专论

Essays

略谈如何欣赏中国古陶瓷

吕成龙

图1　商代早期　原始瓷青釉尊
郑州二里岗商城遗址出土
中国国家博物馆藏

在博大精深的中国古代艺苑中，陶瓷宛如一朵绚丽的奇葩，它历史悠久，光彩夺目，令人叹为观止。

陶瓷是“土与火”的艺术。考古发掘所获得的资料证明，我们的祖先早在距今约两万年以前就已能制造和使用陶器，因此，中国成为世界上最早烧造和使用陶器的国家。

在长期烧造陶器的基础上，到了距今约三四千年前的夏、商时代，以浙江省德清县为中心的东苕溪流域已开始烧造原始青瓷（图1）。经过西周、春秋、战国、秦、西汉的发展，窑工不断改进原料加工和窑炉技术，原始瓷的质量得到不断提高（图2至图5），至一千八百多年前的东汉时期，终于完成了从原始瓷向真正瓷器的过渡，在世界上率先发明了瓷器（图6）。

因此，我们可以自豪地说，中国不仅是世界上最早烧造和使用陶器的国家，而且还在世界范围内率先发明了瓷器。瓷器是中国独享的一项重大发明，堪称对人类文明做出的杰出贡献之一。

陶瓷是中国物质文化的重要组成部分，是一部“变土为宝”的华丽篇章。它历史悠久、自成一体，脉络清晰地向人们传达着古代政治、经济、文化和古人的审美意识。无论是绚丽斑斓的唐三彩、“千峰翠色”般的唐代越窑青瓷、“如冰似玉”般的宋代官窑青瓷、色彩缤纷的明清御窑五彩瓷、色泽优雅的元明清青花瓷、雍容华贵的清代珐琅彩瓷和洋彩瓷，还是五光十色的元明清颜色釉瓷，无不以其永恒的艺术魅力博得世界各国人民的钟爱和称赞。

一方面，中国古陶瓷凭借其自身的实用性、观赏性和独特的古老东方文化的艺术魅力，受到越来越多西方人士的

图2　西周　原始瓷青釉四系罐

图3　春秋　原始瓷青釉印纹罐
萧山博物馆藏

图4　战国　原始瓷青釉鼎
萧山博物馆藏

图5　西汉　原始瓷青釉双系瓿
萧山博物馆藏

图6　东汉　青釉四系罐
山东博物馆藏

喜爱；另一方面，中国古陶瓷所蕴含的深厚民族性、古人的审美意识和思维方式，也得到众多国内和海外华人的认同。因此，近几十年来，中国古陶瓷成为国内外古董商和收藏家竞相追逐的热点，几乎每一场有关中国古陶瓷的专场拍卖会都能吸引来自世界各地的众多买家。拍卖会上价格竞争之激烈，常令人始料不及。

人们可能禁不住会问，这些由普通陶土或瓷土制作而成的陶瓷器，为什么会比黄金珠宝还贵重？

诚然，中国古陶瓷必定有其自身的美感，那么，中国古陶瓷之美究竟美在哪里？笔者认为中国古陶瓷之美主要体现在造型、釉质和装饰三个方面。

一　造型美

中国古陶瓷素以造型丰富、式样优美而著称于世。由于陶土和瓷土都具有良好的可塑性，因此，与金属材料、石质材料、木质材料等相比，陶瓷材料不但取材容易、价格低廉，而且在塑造形体方面更便于操作，因而具有更大的优越性，更易于普及。但由于时代不同、生产力发展水平的差异以及人们生活习俗和审美趣味有别，致使各时代陶瓷造型呈现不同的风貌。如唐代陶瓷造型之圆润饱满、宋代陶瓷造型之秀丽典雅、元代陶瓷造型之雄浑朴拙、明代永乐宣德瓷器造型之端庄稳重、明代成化瓷器造型之隽秀典雅、明代嘉靖隆庆万历瓷器造型之复杂多变、清代康熙瓷器造型之刚劲挺拔、清代雍正瓷器造型之文雅精细、清代乾隆瓷器造型之严谨规整等。

中国传统瓷器造型可分为以下几大类。

第一类是模仿大自然中物质形态的造型。从新石器时代某些陶器造型如葫芦瓶、鹰形鼎、鸟形鬶等可以看出，中国传统陶瓷造型是从模仿自然界物质形态开始的，以后历朝直至今天这种造型方法都被广泛采用。有人称这种造型方法为“象形取意”[1]。这类陶瓷造型源于大自然，因而使人观之倍感亲切，故深受人们喜爱，在我国陶瓷中占有较大比重，不胜枚举。如荷叶形盘、海棠式盘、葵花式盘、菱花式盘、菊花式盘、梅花式碟、菊花式碗、荷花形碗、莲子形杯、鸟形杯、牡丹式吸杯、楸叶式洗、桃式洗、苹果形尊、石榴式尊、莱菔式尊、牛头式尊、马蹄形尊、橄榄式瓶、葫芦式瓶、柳叶形瓶、鸡腿式瓶、天球形瓶、蒜头形瓶、荸荠形瓶、鱼形瓶、鸡冠式壶、梨形执壶、鸳鸯式水注、菱花式花盆、葵花式花盆、海棠式花盆、鸭式香熏、葵花式盒、菊瓣式盒、瓜式盒等。它们都是以自然界的物质形态为基础，加以概括、变形、夸张而成。

第二类是由各部分组合而成、缺一不可的造型。受中国传统文化中追求大而全、和谐美满理念的影响，中国传统陶瓷的造型特别注重完整性的体现，尤其是瓶、罐、壶、尊之类的造型，一般都由口、颈、肩、腹、胫、底、足等几部分组合而成，缺了其中任何一部分都会使人觉得不完整。有些器物还要加上耳、系、流、柄、盖等其他附件，但均要照顾到上下对照呼应、左右对称均衡的关系。这种对造型完整性的追求，使欣赏者能够得到心平气和的美感。

第三类是规范化、程式化的造型。受中国传统文化中“求大同、存小异”思想的影响，中国传统陶瓷造型还体现出较强的规范化和程式化特点。这类陶瓷的造型强调的是在形体基本模式相同、结构固定的情况下，追求一些细微的变化。

例如，凡是梅瓶，均可用小口、短颈、丰肩、长腹、瘦胫、圈足来表述；凡是玉壶春瓶，均可用撇口、束颈、垂腹、圈足来表述；凡是撇口碗，均可用撇口、深弧腹、瘦底、圈足来表述。这类陶瓷造型都是经过陶工在长期实践中不断修改、反复推敲而成，总体上都给人以形态匀称、比例适度、整体和谐之美感。当然，这类陶瓷造型会因时代不同而出现一些细微变化，给人带来不同的审美享受。以梅瓶为例，唐代梅瓶显得矮胖壮实（图7）、宋代梅瓶显得挺拔秀丽（图8）、元代梅瓶显得浑厚朴实（图9）、明代永乐宣德朝梅瓶则显得沉稳端庄（图10）。

受儒家中庸思想影响，中国传统陶瓷造型在外形轮廓线运用方面，多采用缓柔的自由曲线，很少采用生硬的直线（图11），故在形体上给人以委婉曲折、自由生动之美感[2]。

图7　唐　白釉梅瓶
故宫博物院藏

图8　北宋　定窑白釉刻花梅瓶
故宫博物院藏

图9　元　青花云龙纹梅瓶
故宫博物院藏

图10　明永乐　青花桃竹图梅瓶
故宫博物院藏

图11　清雍正　祭红釉石榴尊

总的来说，中国传统陶瓷造型在形体上主要强调静态展示，各类造型都着重追求平稳、对称、均衡等，不太强调动势，故均给人以含蓄隽永之视觉感受。

二　釉色美

颜色釉陶瓷是中国陶瓷中的一大门类，如果从夏代开始出现的高温青釉算起，中国颜色釉陶瓷的烧造至今已有四千多年的历史。在历代陶工的不断探索下，新的釉色品种层出不穷，至清代康熙、雍正、乾隆时期，可谓盛况空前，体现在烧造技术炉火纯青，釉色品种已达数十种，将中国陶瓷百花园装点得绚丽多姿。

陶瓷颜色釉之所以能产生色彩，主要是由于釉层对光的选择性吸收和散射所造成[3]。众所周知，太阳光是一种包含各种波长的复色光，而人的肉眼所能见到的只是波长介于770 ~ 393纳米的光，也就是可见光谱上所显示的赤、橙、黄、绿、青、蓝、紫等七色光。不同物质对各种波长光的散射和吸收程度不同，于是就产生了各种不同的颜色。人的肉眼所看到的就是物质散射出来的光。

例如对一件红釉瓷器来说，人的肉眼之所以观察到的釉色是红色，是因为釉中所含氧化亚铜胶体粒子对红色以外的其他光线吸收能力很强，而对红色光线则基本不吸收，产生散射，因此人的肉眼看到的就是釉层散射出来的红色光。

各种金属元素的离子或由它们组合而成的化合物的粒子都有发色的本领，陶瓷颜色釉就是利用它们来呈色。

在清代康熙以前，我国传统颜色釉（青釉、黑釉、蓝釉、高温红釉、绿釉、黄釉、紫釉、酱釉、茶叶末釉等）中的着色金属元素主要有铁、铜、钴、锰、镁等。从清代康熙朝开始，随着欧洲画珐琅料的传入，窑工们又逐渐掌握了锑、金等金属元素的呈色机理，创烧出蛋黄釉（亦称淡黄釉、柠檬黄釉、洋黄釉、锑黄釉等）、金红釉（包括胭脂紫、胭脂水、淡粉红等）等著名色釉。

颜色釉的呈色除了依赖釉的配方以外，烧成温度和窑内气氛对釉的呈色也会产生间接影响。

例如含有适量氧化铜的釉，在氧化焰中可烧成绿色，而在还原焰中则可烧成红色。

再如我们经常说传世宋代哥窑瓷器的釉色有青灰、粉青、炒米黄等，其实这些釉的配方一样，之所以会产生不同的颜色，是因为各自在窑内的摆放位置不同、感受到的温度和气氛不同所致。

从严格意义上说，我们几乎不可能找到两件呈色完全一致的颜色釉瓷，对于高温颜色釉瓷尤其如此。

图 12　清乾隆　祭蓝釉梅瓶

图 13　清乾隆　粉青釉葫芦瓶
故宫博物院藏

图 14　清乾隆　茄皮紫釉花插
故宫博物院藏

图 15　明宣德　紫金釉盘
故宫博物院藏

图 16　明永乐二十一年　黑釉双耳香炉
1999 年出土于景德镇市珠山
景德镇市陶瓷考古研究所藏

由上述可知，各种颜色釉瓷，无论是一色釉瓷，还是窑变花釉瓷，大抵都是通过合理的釉料配方、严格控制烧成温度方能使釉产生光彩夺目的美感。颜色釉瓷的美在于人工与自然的巧妙结合。

在颜色釉瓷器上，人工附加装饰已居于次要地位。因此，与各种彩绘瓷相比，颜色釉瓷更能使人领悟中国陶瓷艺术的真谛以及高雅含蓄的内涵。颜色釉瓷的美主要体现在以下几个方面。

1. 单色釉的纯净美

均匀、纯净是人们对单色釉瓷的基本要求。单色釉瓷通体浑然一色，纯洁莹亮。人们在欣赏单色釉瓷时，不禁会惊叹人间妙手巧夺天工、偶得天然神韵之绝技。不同颜色的单色釉瓷能给人视觉带来不同美感，如祭红釉之深沉、郎窑红釉之明艳、豇豆红釉之妩媚、祭蓝釉之静穆（图 12）、粉青釉之淡雅（图 13）、茄皮紫釉之高贵（图 14）、紫金釉之沉稳（图 15）、娇黄釉之尊贵、甜白釉之洁净、黑釉之静谧（图 16）……

2. 窑变花釉的幻化美

颜色釉瓷在烧成过程中出现各种变幻莫测的现象，被称作“窑变”，顾名思义是窑内变化所得。关于窑变，宋代景德镇陶工曾将其视为“怪胎”，认为出现窑变是不祥之兆。至清代则被视作祥瑞之征。如乾隆九年二月初八日督陶官唐英（1682 ～ 1756 年）在奏折中写道：“内务府员外郎管理九江关务奴才唐英谨奏为奏明事。窃奴才……于捌年拾壹月内，奴才在厂制造霁红瓷器，得窑变圆器数种，计共贰拾陆件。虽非霁红正色，其釉水变幻实数十年来未曾经见，亦非人力可以制造。故窑户偶得一窑变之件，即为祥瑞之征，视同珍玩。至霁红一种，出窑之后，除正色之外，类皆黑暗不堪，从未有另变色泽生疏鲜艳者。今现得霁红、窑变各种，理合一并奏进。伏祈皇上睿鉴。谨奏。”[4]

图 17　清雍正　窑变釉如意耳弦纹尊

窑变花釉能给人带来抽象朦胧之美感（图 17），有的清虚淡远，有的扑朔迷离。俗话说“窑变无双”，那种隐隐约约难以言传的奥妙和幽玄，使人产生无穷遐想。

再如茶叶末釉，釉面上密密匝匝的铁、镁结晶仿佛佳茗细末浮于水面，或如繁星闪烁苍穹，被认为是一种能养目的釉（图 18）。

图 18　清乾隆　茶叶末釉四连瓶

3. 缺陷给人带来的奇妙美

窑火能赋予颜色釉美丽的色泽，也会使釉面留下缺憾。但鉴赏者若能站在审美的高度观察其种工艺缺陷，则会产生不可名状的惊喜。

如釉面开片本是因陶瓷胎釉膨胀系数不同而造成的一种工艺缺陷，但窑工可以充分利用这种缺陷，通过合理调整胎、釉配方和控制烧成后期的冷却速度，使釉面产生纵横交错、疏密有致的裂纹，平静的釉面遂产生一种韵律美（图 19）。

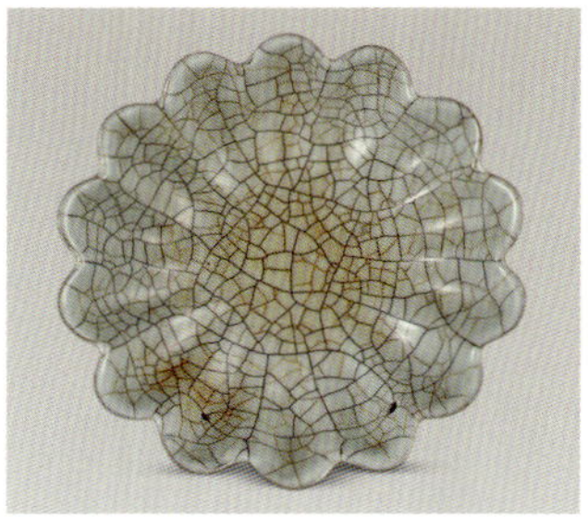

图19　南宋　哥窑灰青釉菊花式盘
故宫博物院藏

图20　清康熙　豇豆红釉锡锣洗

图21　清雍正　祭红釉胆式瓶

图22　清康熙　郎窑红釉观音瓶

再如豇豆红釉瓷器在烧成时常会泛出星星点点的绿斑（图20），这本来是一种工艺缺陷，但正是这种偶然出现的不确定性缺陷，反倒使平凡的釉色产生妙趣横生的多样性，令人回味。

4．釉色与造型的和谐美

不同的釉色只有配以相应的造型方能尽显釉色之美，古代窑工深谙其中的哲理。

如高温铜红釉有祭红、郎窑红、豇豆红釉之分，但并不是所有的器物都适合用这三种釉装饰。

深沉安定的祭红釉适合装饰大小适中的瓶（图21）、罐、壶、炉、洗、盘、碗等；酣畅淋漓的郎窑红釉适合装饰瓶（图22）、尊等稍大一些的立件；而典雅妩媚的豇豆红釉却最适合装饰小巧的瓶、洗、盒、尊（图23）、水丞等小件文具。

再如呈色幽雅的胭脂水釉、淡黄釉每见于小巧的碗（图24、图25）、盘、杯、瓶等器物上；而色彩浓烈的窑变花釉则多施在大件或中等大小的瓶、罐、缸（图26）等类器上。

由此可见，只有将釉色与造型有机结合起来，才能使颜色釉的天然丽质得以充分体现，这似乎与不同体型的人适合穿不同颜色的衣服一个道理。

三　纹饰美

如果将陶瓷的造型比作人的骨架，将釉比作人穿的衣服，那么，纹饰就好比衣服上的花纹。中国传统陶瓷非常讲究装饰，不但装饰手法多样，而且装饰纹样亦很丰富，图案布局更是新颖别致。在装饰技法方面，或刻、划、印、剔、镂、雕、彩绘等单独使用，或综合几种技法共同装饰一件器物。各种技法均有代表性的窑口。

例如北宋耀州窑以刻花技法独领风骚，其刻花青瓷刀锋犀利、线条洒脱、图案清晰，宛如浅浮雕（图27）。

北宋越窑划花青瓷，图案线条纤柔流畅，细如发丝（图28）。

北宋、金代定窑印花瓷器，构图严谨，图案工整（图29）。

北宋当阳峪窑剔花白瓷，地色深褐，图案洁白，颜色对比强烈（图30）。

清代乾隆时期景德镇御窑洋彩镂空转心瓶上的镂空装饰，构思巧妙，透过外瓶上的

图23　清康熙　豇豆红釉太白尊

图24　清雍正　胭脂水釉碗

图25　清雍正　淡黄釉碗

图26　清乾隆　窑变釉缸

图 27　北宋　耀州窑青釉刻划花卉纹注壶

图 28　北宋　越窑青釉刻划鹦鹉纹盘　英国伦敦大维德基金会藏

图 29　北宋至金　定窑白釉印花孔雀牡丹纹盘

图 30　北宋　当阳峪窑白釉剔划缠枝花纹器座　香港艺术馆藏

图 31　清乾隆　洋彩镂空转心瓶

图 32　唐　三彩牵马人和马俑　1981 年洛阳龙门定远将军安菩墓出土　洛阳文物考古工作队藏

图 33　唐　长沙窑釉下褐绿彩花鸟图枕

图 34　元　磁州窑白地黑花人物故事图长方枕

镂空可以窥见内瓶上的图案花纹（图 31）。

唐代三彩陶俑，雕塑技法精湛，形象栩栩如生（图 32）。

唐代长沙窑、宋金元时代磁州窑以及元明清时代景德镇窑彩绘瓷，或在釉下彩绘，或在釉上彩绘，或釉下彩绘与釉上彩绘相结合，将中国陶瓷百花园装点得异彩纷呈（图 33、图 34、图 35）。

在装饰纹样方面，人们喜闻乐见的各种动物、植物、花卉、花鸟、花果、山水、人物、几何、文字（图 36）等无不采用。特别是各种寓意吉祥的图案，更是受到人们广泛喜爱。例如，牡丹寓意富贵，桃子寓意长寿，石榴寓意多子，鸳鸯寓意成双，喜鹊寓意喜庆，鹿寓意禄位，蝙蝠寓意福（图 37），鱼寓意富足有余，鹌鹑寓意平安，灯笼象征五谷丰登。牡丹与缠枝莲相配，寓意连连富贵；牡丹与八吉祥相配，寓意富贵吉祥；牡丹与玉兰、海棠相配，寓意玉堂富贵（图 38）；莲花与鹭鸶相配，寓意科举考试一路连科；枸杞与菊花相配，寓意杞菊延年；葫芦与蝙蝠相配，寓意“福禄”（图 39）；鹌鹑与菊花相配，寓意安居乐业。蜜蜂与猴子相配，寓意世代封侯；松树与仙鹤相配，寓意松鹤延年；戟、磬、瓶相配，寓意吉庆平安；松、竹、梅相配，被喻为“岁寒三友”（图 40），寓意清高。

在图案布局方面，或二方连续，或四方连续，或散点式，不拘一格。

图 35　清雍正　斗彩花卉纹如意耳瓶
故宫博物院藏

图 36　清康熙　青花万寿尊
香港中文大学文物馆藏

图 37　清雍正　釉里红五蝠纹碗

图 38　清雍正　粉彩玉堂富贵图盘口瓶
故宫博物院藏

图 39　清雍正　黄地洋彩蝙蝠衔结带葫芦纹碗
故宫博物院藏

图 40　清雍正　青花釉里红松竹梅竹叶藏诗梅瓶　故宫博物院藏

总之，中国陶瓷以大约两万年延绵不断的历史成为世界工艺美术史上的一大奇迹。其在造型、釉色、纹饰等方面凝聚了不同历史时期社会政治、经济、文化和人们的审美意识。

虽然历史上遗留下来的陶瓷器数量有限，但是它们所给人带来的美感却无限和永恒。随着社会经济的发展和人们对文化需求的不断提高，中国陶瓷必将受到愈来愈多人的喜爱，中国陶瓷所蕴含的博大精深的文化，必将成为未来陶瓷创新发展取之不尽、用之不竭的源泉。

注释

1　杨永善：《陶瓷造型与装饰的关系》，《装饰》2000 年第 1 期。

2　杨永善：《陶瓷造型与装饰的关系》，《装饰》2000 年第 1 期。

3　潘文锦、潘兆鸿：《景德镇的颜色釉》，江西教育出版社，1986 年。

4　铁源、李国荣主编：《清宫瓷器档案全集》，中国画报出版社，2008 年。

A Brief Remark on Appreciation of Chinese Antique Ceramics

Lü Chenglong

Abstract

Throughout the long history of Chinese art, ancient ceramics have held a high and crucial position with their breathtaking splendor.

China was the first country in the world not only to fire and use pottery, but also to invent porcelain. Porcelain, a significant invention uniquely belonging to China, has made an outstanding contribution to human civilization.

In recent decades, almost every exhibition of Chinese antique ceramics held in China or abroad drew a large number of visitors. Chinese antique ceramics have become great attractions which are highly sought after by antique dealers and collectors at home or abroad who rush to auctions to buy those cultural relics through unanticipated and bidding battles. Quite often, a piece of exquisite Chinese antique ceramic can be auctioned very easily for millions, or tens of millions, or even hundreds of millions RMB Yuan.

The fact that Chinese antique ceramics are frequently sold at auctions for high prices and received therefore the earnest attention gives rise to such question: why are those ceramics, made of common and easily accessible material, i.e., pottery clay or white clay, more valuable than gold or jewels? The reason for it is the profound cultural connotations enshrined in Chinese antique ceramics and their aesthetics. Then, in which way do they embody the sense of aesthetics?

In my view, Chinese antique ceramics can be appreciated from three aspects: shape, glaze and decoration.

Keywords

ceramics, appreciation

从清宫档案看清代宫廷用瓷的烧造方式

赵聪月

清代宫廷用瓷的烧造过程，经历了承继、发展、鼎盛、衰落、复兴再逐渐衰落的几个阶段。立国之初，由于朝廷无暇顾及瓷器生产，对景德镇窑场采取了“有命则供，无命则止”的烧造方式。至康熙时期，景德镇瓷业才逐渐得以重视，实行了“官搭民烧”政策，并开始派督陶官统领景德镇窑务，从而促进其发展起来，“查十九年烧造磁器至二十五年工竣，已逾五载之久，而烧成磁器共得一十五万二千余件，动用江省钱粮银一万三百余两”[1]。雍正、乾隆时期的景德镇制瓷业得到了极大的发展并达到鼎盛，这一时期的制瓷技艺娴熟精湛，不仅产量巨大，质量高超，而且釉色品种空前丰富，其胎釉精良细腻，绘画工整考究，造型极尽其巧。嘉庆时期完全继承了前朝风格，但大大减少了烧造年份，皇帝亲自下旨减少内务府用于烧造瓷器的支出，“嘉庆四年，内务府议奏所存磁器甚多，嗣后行令九江关烧造磁器，每年统以五千两银数为率，烧造圆琢磁器。嘉庆十一年，奉旨饬令九江关，按照减半之例，二千五百两银数，尽数烧造，钦此。嘉庆十五年，奉旨九江关十六年分，年例烧造磁器着暂行停止，改烧磁砖”[2]。这为我们解释了嘉庆时期御用瓷器库存数量、品种减少的原因。道光时期，由于道光帝个人的爱好，宫廷御用瓷器烧造的品种、数量较之嘉庆时期均有上升，道光元年（1821 年）即饬令九江关监督“解交大运圆、琢器并天坛、奉先殿等处应用磁祭器以及御茶膳房、寿康宫茶膳房应用磁器”[3]。咸丰以后逐渐衰落，咸丰元年（1851 年）爆发了太平天国运动，致使清王朝动荡不安，此时的景德镇瓷业因时局而每况愈下，最终御窑场于咸丰五年停止生产。同治五年（1866 年），御窑场开始逐渐恢复生产，但仅勉强烧制了大运及同治大婚用瓷。光绪时期，烧造品种略有增加，质量也有所提高。宣统时期，由于时局的变化，景德镇仅为宫廷烧制了两年御用瓷器。通过查阅清宫遗留的档案，梳理其烧造过程，我们能清晰地看到清代御用瓷器的烧造，主要是采用了大运、奉旨传办、年贡及奉文传办瓷器四种方式。

一　大运瓷器

所谓大运瓷器从字义上解释就是指大批运输的瓷器，从实际烧造情况看是指御窑厂每年年底在清宫内务府奏销，按年例不用皇帝另外下旨，按固定的瓷样，定式烧造且统一运至京城，交付清宫瓷库的器物。现常被称作传统品种，一般创烧于康乾盛世，有些陈设器品种则来源于宋、元、明时期的瓷器造型，颜色釉器多是沿用明代形制。但真正形成固定瓷样，按例烧造则始于乾隆十二年（1747 年），据档案记载“内务府大臣具奏呈览，乾隆十二年十二月二十一日奉旨将选定瓷器交唐英，嗣后烧造俱照现今发去样款为定，琢器五十二件样式，尺寸不许更改，其颜色、花纹或于

图1　清乾隆　仿哥釉八卦琮式瓶　故宫博物院藏

图2　清嘉庆　仿哥釉八卦琮式瓶　故宫博物院藏

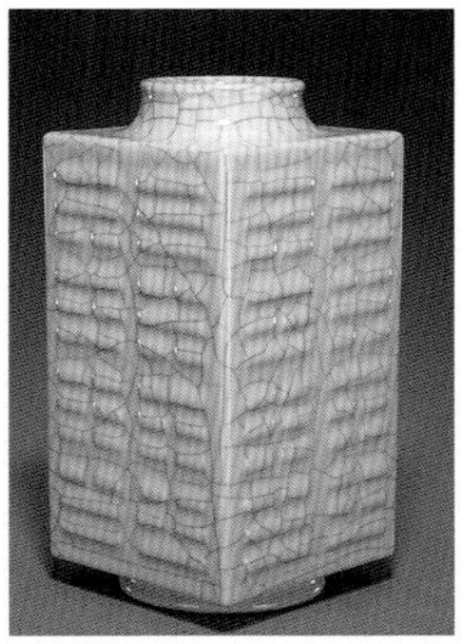

图3　清道光　仿哥釉八卦琮式瓶　故宫博物院藏

图4　清咸丰　仿哥釉八卦琮式瓶　故宫博物院藏

图5　清同治　仿哥釉八卦琮式瓶　故宫博物院藏

图6　清光绪　仿哥釉八卦琮式瓶　故宫博物院藏

图7　清宣统　仿哥釉八卦琮式瓶　故宫博物院藏

此内酌量互相更换尚可。圆器一百六十四件样式，尺寸、颜色、花纹总不许有更换，此外从前奏准样款及该监督新拟样款总不许用，仍于一年定向钱量内酌量撙节，烧造年款俱依新定篆书乾隆年款字样，勿致胶柱鼓瑟，如发去有大明宣德年款者即仍用大明宣德年款也，该监督年节进贡，偶尔随意用洋彩吉言新式之类不在此限，钦此”[4]。乾隆时期由于经济强盛加之乾隆帝对瓷器烧造的重视，创烧出了许多新的品种，有些品种延烧了整个清代。由于这类大运瓷器为定式烧造，画样均放置于御窑厂中，加之窑厂工匠均为世代相传，因此这些器物单从表面上看，每个朝代从造型、釉色及装饰图案并无甚大变化，但如若将清代康熙至宣统九朝器物进行排比，就可看到由精到粗的渐变过程，一般情况下坯胎由坚硬变疏松（扣之声音会由清脆变得发闷，这主要是陶泥淘洗的精细程度不同造成的），胎体由薄变厚（尤以碗口最为明显），胎色由洁白细腻变得灰青，所施釉面薄厚不一：薄者，釉汁稀淡，表面光泽和滋润度不足，显得干涩，缺少油腻感，一般底足处施釉较厚，多出现浪荡釉，这一时代特征，不仅道光、咸丰两朝有，也是清代后期的普遍现象。琢器的造型及釉色均有变化，其中康熙至咸丰时期，变化较少，同治以后造型笨拙，釉色变暗，如琢器中的仿哥釉，已无任何哥釉的特征，变成了粉青釉色（**图1至图7**）。装饰图案的色彩由淡雅变浓艳，尤其是彩器中的艳粉色。装饰图案描绘由精细变得粗率。装饰效果由泾渭分明变得有些模糊。由于胎体的变厚，器物的尺寸有所放大，有些器物的底足足墙变得越来越矮，圈足越来越大。笔者所述以上情况，由于变化极为细小，唯有将其进行排比才能观察得到。

大运瓷器一般分琢器和圆器两种，凡“制造瓶、尊、缸、罐、盆、洗、炉、台等件，俱名为琢器，盘、碗、钟、碟，俱名为圆器”。清代大运瓷器的种类各朝均有变化，查《清宫瓷器档案全集》留有最清晰的烧造清单的是嘉庆十年（1805年）十月档，宫廷将嘉庆九年所烧大运瓷器送往盛京的奏折，其中琢器37种，圆器141种，而据乾隆十二年档记载，乾隆时期烧制了琢器52种，圆器164种之多。道光以后逐年减少，咸丰朝起基本固定为琢器8种，圆器40余种，现以咸丰时期烧造品种为例，列表如下。

咸丰朝大运瓷器烧造品种及数量（《清宫瓷器档案全集》卷三十三第25页）

清单名称	现惯用名称	烧造件数	起始朝代
均釉四方杏元双琯瓶	均（钧）釉四方杏元贯耳瓶	83	乾隆
哥釉四方杏元双琯瓶	哥釉四方杏元贯耳瓶	76	乾隆
天青釉四方太平有象瓶	蓝釉四方象耳瓶	125	乾隆
霁红玉壶春瓶	霁红玉壶春瓶	109	乾隆
哥釉四方八卦瓶	哥釉四方琮式瓶	71	乾隆
青花起线玉堂春瓶	青花赏瓶	53	雍正

续表

清单名称	现惯用名称	烧造件数	起始朝代
青花芭蕉栏杆玉壶春瓶	青花芭蕉玉壶春瓶	101	康熙
花厂官釉太极纸槌瓶	茶叶末釉荸荠瓶	20	乾隆
青双龙茶碗	青花双龙小碗	273	康熙
霁红七寸盘	霁红盘	62	康熙
紫龙白里瓷碗	茄皮紫釉暗刻云龙纹碗	645	康熙
霁红碗	霁红碗	598	康熙
青西莲五寸瓷盘	青花缠枝莲盘	666	康熙
青西莲五寸瓷碗	青花缠枝莲碗	639	康熙
青云鹤八卦中碗	青花云鹤八卦碗	538	康熙
五彩水仙花酒盅	五彩花卉杯	795	乾隆
彩红龙撇口酒盅	白地红龙杯	741	雍正
青夔凤满尺盘	青花夔凤盘	19	乾隆
青花三果中碗	青花三果碗	163	乾隆
填白釉宝烧红团凤中碗	白釉釉里红团凤碗	96	康熙
蓝地彩黄云龙茶盅	蓝地黄云龙碗	35	康熙
青双龙六寸盘	青花云龙盘	125	康熙
霁红六寸盘	霁红盘	193	康熙
青木樨花茶碗	青花缠枝花碗	236	雍正
彩宝莲中碗	斗彩缠枝莲碗	46	雍正
霁青中碗	霁蓝碗	95	康熙
青三友人物六寸盘	青花三友人物盘	127	雍正
紫金釉汤碗	紫金釉碗	126	乾隆
五彩暗水绿龙六寸盘	绿彩云龙盘	18	乾隆
冬青釉红团凤中碗	冬青釉釉里红团凤碗	50	雍正
五彩鸳鸯荷花茶碗	斗彩鸳鸯卧莲碗	131	乾隆
霁青白里茶碗	里白釉外霁青碗	130	康熙
青花八仙碗	青花八仙胭脂水碗	17	雍正
内青花外彩荷花碗	粉彩荷花碗	53	嘉庆
八吉祥碗	斗彩八吉祥折腰碗	20	乾隆
绿花桃黄瓷碗	黄地绿彩桃纹碗	77	康熙
紫龙大黄瓷碟	黄釉碟	76	康熙
紫龙小黄瓷碟	黄釉碟	99	康熙
四号黄瓷碗	黄釉碗	61	康熙
云凤五寸瓷盘	青花双云凤盘	101	康熙
小紫龙瓷碟		25	康熙
二号紫龙瓷碟		69	康熙
彩夔凤串花瓷大碗	粉彩夔凤大碗	48	道光
彩八宝茶碗	粉彩八宝碗	11	乾隆
五彩蚕纹如意七寸盘	粉彩蚕纹盘	36	乾隆
彩红地白竹茶碗	红地白竹碗	84	乾隆
青双龙满尺盘	青花云龙盘	24	乾隆
成窑蓝地彩云龙九寸盘	蓝地黄云龙盘	25	康熙
彩八吉祥串花九寸盘	粉彩八宝盘	20	乾隆

续表

清单名称	现惯用名称	烧造件数	起始朝代
深娇黄暗龙中碗	黄釉碗	24	康熙
娇黄茶盅	黄釉杯	24	康熙
娇黄暗龙墩式碗	黄釉暗龙碗	122	康熙
娇黄暗龙中碗	黄釉暗龙碗	22	康熙
娇黄暗龙撇口汤碗	黄釉撇口碗	24	康熙
青花蚕纹寿字满尺盘	青花蚕纹寿字大盘	12	乾隆
彩龙凤瓷碗	五彩龙凤碗	12	康熙

大运瓷器的烧造是供宫廷内的皇帝、皇后等人使用。琢器一般用于宫中陈设，有些瓶式还用于赏赐。据光绪二十年（1894年）档案记载，为恭备慈禧皇太后万寿，宫廷下旨烧造了厂官釉太极纸槌瓶、均（钧）釉四方杏元双珀瓶、天青釉四方太平有象瓶、青花𢀖线玉堂春瓶、哥釉四方八卦瓶等瓶式用于庆典赏用。圆器的使用是有严格规定的，这与中国的后妃制度有关，中国古代皇帝实行一夫多妻制，皇帝的正妻为皇后，皇后统率后宫，地位极崇，皇后以下有妃、嫔等位，分享不同待遇。据《礼记》载："古者天子后宫立六宫，三夫人、九嫔、二十七世妇、八十一御妻。"意思是帝王身边需要有一大群妻妾，且要有等级高低之分。至秦，开始建立后宫内廷，人数远远超过先前朝代的规模。汉代，后妃有十四个等级，规模庞大。隋唐，制度趋于定型，设有皇后、夫人、嫔、世妇等多个等级，此后历代相承。"清太祖努尔哈赤1616年正式即汗位统""筑城三层，启建楼台。"[5]"宫闱亦有位号，但循国俗称福晋（同下）"，清朝建立以后，皇太极对封建帝制进行了改革，其改革反映到宫中，就是要有一套封建的后妃制度与之相适应，于是"王宫并建，位号即明，等威渐辨"[6]。清入关后，加强了其建设，据《世祖实录》记载"顺治十五年十一月庚子，礼部等衙门会议宫闱女官名数、品级及供事宫女名额，乾清宫设夫人一人，秩一品，淑仪一人，秩二品，婉侍六人，秩三品，柔婉二十人，芳婉三十人，俱秩四品。慈宁宫设贞容一人，秩二品，慎容二人，秩三品，以下勤秩无定数，无品级。又设女官，设六局一司"。康熙以后典制大备，后宫号位定制严明。"皇帝尊圣祖母为太皇太后，尊圣母为皇太后，居慈宁、寿康、宁寿等宫。奉太妃、太嫔等位随居。皇后居中宫，主内治。皇贵妃一位、贵妃二位、妃四位、嫔六位，分居东西十二宫，佐内治。自贵妃以下封号，俱由内阁恭拟进号，钦定册封。贵人、常在、答应俱无定位，随居十二宫，勤修内职。"[7]但后妃的身份并不是一成不变的，会随着其婚后的宫廷生活晋升，而其能否很快晋升，取决于其能否生下皇子，母亲的身份就能给后妃带来荣誉，甚至是政权。对嫔妃来讲，母亲身份的最高奖赏便是其所生皇子能够顺利登基。新登基的皇帝，一般都会将皇太后的称号敬奉给其生母。在清代的24位皇太后中，只有11位进宫时就是皇后，其余都是皇帝的生母或养母。随着后妃制度的建立，后妃所享受的待遇衣、食、津贴及日常用品也随之明确，且按等级分配[8]。而其所使用的瓷器品种、釉色及数量，也有明文规定，"皇太后：黄磁盘二百五十、各色磁盘百、黄磁碟四十五、各色磁碟五十、黄瓷碗百、各色瓷碗五十、黄瓷锺三百、各色瓷锺七十、各色瓷杯百；皇后：黄磁盘二百二十、各色磁盘八十、黄磁碟四十、各色磁碟五十、黄瓷碗百、各色瓷碗五十、黄瓷锺三百、各色瓷锺七十、各色瓷杯百；皇贵妃：白里黄磁盘四、各色磁盘四十、白里黄磁碟四、各色磁碟十五、白里黄瓷碗四、各色瓷碗五十、白里黄瓷锺二、各色瓷锺二十、各色瓷杯百、瓷缸二；贵妃：黄地绿龙磁盘四、各色磁盘三十、黄地绿龙磁碟四、各色磁碟十、黄地绿龙瓷碗四、各色瓷碗四十、黄地绿龙瓷锺二、各色瓷锺十五、瓷缸一；妃：黄地绿龙磁盘二、各色磁盘二十、黄地绿龙磁碟四、各色磁碟八、黄地绿龙瓷碗四、各色瓷碗三十、黄地绿龙瓷锺二、各色瓷锺十二、瓷缸一；嫔：蓝地黄龙磁盘二、各色磁盘十八、蓝地黄龙磁碟四、各色磁碟六、蓝地黄龙瓷碗四、各色瓷碗二十、蓝地黄龙瓷锺二、各色瓷锺十、瓷缸一；贵人：绿地紫龙磁盘二、各色磁盘十、绿地紫龙磁碟二、各色磁碟六、绿地紫龙瓷碗四、各色瓷碗十八、黄地绿龙瓷锺二、各色瓷锺十。常在：五彩红龙磁盘二、各色磁盘八、五彩红龙磁碟二、各色

图 8　清乾隆　里外浇黄锥拱云龙纹碗　故宫博物院藏

图 9　清乾隆　里白釉外浇黄锥拱云龙纹碗　故宫博物院藏

图 10　清乾隆　里白釉外浇黄地绿彩锥拱云龙纹碗　故宫博物院藏

图 11　清乾隆　青花地黄彩云龙纹碗　故宫博物院藏

图 12　清乾隆　绿地紫彩云龙纹碗　故宫博物院藏

图 13　清乾隆　白地五彩云龙纹碗　故宫博物院藏

磁碟四、五彩红龙瓷碗四、各色瓷碗十、五彩红龙瓷锺二、各色瓷锺六；答应：各色磁盘八、各色磁碟四、各色磁碗十、各色磁盅六”[9]（图 8 至图 13）。这些制度在清早期时被严格执行，中期后，由于后妃在宫中地位的提高，其使用的器皿已不能严格按以上宫规执行。清单中的矫黄暗龙中碗、矫黄茶盅、矫黄暗龙撇口汤碗等只有皇帝、皇后及皇太后才能享用。

二　奉旨传办瓷器

图 14　清乾隆　紫地轧道粉彩勾莲开光墨彩诗句壁瓶　故宫博物院藏

图 15　清乾隆　青花地白海水龙纹高足碗　故宫博物院藏

所谓奉旨传办瓷器就是由皇帝亲自下旨，交由景德镇烧制的瓷器，其造型、釉色、装饰花样，甚至有些连数量、款识都是由皇帝钦定。从档案记载看，最早的奉旨传办烧造瓷器，应该始于雍正四年（1726 年），以雍正、乾隆时期为最多，但大批量烧造奉旨传办瓷器，仅见于同治、光绪时期，为同治皇帝大婚及为慈禧皇太后万寿烧制的大婚瓷及万寿用瓷。雍正四年“九月二十二日，郎中海望持出高足宣窑碗一件（口上破纹），奉旨着交与年希尧照样烧些，其碗内款落大清雍正年制，钦此”[10]。“十二月十三日，郎中海望持出红磁白里暗花茶圆二件。奉旨，此茶圆系江西烧造磁器处进来的，釉水颜色俱好，但无落款，胎骨还糙尔，将此茶圆发往江西烧造磁器处，传旨给年希尧，此二件茶圆若补落得款即落款，若不能补落得款便罢。此茶圆二件，内淡红色的更好，烧造时着他仿淡红色的烧造茶圆，其底不必烧红色，仍要白底落款。不独此茶圆，他先带去的样内，好款式的盘、碟俱烧造些，胎骨俱要精细。再，朕闻得磁器胎骨，过三年以后烧造更好，将此缘故亦传给年希尧知道，钦此”[11]等。乾隆七年（1742 年）九月二十三日“司库白世秀、副催总达子来说，太监高玉交御制诗一首，传旨将此诗交与唐英烧造再（在）轿瓶上用，其字并宝尔酌量收小，其安诗地方并花样亦酌量烧造，钦此（于本年十二月十七日司库白世秀、副催总达子，将唐英烧造得御制诗轿瓶十二件持进）”[12]。查故宫库存实物，共有书有乾隆御制诗的乾隆时期壁瓶（轿瓶）138 件，在这些壁瓶上共使用了六首乾隆皇帝在不同时期的诗作，其中“官汝称名品，新瓶制更嘉。随行供啸咏，沿路撷芳华。挂处轻车称，簪来野卉斜。红尘安得近，香籁度帏纱”一诗作于乾隆七年，现故宫库存书有此诗的壁瓶 20 余件（图 14）。乾隆二十四年（1759 年）“十六日，郎中白世秀、员外郎金辉来说，太监胡世杰，交蓝地白花靶碗一件（随堆金漆花紫檀木托），传旨着交江西照样烧造十件，要乾隆年制款，再此靶碗上拱花不真，其新造靶碗上拱花要真，钦此”[13]（图 15）。诸如此类的档案在雍正、乾隆朝比比皆是，以上记载也反映了雍正、乾隆皇帝本人对御用瓷器的关注程度。嘉庆时期，由于经济状况所限，加之嘉庆帝本人的兴趣爱好所致，有关奉旨传办瓷器的记录未见一条。虽然在清宫旧藏品中，道光朝的瓷器库藏数量较之乾隆朝有了大幅减少，但从清宫档案看，道光皇帝还是对宫廷御用瓷器的烧制给予了较多的关注，道光元年（1821 年）即“传旨着交九江关监督照依原交出渣斗大小尺寸烧造十件，俱道光年制款，务于十月内送京，钦此”[14]。道光六年，“八月初七日，库掌常明、太监武进忠来说，太监祥庆交红水大碗样一件，传（旨着）御前大臣禧，寄交九江关监督克蒙额，照样高落矮二分，烧造五彩大碗四十件，要两样花样，得时送京，钦此”等。咸丰时期，由于太平天国运动，作为战略要地的江西也陷入了战乱，景德镇则处在太平军和清兵交战的军事腹地，一直战争不断。自咸丰三年（1853年）六月起，太平军“入江西取九江湖口进围南昌”并“分军入抚江西腹地”[15]，直至咸丰十一年（1861年）正月“左宗棠兵复饶州既都梁”[16]。由此看来，御窑厂在咸丰朝的前四年只烧制了较之前朝大幅减少的大运瓷器及一些传办祭器和年节贡瓷，咸丰五年起因制瓷业倍受经费及战乱影响，清宫御用瓷器已处于停烧状况。直至同治三年（1864年），宫廷派员赴景德镇，“查勘厂署原有房屋一百余间，向系工匠做造瓷坯、住值之所，现在仅存基址，工匠栖身无所，当即饬令，先就原基赶紧起造数十间，一面购买物料，招集工匠，先搭棚厂，暂行栖身，择于十二月十四日开工做造，限来年二月内一律齐全，接办大运圆琢瓷件”[17]。由此景德镇御窑场的瓷器烧造逐渐恢复，随后进入了奉旨传办瓷器烧造的小高峰，同治六年为恭办同治皇帝大婚，宫廷下旨烧造了大婚用瓷。“专旨着总管内务府大臣瑞常明善，传知造办处，照交下应预备皇后所用等项活计画样”[18]，此画样正是景德镇奉旨传办烧造的同治大婚用瓷，共二十三种图样，每个图样成套烧造，要求烧造海碗四十件、大碗四十件、中碗四十件、汤碗四十件、饭碗六十件、怀碗四十件、九寸盘四十件、七寸盘四十件、五寸盘四十件、四寸碟四十件、三寸碟四十件、二寸五碟四十件、酒盅四十件、羹匙四十把、茶盅二十个、大茶盅二十个、盖碗二十个、茶缸二十件、二寸五见圆奓斗五对、二寸见圆粉盒四件、二寸五见圆唄头缸四件、一寸见圆胭脂盒四件及尺寸、形状不同的花盆三对和造型不同的水仙奁一对，共计10072件。烧造这批器物的二十三种图样，现均存于故宫博物院图书馆，而器物则藏于瓷器库房内，经核查仅藕色地锦上添花茶缸样、绿地五彩福寿茶缸样及粉地蓝八卦海水江芽茶盅样没有库存实物，其他图样均有器物在库。由于光绪大婚时也动用此批大婚用瓷，因此库存中已无同一图样的整套器物。同治十二年，为预备慈禧皇太后四十大寿，宫廷开始修葺长春宫并下旨烧造了“永庆长春、大雅斋及天地一家春”款瓷器，关于此款瓷器的烧造，清宫档案有明确记载，其画样画于“同治十二年十二月十八日太监张得禄来说，长春宫总管陈进才传旨，着造办处画做各式大小花瓶纸样八个，各式元花盆纸样七件，再烫合牌胎长方花盆样五件，各式合牌胎水仙盆样三件，俱四面满各色花卉代翎花虫草要细要好，赶紧成做，钦此”[19]。档案中要求此批器物限同治十三年（1874年）九月呈进，如按“大雅斋”款瓷器烧制清单计算，应烧器物5196件，而实际烧制完成时间为光绪元年及光绪二年，分两次解京进宫，且数量只完成了4299件。故宫博物院藏署“永庆长春”“大雅斋”与“天地一家春”三款的瓷器分为三种情况：第一，三款作为一体出现在同一个器物上，主要是一些盘、碗、盖碗、高足碗、奓斗、盖盒、羹匙等尺寸较小的日常生活用品；第二，署“大雅斋”及“天地一家春”两款的，主要是造型较大的鱼缸、花盆及底足无法书款的高足碗、盅；第三，花瓶上只署“永庆长春”款识。其款识的书写大致相同，“大雅斋”“天地一家春”以红彩书于器表，“永庆长春”则以红彩书于足底。此类器中的鱼缸、盘、高足盘、碗、盖碗、茶碗、奓斗、盖盒及羹匙，其装饰的图案均分五种，分别为绿地墨彩画秋菊、秋葵纹，白地粉彩绘荷莲纹，耦合地粉彩绘虞美人纹，绿地粉彩绘藤萝纹及黄地墨彩绘芙蓉花纹。而花盆、花瓶则装饰有不同色地，不同花卉图样。署“永庆长春”款的花瓶共计19件，除4件白地蒜头瓶外，均为色地粉彩器，有绿地、黄地、藕合地及浅藕合地等，按器形分为蒜头瓶、葫芦瓶、高足瓶、螭龙耳瓶、狮耳瓶、象耳瓶等，其装饰图案均为花卉及虫鸟，主要有牡丹、藤萝、海棠、荷莲、梅花、桂花等，款识均是在圈足内红彩书“永庆长春”楷款。署“大雅斋”及“天地一家春”两款的鱼缸仅存4件。鱼缸器形高大，口径达70厘米，胎体厚重，施彩均匀，画工精细，为晚清瓷器中的精制之作。花盆共计35件，分为圆形及长方形两种，均以色地粉彩装饰，描绘图案为花卉虫鸟或桃实，尺寸较小者均配以盆奁。高足碗、盘，按装饰图案分为四种，分别为绿地墨彩画秋菊、秋葵纹，白地粉彩绘荷莲纹，耦合地粉彩绘虞美人纹及绿地粉彩绘藤萝纹。同署“大雅斋”“天地一家春”和“永庆长春”三款的瓷器最多，共计141件，除花盆所装饰的图案不同外，其他盘、碗、奓斗、盖盒、盖碗、茶碗及羹匙的装饰图案均为上文所述的5种图案。花盆按造型分腰圆式、扇面式、方胜式及圆形4种，花盆内均施松石绿釉，口沿处以蓝料彩绘连续不断的回纹，外腹部以不同的色地描绘不同花卉，下承四足。除此之外，光绪时期为预备慈禧皇太后五十、六十、七十大寿及光绪皇帝大婚，均烧造了奉旨传办瓷器。宣统时期，宣统皇帝已无暇顾及此事项。

图16　清乾隆　黄地轧道粉彩开光三羊图碗　故宫博物院藏

图17　清道光　紫地轧道粉彩开光五谷丰登图碗　故宫博物院藏

图18　清道光　蓝地轧道粉彩鹊桥仙渡图碗　故宫博物院藏

图19　清嘉庆　粉地轧道粉彩丹桂飘香图碗　故宫博物院藏

图20　清嘉庆　蓝地轧道粉彩菊花纹碗　故宫博物院藏

图21　清道光　黄地粉彩花卉纹碗　故宫博物院藏

三　年贡御瓷

“任士作贡，自古有之”，也就是说地方大员定期或年节要向皇帝进贡特产。清承旧制，每岁凡逢年节、帝后万寿时，各省督抚大臣、地方官员及边远少数民族王公大臣，均要进献方物给皇帝，向有年贡、例贡及岁贡之物[20]。年贡一般分年节、端阳、中秋、万寿四贡，嘉庆四年“停止督抚、盐政中秋节贡”，嘉庆后仅有年节、端阳、万寿三贡。由于年贡瓷是九江关监督在御窑厂专门为皇帝精心烧造的御用器皿，因此其纹饰及造型均有别于大运瓷器，且质量要优于大运器皿。年节贡一般于每年的十二月底抵京，题材多为喜庆吉祥之类；端阳节，为每年的五月五日，据《荆楚岁时记》载，因仲夏登高，顺阳在上，五月正是仲夏，它的第一个午日是登高顺阳的好日子，故称五月初五日为“端阳”，此节贡一般于四月底前抵京，内容多是吉祥、祈祷平安及装饰辟邪之物；万寿节一般为皇帝生日前几天抵京，内容多与福寿有关。对于每个年节贡瓷上的装饰图案，乾隆八年（1743年），乾隆帝曾下御旨“太监胡世杰交御用青花白地膳碗一件，传旨着交唐英烧造，其碗大小、厚薄、深浅、款式俱照此膳碗，外边俱烧五彩各色地仗花样，各按时令分别吉祥花样，碗内仍照外边花样俱要青花白地。年节用三羊开泰（图16），上元节用五谷丰登（图17），端阳节用艾叶灵符，七夕节用鹊桥仙渡（图18），万寿用万寿无疆，中秋节用丹桂飘香（图19），九月九用重阳菊花之类（图20），寻常赏花用万花献瑞（图21），俱按时令花样烧造五彩，要各色地仗，每十件地仗要一色，按时令每样先烧造十件，钦此”[21]。此条档案记载虽属传办方式，但从后期督陶官所贡器物看，基本符合以上各个年节所含寓意。从档案记载看雍正时期地方官员进贡之物多为宋、明之瓷，并非本朝所烧之器。自乾隆二年起，督陶官开始进贡本朝所烧器物，但数量及次数均较少，自乾隆十六年起逐年增加，嘉庆、道光时期九江关监督所贡器物最多，尤以道光时期为甚。嘉庆六年（1801年），农历十二月二十六日，督陶官阿克当阿恭进：“（交毓庆宫）霁青描金歌舞升平太平尊成对（随像生花），（交佛堂）黄地洋彩五供成分，（交佛堂）黄地洋彩八宝成分，（交佛堂）松绿地洋彩宝塔成对，（交佛堂）洋红地洋彩宝瓶成对，（交佛堂）金地拱花藏轮成对，（交佛堂）绿地拱花奔巴壶成对，（交圆明园）洋彩太平有象成对，（安养心殿赏人用）红地洋彩三羊开泰吉庆尊成对，（安养心殿赏人用）黄地洋彩岁岁平安如意尊成对，（安养心殿赏人用）绿地洋彩龙凤呈祥鱼尾尊成对，（安养心殿赏人用）五彩五古丰登太极瓶成对，（安养心殿赏人用）五彩群仙庆祝双喜瓶成对，（安养心殿赏人用）霁青描金福寿柳叶瓶成对，（安养心殿赏人用）青花九龙呈瑞玉堂春成对，（安养心殿赏人用）洋彩瓜瓞绵绵观音瓶成对，（交圆明园）影青釉把碗十件，（交圆明园）天鸡红龙把碗十副。”[22] 由此贡单可以看出嘉庆时期每年进贡器物之多，通过查看档案，嘉庆时期九江关监督所贡器物，以佛前用器为最多。道光时期，皇帝对年贡御瓷非常重视，对于九江关监督所呈进器物的式样、釉色均提出了要求，“道光二年五月十五日，总管内务府大臣禧常，面奉谕旨，九江关所进磁器，颜色花样均属不佳，着寄信九江关监督，嗣后呈进磁器，素色着仿古用粉窑、哥窑及青花白地者，其彩色着用霁红色并五彩花样者，不得过艳，其洋彩及鼓出花样之件，着无庸呈进，如本年年节，应进磁器，业经烧造，改辨不及，仍准其照旧呈进，俟明年端阳节再行遵照所改颜色、式样呈进，钦此”[23]。道光十三年（1833年）道光帝亲下御旨，开始烧造“慎德堂制”款瓷器，这批署有“慎德堂制”瓷器最能代表当时制瓷最高水平，其烧造情况较为复杂，烧制之初应属奉旨传办，自第二年起，道光皇帝下旨改为年贡御瓷，这在清宫档案中有明确记载，道光十三年“八月十九日，主事那隆阿、太监张得兴来说：太监沈魁交金鱼荇草瓷奓斗样一件，外黄里白暗龙黄瓷盅样一件，青花白地瓷碗样一件。传旨瓷奓斗一件，着照此样要黄瓷里白烧造六十件，内慎德堂制款三十件，湛静斋制款三十件，俱要楷书字。暗龙黄瓷盅一件，着照此样烧造四十件，要湛静斋制款，俱要楷书。青花白地碗一件，着照此样要里外俱黄色，烧造四十件湛静斋制款，俱要楷书钦此”[24]。由此记载可以说明“慎德堂制”款瓷器，最迟于道光十三年开始烧制，而道光十四年“二月二十二日，主事那萨阿首领武进忠来说，太监沈魁传旨，十四年年贡起，九江呈进瓷器款，慎德堂制要红字，钦此”[25]。故宫博物院库存藏署“慎德堂制”瓷器，共计357件，其中宫中旧藏298件，其造型、品种多样，多为日用器皿，有少量的陈设器。主要品种为碗、盖碗、盘、瓶、羹匙、渣斗、鸟食罐、罐、花盆、盆、花插、器物座等。从清宫档案记载可知，咸丰元年、二年九江关监督曾五次向咸丰帝恭进了御瓷，共计638件，器形有瓶、尊、花盆、盖罐、盖碗、渣斗、羹匙及碗、盘、碟、茶盅。从故宫博物院现有藏品看，除整器以青花装饰的制品、羹匙及黄釉碗外均大量使用了金彩描绘，其金彩色调不及乾隆鲜亮。同治时期九江关监督疲于完成大运及奉旨、奉文烧造任务，未见进贡瓷器的记载。光绪时期，仅见光绪十二年庆典进贡清单，为王公贵族所进，非御窑场所烧器物。宣统时期未见贡单，只存瓷器。

四　奉文传办瓷器

奉文传办瓷器包括有御膳房、御茶房所需日用器及宫廷祭器，主要是祭器，祭器即指祭祀时用的器具。清代宫廷的祭祀包括祭天、祭神、祭祖，是宫廷中重要的礼仪活动，包括了大祀、中祀、群祀的朝廷传统祭祀、满族特有的祭祀堂子和坤宁宫祭神及与汉族相似的祭祖活动，如祭太庙、祭奉先殿和祭陵等。其祭祀时使用的瓷质祭器，清承明制均交由江西景德镇烧造。明洪武二十六年定“凡烧造供用器皿等物，须要定夺样制，计算人工物料，如果人匠赴京，置窑兴工，或数少行移饶、处等府烧造”[26]。“嘉靖九年定四郊各陵祭器：圜丘青色、方丘黄色、日坛赤色、月坛白色，行江西饶州府如式烧解。”[27] 凡坛庙陵寝需用祭器，照太常寺图式颜色数目，颁发江西烧造解部[28]。太常寺是封建社会中掌管礼乐的最高行政机关，秦时称奉常。汉景帝六年（前151年）改称太常（《汉书·百官公卿表》）。汉以后改称太常寺、太常礼乐官等。《隋书·百官志》：“太常，掌陵庙群祀，礼乐仪制，天文术数衣冠之属。”历代大体相同。清代之太常寺于顺治元年（1644年）初设置，属礼部。按雍正时定制，清代烧造的祭器是由内务府传办交景德镇烧造的，每年所烧器物及数量不尽相同，大体是按器物的使用状况来决定。据乾隆二年档记载：“总管内务府谨奏，为请旨事，敬查坛、庙、奉先殿祭祀所用磁、樽、爵、笾、豆、盘、毛血盘、羹碗，悠关甚重。从前此项磁器俱由内库备用，但现今库内此项磁器不全理合，预行烧造。除现今所有蓝磁樽，白磁樽爵外，应烧造黄磁樽一百件，爵二百支，毛血盘一百件，笾、豆、盘四百件，羹碗一百件，蓝磁爵二百支，毛血盘一百件，笾、豆、盘四百件，羹碗一百件，白磁毛血盘一百件，笾、豆、盘一千件，羹碗一百件，应请交与江西烧造磁器处员外郎唐英等，令其敬谨加厚烧造，赍送可也。为此谨奏请旨，乾隆二年五月十五日。”其传办祭器只烧了两年。嘉庆时期虽然停烧了大运瓷器，但祭器的烧造并未停止。而咸丰五年也曾传办烧造祭器，但因战乱未能完成，“查咸丰五年十二月初二日，奉总管答开恭照礼部具奏，十月十九日大行皇太后神牌升祔白瓷樽一件，供果小磁盘十二件，供鲜大白瓷盘一件，供鲜大瓷碗一件，盛银勺小白瓷盘一件，膳房瓷登一件，供鲜大白瓷盘一件，供肉小白瓷盘三件，赶紧解京，以备应用等因。当因时值隆冬，泥坯冻结，须俟春融开工照式赶办，即经其文呈覆总管内务府在案，讵自本年开春以后，逆匪窜扰抚州建昌等郡，景镇界连，人心震恐，工匠纷纷迁避，职关屡督厂役设法招募，无如已避者迄未覆业，在镇者仍多惊散，所有奉文饬烧前项瓷器一时骤难制办”[29]。烧制完成且送至京城的是咸丰元年、二年为寿皇殿、太庙、西陵、三坛及奉先殿所造之器，共计1195件。釉色以白釉为主，还有酱釉、黄釉及天青釉。器形包括了樽、罐、爵、登、簋、盘、碗、茶碗等祭祀用器。白釉盘、碗大部分是为寿皇殿及奉先殿供鲜、供果、供肉或盛酱所用。同治、光绪、宣统时期会随各处所需及器物破损情况烧造。

五　有关四种方式的款识

大运瓷器的款识，康熙至宣统均为青花六字款，其中康熙、雍正时期的款识较为多样，既有楷书也有篆书，多为青花双圈内六字楷款，乾隆、嘉庆、道光三朝为六字篆款，咸丰、同治、光绪、宣统三朝均为六字楷款，仅见乾隆时期的黄地绿彩团龙纹碗及黄地绿龙花鸟纹碗为青花六字楷款，极个别的仿古琢器有刻款。奉旨传办和年节贡瓷的款识大多为红彩，但以道光、咸丰、同治三朝最有规律，道光时期为红彩六字篆书款，咸丰时期均为红彩六字楷书款，而同治时期传办的大婚瓷，则为红彩四字楷款。奉文传办瓷器款识基本同于大运瓷器。

综上所述，清代宫廷于建国初期，在景德镇设立御窑场，采用了大运、奉旨传办、年节御贡及奉文传办瓷器四种方式烧造宫廷用瓷。笔者通过查阅档案，并认真梳理各时期大运瓷器清单，奉旨传办瓷器、奉文传办瓷器奏折文稿及年节御贡瓷器贡单，结合库存实物，对于清代各朝宫廷所烧器物的品种、数量的变化过程及变化原因，有了清晰的认识。单从库存实物看，奉旨传办器、年贡御瓷质量上要优于大运瓷器、奉文传办瓷器。而大运瓷器、奉文传办瓷器数量上要多于奉旨传办瓷器及年贡御瓷。通过了解其烧造方式，为我们解释了各时期宫廷用瓷产生不同的原因。通过对清代宫廷用瓷烧造方式的研究，为我们分类研究清代各朝瓷器的时代特征及新品种创烧原因，提供了新的思路。

注释

1 《清宫瓷器档案全集》卷一第，第 63 页，中国画报出版社，2008 年。
2 《清宫瓷器档案全集》卷三十，第 45 页，中国画报出版社，2008 年。
3 《清宫瓷器档案全集》卷三十，第 233 页，中国画报出版社，2008 年。
4 《清宫瓷器档案全集》卷三，第 86 页，中国画报出版社，2008 年。
5 赵尔巽：《清史稿》列传卷一，第 8897 页，中华书局，1976 年。
6 赵尔巽：《清史稿》列传卷一，第 8897 页，中华书局，1976 年。
7 （清）鄂尔泰、张廷玉：《国朝宫史》上册，第 138 页，北京古籍出版社，1987 年。
8 王佩环：《清宫后妃》第三章，辽宁大学出版社，1993 年。
9 （清）鄂尔泰、张廷玉等：《国朝宫史》下册，第 390 页，北京古籍出版社，1987 年。
10 《清宫瓷器档案全集》卷一，第 54 页，中国画报出版社，2008 年。
11 《清宫瓷器档案全集》卷一，第 57 页，中国画报出版社，2008 年。
12 《清宫瓷器档案全集》卷二，第 195 页，中国画报出版社，2008 年。
13 《清宫瓷器档案全集》卷六，第 153 页，中国画报出版社，2008 年。
14 《清宫瓷器档案全集》卷三十，第 180 页，中国画报出版社，2008 年。
15 印鸾章：《清鉴》下册，第 600 页，中国书店。
16 赵尔巽：《清史稿》卷二十一，第 764 页，中华书局，1976 年。
17 《清宫瓷器档案全集》卷三十四，第 345 页，中国画报出版社，2008 年。
18 《清宫瓷器档案全集》卷三十五，第 102 页，中国画报出版社，2008 年。
19 中国第一历史档案馆：《清宫内务府造办处活计档》胶 41。
20 林永匡、王熹：《清代皇室与年例岁贡》，《故宫博物院院刊》1990 年第 4 期。
21 《清宫瓷器档案全集》卷二，第 272 页，中国画报出版社，2008 年。
22 《清宫瓷器档案全集》卷二十七，第 119 页，中国画报出版社，2008 年。
23 《清宫瓷器档案全集》卷三十，第 232 页，中国画报出版社，2008 年。
24 《清宫内务府活计档》中国第一历史档案馆，编号 2986。
25 《清宫内务府活计档》中国第一历史档案馆，编号 2988。
26 王光尧：《中国古代官窑制度》第 148 页，紫禁城出版社，2004 年。
27 《明会典》卷二〇一工部二十一“器用”。
28 （清雍正）《大清会典》卷二〇〇工部“窑冶”条。
29 《清宫瓷器档案全集》卷三十三，第 239 页，中国画报出版社，2008 年。

A Brief Summary of Imperial Porcelain's Production in the Qing Dynasty

Zhao Congyue

Abstract

The production of imperial porcelains in the Qing Dynasty underwent several stages: succession, development, flourishing, decline, revitalization and decay. As I've found from imperial archives, the imperial porcelains in the Qing Dynasty mainly fell into four categories: *Da Yun* (fired in mass production), *Chuan Ban* (fired upon imperial orders), annual tributes and sacrificial utensils fired upon imperial orders. The so-called "*Da Yun* porcelain" literally means porcelain transported in large-volume, while in reality, it refers to porcelain fired annually according to fixed models and transported to the capital city without Emperor's approval. *Da Yun* porcelains, which are usually classified as traditional variety nowadays, were in general manufactured in the prosperous age ruled by Emperors Kangxi and Qianlong. While the shapes of some porcelains for display originated from Song, Yuan and Ming Dynasty, glazed porcelains mostly followed the shapes that were common during the Ming Dynasty. Unlike *Da Yun*, *Chuan Ban* porcelains were usually fired in Jingdezhen, Jiangxi, upon imperial orders which confined shape, glaze, decoration, sometimes even quantity and inscription. Porcelains as annual tributes refer to those porcelains offered to emperors on special occasions by supervisors of the Imperial Porcelain Manufactory at their own cost—and this had been a long-standing tradition. The last category, ritual utensils, were porcelains used for important rites: state rituals such as heaven ceremony or ancestor worship, traditional Manchu rites such as sacrifice to heaven or other divines in the *Kunning* Palace and other ritual-based ceremonies of Han ethnic group such as ancestor worship in *Tai Miao* (Imperial Divine Hall), *Feng Xian Dian* (Hall of Worshiping Ancestors) or Mausoleums. All ritual utensils were manufactured in Jingdezhen upon imperial orders communicated by *Nei Wu Fu* (the Imperial Household Department). The variety as well as the quantity of ritual utensils to be fired varied from year to year and were generally determined by their actual purpose of usage. Although these four categories of imperial porcelains were highly distinctive in their quantity, quality and inscription, yet they were harmonized in certain rules. Besides, the Porcelain Storehouse in the Palace Museum has a large collection of those porcelain objects, which are easily to be classified on the basis of archives recorded in the Qing Dynasty. All these facts provide us new ideas for research.

Keywords

imperial archives of the Qing Dynasty, *Da Yun*, *Chuan Ban*, imperial tributes, ritual utensils

故宫博物院明清外销瓷收藏及影响

孙悦

外销瓷（export porcelain），或曰贸易瓷（trade porcelain），一般是指出口到海外市场的中国陶瓷产品。这些"外销"世界的陶瓷，有些在生产之前即为专供国外市场而特制；有些则是供应国内市场的一般民窑，随后被转销至国外市场。另外，外销瓷虽属一种商品，但明清时期的中国瓷器有的是以对朝贡国的赏赉、对外国使团的回赠等形式流入外国，并不局限于商业途径。因此，本文涉及的外销瓷概念含义相对宽泛，包含以各类形式流布于海外的官民窑瓷器。

一　明清时期中国陶瓷的外销

明清时期，陶瓷器的外销既是海外贸易的一部分，也属于朝贡体系下的一种政治外交品。外销瓷，兼有商业与国政上的价值和独特意义。因此，随着朝廷外交政策的不断变动和海事开禁政策的更迭，陶瓷对外输出的情形也代有所变。

明初洪武年间，朝廷实施严格的海禁政策，规定"禁滨海民不得私出海"，"片板不许入海"[1]。当然，这种严苛的海禁只是针对民间的私人海外贸易，官方的朝贡贸易则不受限制。明初政府给予前来朝贡的外国使团丰厚的礼品，这些赏赉之物中，就包括有大量瓷器。如"（洪武七年）命刑部侍郎李浩赉赐（琉球）文绮、陶铁器，且以陶器七万、铁器千，就其国市马"[2]。洪武十六年"复遣使赐织金文绮三十二，瓷器万九千。其（真腊）王遣使来贡。十九年遣行人刘敏、唐敬偕中官赉瓷器往赐"[3]。可见当时明廷赏赐给朝贡国的各类陶瓷器数量巨大。

永乐三年（1405 年）始，永乐皇帝命太监郑和出使西洋，至宣德八年（1433 年），前后历时 29 年，先后 7 次远航西洋。郑和船队遍访亚非 30 余个国家和地区，并与它们建立了友好的关系。船队每到一处，便与当地进行互市。其中，瓷器是船队进行交易的主要产品。《星槎胜览》中记载的沿途各国与中国进行瓷器贸易之处，计有"青花白瓷器三处：锡兰山、古里、天方；青白花瓷器六处：暹罗、柯枝、忽鲁谟斯、榜葛剌、大唄喃、阿丹；青白瓷器四处：旧港、满剌加、苏门答剌、龙牙犀角；瓷器十处：花面、剌撒、三岛、苏禄、佐法儿、竹步、木骨都束、溜洋、卜剌哇、阿鲁；大小瓷器一处：旧港；瓷碗三处：淡洋、吉里地闷、琉球；青碗一处：交栏山"[4]。从这些记载可知，明初时期的陶瓷贸易品种是以浙江龙泉青瓷和景德镇青花瓷器为主。

郑和下西洋结束之后，明廷再度关闭海外贸易。然而，明代中期以来的海禁政策并未完全杜绝中国同外国的私人贸易往来。特别是中日之间，由于地利之便，包括瓷器在内的各类走私品贸易颇为频繁。据《见只编》记载，"大抵日本所须，皆产自中国……如饶（景德镇）之瓷器，湖（湖州）之丝绵，漳（漳州）之纱绢，松（松江）之棉布，尤为彼国所重”[5]。

不仅亚洲，此时的欧洲商人也开始涉足中国陶瓷贸易。1514 年，葡萄牙人来到广州附近的屯门岛（Tunmen、或 Tamao，今深圳南头附近）购买了一些瓷器。这是葡萄牙殖民者第一次来到中国，不仅意味着欧洲与中国直接贸易关系的开始，也意味着中西瓷器贸易的开端[6]。嘉靖时期（1522 ~ 1566 年），葡萄牙人已经开始采用订货方式从中国购买瓷器[7]。当然，中葡之间的贸易形式在当时仍属走私性质，交易地点主要集中活跃在福建漳州、泉州，浙江舟山，广东广州等东南沿海一带。

隆庆元年（1567 年），为了抑制走私、增加税收，明朝政府开放福建漳州地区的月港作为对外通商的关口，允许民间与东西各国进行贸易，史称“隆庆开关”。从此，官方对外贸易量激增，日本、葡萄牙、西班牙、荷兰等东西洋各国商人开始往来中国进行商贸活动，大量的中国瓷器出口到海外。据统计，隆庆元年便有 50 艘船只出航到东西洋各国贸易，在万历时期，出航的船舶数量更胜，鼎盛时达到 137 艘之众[8]。

不仅海路，陆路也是瓷器外销的途径之一。沈德符《万历野获编》中述其事云：“余于京师，见北馆伴（当）、馆夫装车，其高至三丈余，皆鞑靼女真诸虏，及天方诸国贡夷归装所载。他物不论，即瓷器一项，多至数十车。予初怪其轻脆，何以陆行万里。既细叩之，则初买时，每一器内纳少土及豆麦少许，叠数十个，辄牢缚成一片。置之湿地，频洒以水，久之则豆麦生芽，缠绕胶固。试投之荦确之地，不损破者，始以登车。临装驾时，又从车上掷下数番，其坚韧如故者，始载以往，其价比常加十倍。”[9] 此条笔记详细记录了万历时期中国瓷器经由陆路远销北方各地和西亚诸国的情形，以及当时外销瓷的包装、运输方式。

17 世纪以来，东西方的陶瓷贸易发生了新的变化。1600 年，英国东印度公司率先成立。紧接着，荷兰于 1602 年，丹麦于 1616 年，葡萄牙于 1628 年，法国于 1664 年，瑞典于 1731 年相继成立了本国的东印度公司。中国与欧洲的陶瓷贸易，基本由这些东印度公司所操控。其中荷兰东印度公司（Vereenigde Oostindische Compagnie，简称 VOC）影响最大，在 17 ~ 18 世纪的中欧陶瓷贸易中占有主导地位。

荷兰东印度公司在成立之初，欧亚的贸易活动还几乎是被葡萄牙人所垄断，荷兰人并未有机会在中国建立据点同中国直接进行贸易。因此，荷兰人最初的贸易活动都是伴随着海盗式的抢劫。1602 年和 1604 年，荷兰俘获了两艘满载中国外销商品的葡萄牙商船“圣 · 雅各”号（San Jago）和“圣 · 凯瑟林娜号”（St. Catharina）。这两艘商船上运载着超过 10 万件中国瓷器，主要是“克拉克”风格的青花瓷器。这些瓷器在阿姆斯特丹拍卖，吸引了欧洲各国的王室成员前来参拍，引起巨大轰动，公司获利丰厚[10]。有学者统计，在 1602 ~ 1682 年间荷兰东印度公司从中国进口的瓷器总数便达 1200 万件以上[11]。这个数字仅从东印度公司档案中的发货单统计得出，实际的瓷器出口应该远大于此数。

1644 年明清鼎革。入主中原的清廷为了政局稳定，实施了较明代更为严格的海禁。顺治十二年（1655 年）规定：“海船除给有执照、许令出洋外，若官民人等擅造两桅以上大船……皆交刑部分别治罪。”第二年又发布谕令：“今后凡有商民船只私自下海，将粮食货物等项与逆贼贸易者，不论官民，俱奏闻处斩。”[12] 在清初禁海令颁布时期，中国与西方的瓷器贸易受到很大影响。荷兰东印度公司转而和日本往来密切，从日本订购了大量瓷器。而一些中国瓷器，也会通过日本转手再行销到欧洲。如东印度公司档案显示，1669 年的一艘中国货船就带有 70000 件瓷器从中国出发，经日本东京抵达印尼爪哇岛的贸易城市万丹（Bantam），与荷兰东印度公司在此设立的贸易点完成交易[13]。

在经历了王朝更迭之后，国家趋于稳定，清朝政府也意识到发展贸易的重要性。1683 年清王朝平定台湾后，决定开放海禁。1684 年康熙帝发布谕令：“向令开海贸易，谓于闽、粤边海民生有益，若此二省民用充阜，财货流通，各省俱有裨益。且出海贸易，非贫民所能，富商大贾，懋迁有无，薄征其税，不致累民，可充闽、粤兵饷，以免腹里省分转输协济之劳。腹里省分钱粮有余，小民又获安养，故令开海贸易。”[14] 正式开放了粤海关（广州）、闽海关（福建漳州）、浙海关（浙江宁波）、江海关（今上海）作为管理对外贸易和征收关税的机构。自此，中国陶瓷的对外贸易开始在现代海关制度的框架下进行。乾隆二十二年（1757 年），乾隆下令关闭其他三处海关，只留广东粤海关一处与外国通商，加大了锁国力度，陶瓷外销因而受到影响。再者，由于欧洲在18世纪初期掌握了制瓷技术，各国纷纷建立了本国的瓷厂，中国本土瓷业又无所发展甚至每况愈下。因此，在乾隆朝之后，中国瓷器外销的数量和质量都有所下降，不复康乾时期的盛况。

二　故宫博物院藏明清外销瓷

故宫博物院的陶瓷类文物收藏，以明清官窑和历代名窑为主，外销类陶瓷并非主流。然而，外销瓷作为民窑器的一种，在清宫之中也有使用。此外，通过文物征集、拨交、各界人士捐赠等方式，陆续有一些明清外销瓷器入藏故宫。归结其来源，主要有以下几个方面：

（一）清宫旧藏

如前所述，有些明清“外销”瓷器是以朝廷赏赐、馈赠等形式或官方有组织的贸易活动而流入海外，属于朝贡体系下的一种政治外交品。这类瓷器在清宫旧藏之中有同类风格的器物留存。如明初永乐、宣德时期的青花瓷器，龙泉青瓷等。可以看到，这些瓷器与亚非各国出土的明初瓷器相类似，应是郑和船队所携带的同类器物。特别是一些如折沿盆、宝月瓶等带有伊斯兰风格的器形，在当时也应主要用来赏赐使团或进行下西洋贸易之类的“外销”之用。

故宫博物院收藏有一批“转变期”风格的瓷器。所谓转变期，一般是在1620年至1683年之间的瓷器。由于明代嘉靖时期开始实行“官搭民烧”，官窑与民窑的界限逐渐模糊。自明末直至清康熙二十三年（1684年）重新开放海禁之前，这段时期的官、民窑风格接近，常常是以质量优劣而区分。一些质地上乘的民窑或外销器，亦可进入宫廷。同样的，宫廷之内使用的同款、同纹器形，也会出现在陶瓷贸易市场。因此，这些转变期瓷器，亦可视为广义的外销瓷。故宫博物院所藏的各类崇祯、顺治乃至康熙时期的一些青花、五彩器，荷兰东印度公司的贸易货单中亦多有所见。这些瓷器均有外销性质，并非纯粹意义上的官窑器。

此外，故宫博物院还藏有一些清代雍正、乾隆、嘉庆时期的外销瓷（图1）。这些瓷器的具体来源不得而知，但明清时期，宫中已有使用外销类瓷器的先例。2014年故宫考古所在紫禁城南大库工地进行考古发掘，共发掘出土了时代自明洪武至晚清光绪时期瓷片数万片。其中有不少民窑瓷片，特别是出土了万历克拉克风格的青花开光花瓣口大盘[15]。这证实了克拉克瓷并非专为外销生产，同时也供应国内市场。从这些瓷片亦可推断，清宫旧藏中存在有外销风格的民窑瓷器，应是宫中服役人员的生活用瓷。

（二）韩槐凖捐献

图1　清嘉庆　青花山水人物图腰圆盆　故宫博物院藏

韩槐凖（1892～1970年），字位三，又名愚趣斋主，海南文昌人，早年赴南洋一带谋生，是我国著名的爱国华侨，生前曾受聘为中国文史研究馆馆员兼故宫博物院瓷器顾问。从1956年至1962年，韩槐凖先生将数十年历尽艰辛、奔波于东南亚各国所搜集的中国陶瓷及其他文物和资料等两千余件装箱运至北京，分批捐赠给故宫博物院。其中陶瓷器有300余件，属于外销类的陶瓷有100余件。这是故宫博物院首次成规模地收藏外销类瓷器，填补了院藏空白。

韩槐凖先生长期生活工作于东南亚地区，其收藏的外销瓷，也以明清时期销往东南亚的瓷器类型为主。在明代后期的瓷器贸易中，虽然欧洲商人充当了东亚贸易的重要角色，但并非所有欧洲人购买的中国瓷器都流入到欧洲市场。有学者统计，中国出口的这些外销瓷仅有16%运往欧洲，其余部分分别被出口到了日本和东南亚地区[16]。韩槐凖捐

图2　明中期　漳州窑红绿彩阿拉伯文盘
故宫博物院藏

图3　明万历　青花花卉纹瓜棱瓶
故宫博物院藏

图4　清康熙　青花凸莲瓣花卉纹军持
故宫博物院藏

图5　清同治　宾乍隆神怪故事图器盖
故宫博物院藏

图6　清　青花山水亭台图瓷盘
故宫博物院藏

赠的这批瓷器，基本涵盖了明清外销瓷的主要品种，如青花、五彩、粉彩等。窑口主要有景德镇窑和福建漳州窑，皆是明清时期外销瓷的主要品种。与欧洲常见的外销瓷相比，这批瓷器反映出更多的东南亚地区生活元素。如明代漳州窑红绿彩阿拉伯文盘（图2）反映出东南亚地区普遍信奉伊斯兰教的史实。此外，明万历青花花卉纹瓜棱瓶（图3）、清康熙青花凸莲瓣花卉纹军持（图4），均在瓷器上镶嵌了银饰。而以金属装饰瓷器，正是伊斯兰世界对中国瓷器再装饰的主要方式。

除16～18世纪中国外销瓷贸易巅峰时期的作品之外，韩槐準的捐献品中还有不少19世纪的外销瓷。这体现出清代中晚期，中国外销瓷器仍在东南亚有着广大的市场和影响力。其中一件清代同治时期的器盖，是中国景德镇窑产品，由泰国工艺师设计具有泰国风格的图案纹饰并进行彩绘，再运回中国景德镇烧成（图5）。这类瓷器在泰国被称为“宾乍隆”[17]。这件瓷器体现了19世纪后半叶泰国瓷器绘制工艺水平，也反映出中泰两国在瓷器工艺技术方面的交流。

（三）罗桂祥捐献

1987年，香港实业家、收藏家罗桂祥先生捐赠了13件清代青花外销瓷[18]。这些青花瓷器均来自乾隆时期的一艘重要沉船“哥德马尔森”（Geldermalsen）号。

“哥德马尔森”号又称“南京号”，是一艘荷兰东印度公司的商船。1751年，满载203箱瓷器的商船从中国广州起航准备返回欧洲，1752年1月途经印度尼西亚附近海域时沉没。1984年7月，英国人迈克·哈彻的打捞公司组织实施打捞，共出水20余万件瓷器。1986年4月，这批瓷器在荷兰阿姆斯特丹举行公开拍卖，引起世界广泛关注[19]。

罗桂祥先生捐赠的十余件瓷器，是这批沉船瓷的代表作。其中一件青花山水亭台图瓷盘（图6），绘制了亭台、树石、飞雁、孤舟等画面，这是“哥德马尔森”号沉船瓷的典型产品，也是流行于乾隆、嘉庆时期外销瓷的常见图案。

（四）沃尔沃公司捐赠

2005年，故宫博物院举办了“世纪藏瓷、情归华夏——瑞典藏中国陶瓷展”。展览主办方、赞助商之一的沃尔沃集团出资购买了展品中的18件中国外销瓷器，无偿捐赠给故宫博物院。18件器物分别为青花鸡纹盘、粉彩描金徽章纹杯碟、粉彩描金徽章纹大盘、粉彩描金徽章纹单柄壶、矾红彩描金徽章纹碗、青花山水楼阁人物图花口盘、青花山水人物图长方花口盘、粉彩描金帆船纹花口盘、黑彩描金花卉纹大碗、五彩瑞兽纹瓜棱执壶、蓝彩描金徽章纹八方盘、粉彩孔雀牡丹纹汤盘、黑彩描金徽章纹盘、粉彩描金徽章纹盘（2个）、青花矾红描金石榴纹盘、粉彩描金牡丹垂柳纹折沿盘、粉彩描金样盘。

图 7　清　粉彩描金徽章图杯碟　故宫博物院藏

这批瓷器之中，有一些属于“哥德堡号”沉船瓷器。1745 年，名为“哥德堡号”的瑞典商船从中国返回瑞典哥德堡港时，据港口仅 900 米处不幸触礁沉没。一批清代外销瓷器从此沉入海底。打捞工作从当年开始，一直持续到 1991 年。其中 1986 年至 1991 年的打捞中，打捞出 6 吨的瓷器碎片和将近 300 件完整瓷器 [20]。

这批瓷器属于典型的外销至欧洲的器物。其中一些是为欧洲的餐饮、生活习惯而制作的特殊器形。另外，这些瓷器中有的带有徽章图案，是所谓“纹章瓷”。比较有代表性的如一套咖啡杯碟（图 7），杯身和盘心分别绘有蓝地金彩字母 G 和月桂树围绕的文字“D.19AUG.1772”。这是为纪念瑞典国王古塔夫三世发动的“荣誉革命”事件而特别订制的。这一纹章标志还被复制，用于瑞典大使馆 [21]。

（五）其他途径入藏

除上述几个主要的捐赠者外，故宫博物院历年文物征集中亦收购有明清外销瓷多件。如 1986 年故宫博物院陶瓷专家冯先铭、耿宝昌先生在比利时购买的 4 件清康熙时期外销瓷。此外，国家文物局、文联局等机构于 20 世纪五六十年代多次拨交了数批清代康熙、雍正、乾隆时期外销瓷，以补充丰富故宫博物院陶瓷的收藏门类。

三　明清外销瓷的意义和影响

中国作为瓷器的发源地，行销各地的瓷器对世界陶瓷史、艺术史和经济贸易史的重大影响显而易见。在亚洲、非洲、欧洲各国，高质量的中国瓷器深受世界各地的青睐，也引得各地的陶业作坊争相仿制。亚洲的日本、朝鲜、越南、泰国等，本地窑业都不同程度地受到中国陶瓷的影响。中亚地区，14 至 18 世纪掀起了对中国青花瓷器和龙泉青瓷仿制的热潮。在 17 ~ 18 世纪，西方世界更是掀起了以收藏、陈设中国艺术品为时尚的“中国风”。陶瓷作为代表中国元素的艺术品，在欧洲世界备受青睐。从王公贵族到普通市民，都以拥有中国瓷器为时尚，影响了欧洲艺术的审美风尚。1709 年，在德国小镇迈森（Meissen）奉命研制瓷器配方的炼金术士伯特格，通过对中国瓷器的仿制、研究，终于烧造成功了欧洲历史上第一件硬质瓷器，打破了中国瓷器对世界的垄断。

然而，文化的交流总是互通互鉴。中国瓷器远销各国的同时，来自世界各地的一些外来技术和工艺，也推动了中国陶瓷的发展。归纳而言，对于中国陶瓷业的影响主要有以下几个方面：

（一）技术传播

明清时期中国陶瓷的很多品类，其原料都来源于外国。最典型者如明代初期青花瓷所用的钴料“苏麻离青”，来自伊朗喀珊 (Kashan) 地区 [22]。明中后期的回青料，则来自西域 [23]。

清代康熙时期，传教士带来了珐琅颜料，康熙皇帝下令将之用于瓷胎之上，烧造成功了珐琅彩瓷。此外，康熙、雍正、乾隆时期的种种颜色釉，如胭脂红釉、锑黄等，均来自西方 [24]。

（二）艺术互通

明代初期，郑和船队中携带的许多瓷器，如折沿盆、宝月瓶、花浇、八角烛台等，其造型均源自阿拉伯地区的金属器、玻璃器。这些带有伊斯兰风格的器形，不仅丰富了明代的官窑瓷造型，对清代官窑也产生很大影响。雍、乾时期的许多官窑器，正是模仿此类器形。此外，中亚伊斯兰地区的艺术品中常用的几何纹样叠加的构图方式、植物化装饰等，都对明代青花瓷的装饰纹样产生显而易见的影响。明代嘉万时期的《江西大志》中提及的“回回花罐”“回回宝相花”等，即是这类伊斯兰装饰风格的纹饰图案[25]。

由于明末清初的海禁，荷兰东印度公司转向日本订购瓷器，日本瓷器迅速占领欧洲市场，在欧洲拥有了固定的客源，甚至对欧洲人的陶瓷审美观产生了一定影响。1683年清廷重新开放海禁之后，荷兰商人曾在景德镇订烧一定数量的仿日本伊万里风格的瓷器，称为“中国伊万里”(图8)。

到了清代，随着西方订制瓷器的大量出现以及欧洲本土瓷器的发明，一些带有西方元素的纹饰，开始流行于中国民窑乃至官窑器物之中。当时欧洲迈森瓷厂的“蓝色洋葱”纹饰，英国伍斯特（Worcester）瓷厂的“松果纹”“栏杆纹”，考格利（Caughley）瓷厂的“柳叶纹”等纹饰，在乾隆之后的中国民窑瓷中都有仿制。17 ~ 18世纪风靡欧洲的巴洛克和洛可可艺术风格，本身有借鉴“中国风”的因素，其兴盛之后，艺术风格又反作用于康雍乾时期的官窑瓷器。特别是洛可可艺术中那种一味追求感官刺激、卖弄炫技的艺术表达方式，与乾隆官窑器中那种装饰繁复、鬼刻神镂的风格异曲同工。

图8　清康熙　五彩花卉图瓜棱盖罐
故宫博物院藏

（三）文化交融

新技术、新材料的传入，丰富了中国原有的陶瓷品类，也创造了新的器形和纹饰。进而，在一些器物的功用乃至命名方面，也对中国固有的称谓带来变化。比如，明代永宣时期的折沿盆，本是借鉴伊斯兰地区回教徒净手盆的器形。到了乾隆时期，清宫造办处档案中则有称这类器物为“洋帽洗”[26]。此器形宽沿深腹，形似欧洲人带的一种帽子，可谓实至名归。奇怪的是，久在深宫的造办处人员何以得知此器形类似洋帽？这或许与荷兰商人对另一类中国外销瓷的命名有关。查阅东印度公司档案，荷兰人将一种腹部略深、口沿扁平的大碗称之为Klapmuts（英文clapmutsen），即“洋帽碗”。明末清初之际，这类“洋帽碗”器形颇为流行，每年都有大量出口到欧洲（图9）。以1640年为例，当年荷兰东印度公司便订购了10032件洋帽碗[27]。欧洲商人对这类器形赋予的新名称，影响到国人的认知，以至于宫中造办处的官员也将旧藏的明代折沿盆称之为“洋帽洗”了。

图9　清康熙　青花回文开光花鸟纹
折沿碗　故宫博物院藏

小结

明清时期，随着大航海时代的到来，中国瓷器的外销经历了从兴起、鼎盛到衰落的过程。辉煌时期，这些精美的陶瓷产品曾遍布欧、亚、美、非各大洲，为世界各国提供了饮食、陈设用具，其代表的东方生活方式和承载的美学内涵，引领了世界审美风尚。同时，以陶瓷贸易为载体的东西方文明交流互鉴，也促进了中国陶瓷自身的发展，使得明清时期的陶瓷品类和造型更趋丰富，呈现出东西兼容、异彩纷呈的艺术风貌。

注 释

1 《明史》卷二百五列传第九十三“朱纨传”，第 5403 页，中华书局，1974 年。

2 《明史》卷三百二十三“琉球”，第 8361 页，中华书局，1974 年。

3 《明史》卷三百二十四“真腊”，第 8394 页，中华书局，1974 年。

4 中国硅酸盐学会编：《中国陶瓷史》第 409 页，文物出版社，2004 年。

5 （明）姚士麟：《见只编》卷上，见《丛书集成初稿》三九六四，第 123 页，中国书店，1985 年。

6 [英] R.B. 沃纳姆：《新编剑桥世界近代史》（明 · 第三卷），第 721 页，中国社会科学院世界历史研究所，中国社会科学出版社，1999 年。

7 1528 年，葡萄牙海军军官惹尔日 · 卡布拉尔（Jorge Cabral）便在马六甲订购中国瓷器。见王冠宇《早期来华葡人与中葡贸易——由一组 1552 年铭青花玉壶春瓶谈起》，《南方文物》2017 年第 2 期。

8 隆庆开关后出航到东西洋的船舶数量，见日本学者松浦章《17 世纪初欧洲人看到的中国船南海交易》，载《东方学》第 85 辑，1994 年。

9 （明）沈德符：《万历野获编》第 781 页，中华书局，1959 年。

10 Thomas Volker, *Porcelain and the Dutch East India Company, as Recorded in the Dagh-registers of Batavia Castle, those of Hirado and Dashima, and other contemporary papers,1602-1682,* Leiden, 1954, p.22.

11 叶文程：《宋元明时期外销东南亚瓷器初探》，载《中国古外销瓷器研究论文集》第 69 页，紫禁城出版社，1988 年。

12 《大清会典 · 康熙朝》卷一百十八“关津”。

13 Thomas Volker, *Porcelain and the Dutch East India Company, as Recorded in the Dagh-registers of Batavia Castle, those of Hirado and Dashima, and other contemporary papers,1602-1682,* Leiden, 1954, p.209.

14 《清实录 · 圣祖仁皇帝实录》卷一百十六“康熙二十三年”，中华书局，1986 年。

15 李季、王光尧、冀洛源、单莹莹、王翃、赵瑾、唐雪梅、纪东歌、陈鹏宇、见骅、刘思桐、霍云、吕进、李绚丽、张敏航：《故宫南大库瓷片埋藏坑发掘简报》，《故宫博物院院刊》2016 年第 4 期。

16 Chuimei Ho, “The Ceramic Trade In Asia, 1602-1682” , In *Japanese Industrialization and the Asian Economy*, edited by A. J. H. Latham and Heita Kawakatsu, London: Routledge, 1994, p.39.

17 董健丽：《东南亚遗珍——故宫博物院藏韩槐準捐献的外销瓷》，《福建文博》2019 年第 3 期。

18 吕成龙：《罗桂祥捐献的瓷器》，《紫禁城》1989 年第 3 期。

19 Michael Hatcher, *The Nanking Cargo*, London: Hamish Hamilton Ltd, 1987, p.105.

20 故宫博物院编：《瑞典藏中国陶瓷》第 50 页，紫禁城出版社，2005 年。

21 故宫博物院编：《瑞典藏中国陶瓷》第 63 页，紫禁城出版社，2005 年。

22 Moujan Matin and Mark Pollard, *Historical Accounts of Cobalt Ore Processing from the Kashan Mine Iran*, The British Institute of Persian Studies, 2015, Volume LIII, p.171.

23 （明）宋应星：《天工开物 · 回青》第 230 页，中国社会出版社，2004 年。

24 段鸿莺、刘瀚文、杨玉洁、赵丛山、李越、曲亮、雷勇：《故宫宁寿宫装饰彩瓷嵌片釉彩料的分析研究》，《文物保护与考古科学》2019 年第 3 期。

25 相关研究见翟毅：《明代青花瓷上的“回回花”》，《紫禁城》2016 年第 11 期。

26 乾隆三年六月二十五日，七品首领萨木哈、催总白世秀来说，太监高玉交……宣窑青花洋帽洗一件。乾隆八年闰四月初八日，亦有司库白世秀、副催总达子来说，太监高玉交……宣窑洋帽洗一件，传旨，着俱各配架座，钦此。分别见于《清宫内务府造办处档案总汇》第 8 册第 281 页、第 11 册第 313 页。

27 Thomas Volker, *Porcelain and the Dutch East India Company, as Recorded in the Dagh-registers of Batavia Castle, those of Hirado and Dashima, and other contemporary papers,1602-1682,* Leiden, 1954, p.46.

Collections of Chinese Export Ceramics in the Palace Museum and Their Impact

Sun Yue

Abstract

Accompanied by the advent of the Age of Discovery, Chinese export ceramics underwent a process of emergence, prosperity and decay in the Ming and Qing Dynasties. During the glorious days, having been the embodiment of oriental lifestyle and aesthetics, Chinese ceramics with finest craftsmanship were found in Europe, Asia, America and Africa, providing for all countries tableware as well as displays and leading the world aesthetic trend. Meanwhile, the cultural exchange and the mutual appreciation between the East and the West based on ceramics trade promoted in turn the development of Chinese ceramics production itself so that ceramic categories were increased and shapes were enriched with a culturally harmonized and colorful artistic style.

The main collection sources of Chinese export ceramics in the Ming and Qing Dynasties in the Palace Museum are historical relics of the Imperial Court, donations from Han Huaizhun, *Luo Guixiang* and Volvo Group, cultural relics collected by the Palace Museum, or consignment from the State Administration of Cultural Heritage and the Federation of Literary and Art Circles. Although the number of collected items is relatively small, the full range of their categories yet reflects basic scene of Chinese export ceramics in the Ming and Qing Dynasties.

Keywords

Ceramics, Export, the Palace Museum

明清时期陶瓷祭祀用器溯源

唐雪梅

图1　明嘉靖　黄釉、白釉、祭蓝釉盘　故宫博物院藏

“郊祀社稷，所从来尚矣。”[1]祭祀用器是国家礼制的实物化体现。明清两代作为中国古代传统社会的最后两个王朝，政治制度和礼乐制度一切遵从前代，而表现制度礼法的器物自然也不可避免地继承前代的内容。从传世资料看，明清时期，陶瓷祭祀用器在各类祭祀活动中均扮演十分重要的角色。学界对于这一时期陶瓷祭祀用器的探讨，也有着较为丰硕的成果[2]。然而若追溯其来源，当与元代礼制与祭器使用有很大关系。元代的祭祀体系又深受宋、金时期礼制影响。本文依据文献记载、考古发现及传世实物，以陶瓷祭祀用器为落脚点，由明清上溯至元代，又及宋、金，探讨明清时期陶瓷祭祀用器的来源问题。

一　明清时期陶瓷祭祀用器的基本面貌

关于明清时期陶瓷祭祀用器的面貌，有着较为丰富的文献与实物资料。明代，从文献记载看，有《大明会典》“洪武元年令，太庙器皿易以金造，乘舆服御诸物应用金者以铜代，二年定祭器皆用磁”，记载了明代使用瓷质祭祀用器的开端。《明史》中太祖诏制太庙祭器云：“礼顺人情，可以义起。所贵斟酌得宜，随时损益。近世泥古，好用古笾豆之属，以祭其先。生既不用，死而用之，甚无谓也。孔子曰：‘事死如事生，事亡如事存。’其制宗庙器用服御，皆如事生之仪。”[3]嘉靖时期，对祭祀用器进行了改制，规范了祭祀用瓷的种类、颜色及对应的祭祀地点：“（嘉靖）九年定四郊各陵瓷器，圜丘青色，方丘黄色，日坛赤色，月坛白色，行江西饶州府如式烧解。计各坛陈设，太羹碗一、和羹碗二、毛血盘三、着尊一、牺尊一、山罍一、代簠簋笾豆瓷盘二十八。”[4]万历《大明会典》中更明确标注了“登、铏以磁碗代，簠、簋、笾、豆以磁盘代，凡坛庙同”[5]。表明了明代一贯有以碗、盘等日用形制器物来代替部分复杂祭祀用器的做法。且从嘉靖时期起，更明确了各种场合祭祀用瓷器的釉色以及瓷器烧造种类，这从故宫博物院藏传世器物中可以得到验证（**图1**）。景德镇御窑遗址的考古发掘成果，则从实物的

图 2　明早期　单色釉碗、盘　景德镇御窑遗址出土

图 3　清乾隆　白釉祭礼器　故宫博物院藏

角度表明（图 2），明代早期的祭器和日用饮食器在器形方面没有严格的区别，因此一些碗、盘、罐等类也可能与祭祀相关[6]。

清代，文献明确记载有"乾隆十二年谕：国家敬天尊祖……考之前古，笾、豆、簠、簋诸祭器，或用金玉以示贵重，或用陶匏以崇质素，各有精义存乎其间，历代相承，去古浸远。至明洪武时更定旧章，祭器祭品悉遵古，而祭器以瓷代之，惟存其名……联思坛庙祭品，既遵用古名，则祭器亦应悉仿古制，一体更正，以备隆仪"[7]。可知以乾隆十二年（1747 年）为界，此前因循明之旧制，此后则进一步规范了礼制，并丰富了瓷制祭祀用器的形制。从故宫博物院清宫旧藏的清代瓷祭祀用器来看（图 3），簠、簋、笾、豆等各色造型仿古的祭器也是在乾隆时期才有烧造，并一直延续至清末。

由此，明清时期对于瓷质祭祀用器的使用可划分为两个大的阶段：第一个阶段为明代至清乾隆十二年以前，基本以碗、盘、罐等器物代替簠、簋、笾、豆、尊类比较繁复的祭祀用器，瓷质祭器的风格简洁质朴。第二阶段为乾隆十二年以后，乾隆皇帝对祭祀用器做了较为详细的改制，此后国家祭祀用瓷器均仿三代古制之造型，变得复杂而规范。

二　明代陶瓷祭祀用器受元代礼制影响

明清时期，陶瓷祭祀用器已成为各类祭祀活动中的重要用器，其面貌与元代陶瓷祭祀用器的发展有着最为密切的关系，可谓深受其影响。明代从洪武二年（1369 年）起规定"祭器皆用磁"，但用器简洁质朴。一些器物虽然性质上属于祭祀用瓷，形制上却与日用器无异，多为碗、盘之类。追溯以普通日用形制的器物作为祭祀用器这种做法的源头，却并非始于明代，是为受到元代礼制影响的结果。

越来越多的考古证据表明，元代陶瓷祭祀用器中，除了簠、簋、豆、爵、尊等这些明确为祭礼器的器物，以及文献中记载陶瓷炉（鼎）、瓶这类器物应属祭祀用器外[8]，一些碗、盘类器物，以及盒、烛台等陶瓷器也与其他随葬的陶瓷模型明器及日用器性质不同，应与祭祀行为相关。

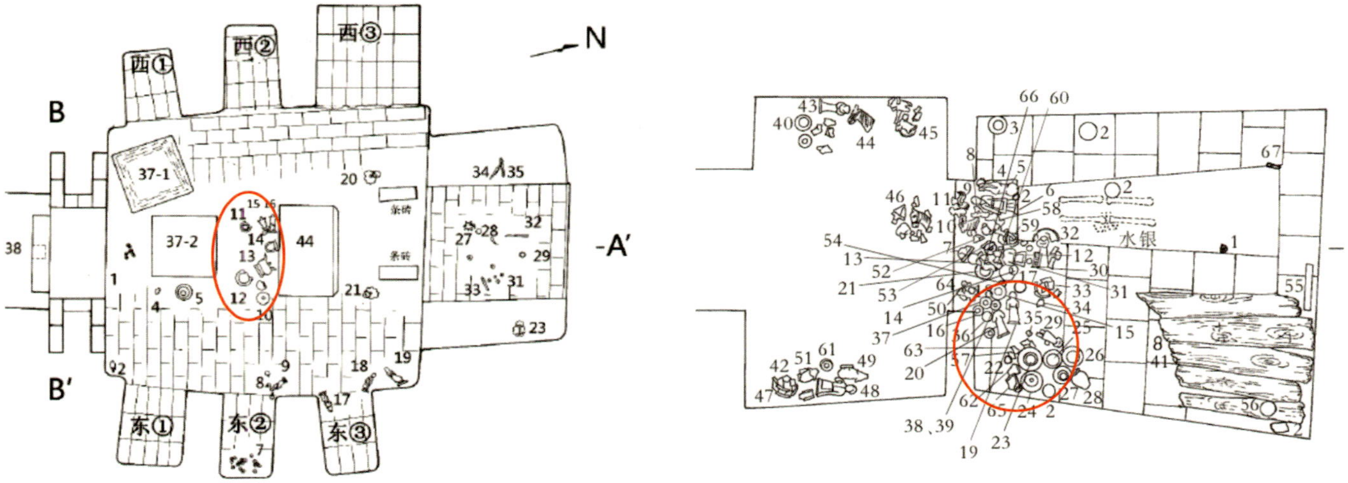

图4　西安刘黑马墓（左）、西安曲江缪家寨元代袁贵安墓（右）祭祀供器出土位置

以文献明确记载的香炉、瓶等元代陶瓷祭祀供器为出发点，观察元墓出土器物的摆放位置及其组合关系，为我们提供了以考古出土实物为据扩充元代陶瓷祭祀供器种类范围的可能。通过梳理部分器物出土位置明确的元代墓葬信息，可以看到出现在陶瓷炉、瓶类附近位置的器物组合具有重复性（图4、图5）。

典型墓葬如西安刘黑马墓[9]，其出土陶香炉位于墓室中部的石函前，在香炉周围集中分布有陶盒、烛台、刻花盘及碗、盏等器物。西安曲江缪家寨元代袁贵安墓[10]出土陶炉、瓶组合附近区域，除陶盒、烛台、碟外，还有盖罐、单耳杯等。西安曲江元代张达夫及其夫人墓（M6）比较特殊，在墓室东西侧各设一处供桌，供桌之上及周围集中摆放陶瓷器，这从出土位置上就表明了一些器物应属于祭祀用器的性质。其中，炉、簠、簋分位于西侧供桌，附近器物有青瓷碗、碟等，东侧供桌附近集中分布了烛台、单耳杯、匜、盏托、玉壶春瓶等陶瓷器。

综合以上几个典型墓葬中的器物组合，可知陶瓷盒、碗（盏）、盘（碟）、烛台、罐、单耳杯等几类器物在供桌区域及炉、瓶附近重复出现，表明其可能被视为祭祀用器使用。此外，汪懋昌墓中“一些陶器出自室后棺侧陶案上，且罐及盒内均有粮食及肉食品等痕迹”[11]，亦可佐证盒、罐类器物具有祭祀供器的性质。

通过对考古证据的梳理，可见陶瓷碗、盘（碟）、烛台、罐、盒等器物凭借其相对固定的出土位置与器物组合，表明了它们与祭祀活动的关联。这为元代已经将一部分与日用器形相同的器物作为祭祀用器使用提供了实物证明。

明初制度多承袭元代。明太祖在元代基础之上，即位不久便设承宣布政司取代行中书省，将地方权力向中央集中，就是这种承袭的重大表现。在礼制问题上亦是如此。文献记载元代祭祀“衣冠尚质，祭器尚纯”[12]，表明了元代对于祭祀礼制建设的整体基调。通过前文的考证，可知元代碗、盘、罐一类即已参与到祭祀活动之中，这类器物形制简单而不具备特殊性，反而令其使用性质具有了更多的可能。明代的陶瓷祭祀用器以碗、盘代替登、铏及簠、簋、笾、豆一类，显然也是承袭元代制度的结果。

三　清代陶瓷祭祀用器受元、明礼制影响

文献与传世器物均表明，清乾隆十二年之前，清代礼制沿袭明代旧制。乾隆十二年，皇帝下令规范礼制、“更正”

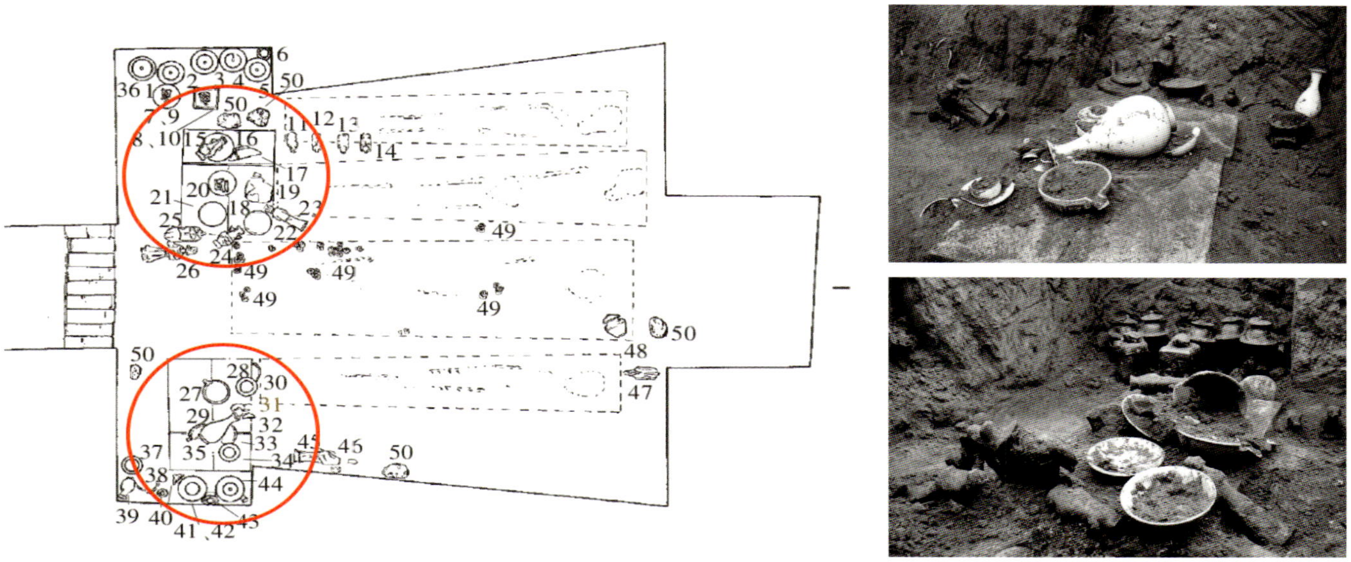

图 5　西安曲江元代张达夫及其夫人墓（M3）祭祀供器出土位置及出土状态

祭祀用器，此后祭祀用器依然用瓷，然而造型却恢复了效仿三代古器的面貌，风格转向复杂规整。同明代及清初一样，仿古的祭祀用器做法也非乾隆皇帝所创。诸多考古发现表明，元代，各式仿古陶瓷祭祀用器已经在今甘肃、陕西、河南这一区域流行开来。

通过对今甘肃、陕西、河南这一区域元代纪年墓葬的梳理，观察陶瓷类器物组合，可以明确元代仿古造型陶瓷祭礼器的使用与发展状况。

我们以随葬器物组合为依据，可将典型纪年元墓分为三组：第一组的陶器组合包括香炉（鼎）、瓶、盒、蜡台、盏托、匜、罐、盘、仓、灶及陶俑等。属于这一组的纪年墓有西安刘黑马墓、西安曲江段继荣墓、西安曲江袁贵安墓、西安南郊王世英墓[13]、洛阳道北王英墓[14]、西安曲江李新昭墓[15]等。第二组的陶器组合包括香炉（鼎）、瓶、簠、簋、蜡台、罐、仓、灶及陶俑等。属于这一组的纪年墓有甘肃汪世显家族汪懋昌墓、西安张达夫及其夫人墓等。第三组陶器组合包括香炉、鼎、爵、尊、簠、簋、敦、豆等。属于这一组的纪年墓有洛阳王述墓[16]、赛因赤答忽墓[17]等。

通过纪年墓提供的年代信息，可知在第一组墓葬中，年代最早的纪年墓是 1262 年的西安刘黑马墓，最晚为 1325 年的西安曲江李新昭墓。第二、三组墓葬中最早的纪年墓是 1329 年汪懋昌墓，最晚的是 1365 年赛因赤答忽墓。

观察其中的陶瓷祭祀用器（表一），可见第一组墓葬中基本为一炉、二瓶以及盒、碗、盘、烛台、罐、单耳杯的组合形式。从第二组开始，除炉、瓶等第一组中的器物组合外，又增加了簠、簋类的祭礼器，但这一组中簠、簋的造型均以聂崇义之《三礼图》中所描绘的器物形制为蓝本，与传统三代青铜礼器不同。第三组墓葬中，有陶鼎及诸多仿三代青铜祭礼器造型陶器组合，且随葬品以祭礼供器占大宗。

显然，元代祭祀用器的形制远不如清代之规范。从上述的元代典型纪年墓来看，可知元代陶瓷祭祀用器经历了一个逐渐成熟的过程，仿古的礼器组合从无到有、从谬误到规范。这与时人对于三代之礼器的认知有关，其背后应是元代统治者对儒家文化的认同。观察几个时间节点，不难发现对陶瓷祭礼器的使用从忽必烈时期始见，至文宗后又有所变化，直至元末可谓发展至高潮阶段。元代统治者中，以忽必烈为元统治者重视儒家思想之始。至文宗时期，不仅崇儒，更见文献记载亲祀昊天上帝于南郊，以太祖配享。

然而正是源于元代在接受儒家思想的进程中对于礼制的不断探索，才使得明清礼制有本可依，并不断发展。清乾

表一　典型纪年元墓年代、分组与陶瓷祭祀用器组合

墓葬分组	典型纪年墓葬	随葬陶制祭祀供器情况
第一组	1295 年 西安曲江缪家寨 袁贵安墓	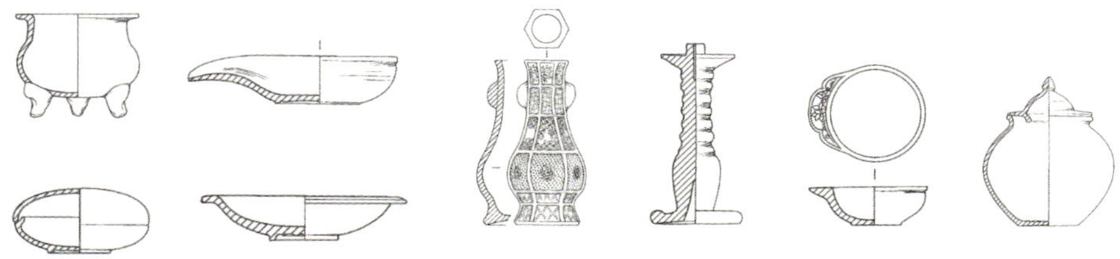
第二组	1339 年 西安张达夫 及其夫人墓	
第三组	1365 年 赛因赤答忽墓	

隆十二年以后的礼器定制，效仿三代礼器制度，其用器之规范，自然与清代对三代礼制的认知相关，却也绝非一代之功。仿三代祭礼器形制之器物在元赛因赤答忽墓中已经有所显现，便是清代祭祀礼器制度受元代影响的最好证明。

四　宋、金礼制对于元代陶瓷祭祀用器的影响

观察为明清时期陶瓷祭祀用器带来深刻影响的元代祭祀系统，可知其具有复杂多元的特点：有炉、瓶组合，有仿古造型的各式祭礼器，也会以简单的碗、盘、罐、盒等器物作祭祀用。这种局面的形成，是元代统治者对于儒家思想文化的渴求程度与其掌握程度不符的表现，同时与宋、金礼制的影响有很大关系。因此，追溯明清时期祭祀用器的来源，不能止步于元代，还应看到元代所受宋、金传统的影响。

元代墓葬中所见陶瓷祭祀礼器组合的形式，在宋代蓝田吕氏家族墓中已有所显现[18]（图6）。吕氏家族墓中随葬有

图 6　蓝田吕氏家族墓出土石、瓷质祭礼器[19]

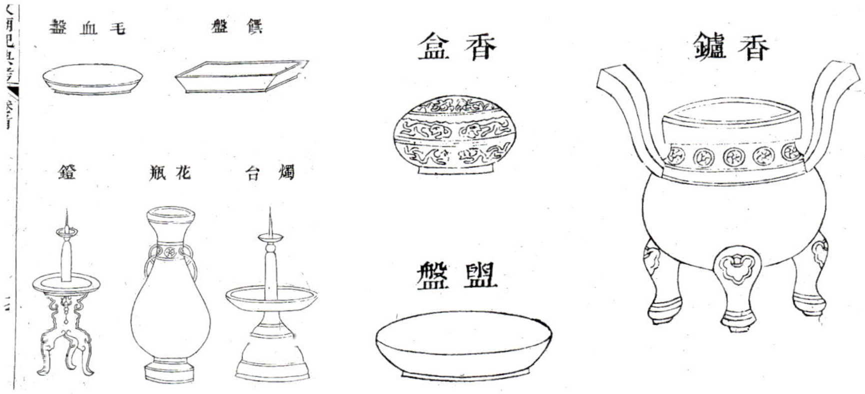

图 7　与元代祭祀用器相近的孔庙祭祀礼器[22]

瓷质以及石质祭礼器组合，其中多数在造型上与三代传统青铜礼器仍然有差别，却已呈现出祭礼器组合的形式，部分石器上还刻有铭文，颇具三代礼器之古风。如此，元代墓葬中出现陶瓷祭礼器组合的现象绝非偶然，在宋代吕氏家族墓中已现端倪。

种种迹象表明，作为汉地本土文化的儒家思想，却在金元时期拥有很高的地位。金元时期不仅数次修缮曲阜孔庙，金代于上京就已敕建孔庙，元代甚至曾命云南诸路皆建学以祀先圣[20]，可见其统治者利用儒家思想统治汉地的强烈愿望。

由于赋予了儒学更加崇高的地位，金代对儒家思想文化的重视与利用，对元代乃至后世影响同样不可小觑。在孔庙祭祀用器中，除青铜彝器与簠、簋、笾、豆等常见礼器外，还见有毛血盘、香炉、香盒、花瓶、烛台等器物，并明确记载毛血盘为瓷质[21]（**图7**）。可以看到，元代祭祀用器与部分孔庙祭器十分相近，尤其瓷质毛血盘作为元代祭祀礼器有明确文献记载。而炉、瓶、盘、烛台的器物组合，也与元墓中常见的祭祀器物组合相同。可见在元代祭祀用器的系统中，有借鉴孔庙祭祀用器的成分，显然受到了金代以来孔庙祭祀制度的影响。

从某种程度上而言，元代所承袭的宋、金之制，并非其礼制中的主流部分。但元代复杂多元化的礼制系统，却正是在这样的背景之下，逐步摸索着建立起来的。这套世俗化的实用体系，承载了对儒家文化与理学思想的传承，对之后的明代乃至清代的礼制建设和祭祀用器的规范都产生了巨大的影响。

小结

由明至清，礼制不断被完善、祭器的使用也逐渐规范，对陶瓷祭祀用器的使用更是达到了高峰。然而礼制的建设与发展绝非一朝一代之功，明代礼制与器用深受元代影响、清初又承袭了明代制度，此时的陶瓷祭祀用器质朴简洁，这与元代祭祀活动中对碗、盘、罐等器物的使用有直接关系，是明代承袭元代世俗化的质朴祭祀的体现。

直至清乾隆十二年，皇帝重新规范了礼制与祭器的使用，这时的陶瓷祭祀用器以仿自三代礼器的造型组合出现，风格变得复杂规整。然而这样的器物组合也早已在元代贵族墓葬中已被逐步呈现出来。元代吸纳儒学思想探索出来的祭祀规制，被清代所继承。

传承于明清的元代礼制与祭器系统，又是在深受宋、金时期部分礼制的影响下形成的。蓝田吕氏家族墓中的祭器以及孔庙祭祀用器的面貌，足以说明元代祭祀用器相对混乱又多元化风格的来源。宋、金时期制度的影响在直接作用于元代礼制的同时，也必然间接触及明清。由宋、金经元至明清，礼制建设与祭祀礼器的使用虽形式万变，却不离儒家文化、理学思想之宗，体现着其在中华文化形成中的重要作用。

元代与清代都是庞大的非汉族政权，不同的是，元代的统治者似乎始终未能完全接受汉人的文治政权意识。这种“倒退的政治”[23]也使得礼制在元代被充分的世俗化。从这个角度来说，明代祭祀用器的面貌，是继承了世俗化的元代制度的表现，清初又沿袭了明代旧制。如此，则乾隆皇帝对于礼制与祭器规范的重新审视，绝不仅是器用与制度的恢复，它预示着统治者从对儒学的被动接受真正转向了文人风格。同样作为非汉族政权，清代祭祀体系受元代影响却与之大不相同，变得极为规整，展现出统治者思想乃至性质的变化。从这一点来说，清代没有重蹈元代覆辙，元代的忽必烈仍是“大汗”，而清代的乾隆皇帝，早已成为了统治中国的帝王。

注释

1 （汉）班固撰，（唐）颜师古注：《汉书》卷二十五上·郊祀志·第五上，第1191页，中华书局。

2 陆明华：《明清皇家瓷质祭器研究》，《上海博物馆辑刊》1990年；王光尧：《清代瓷质礼器略论》，《故宫博物院院刊》2003年第2期；刘新园：《明宣宗与宣德官窑》，《南方文物》2011年第1期；郭家彦：《皇朝礼器》，香港中文大学文物馆，2019年。

3 （清）张廷玉等撰：《明史》卷五十一·志第二十七·礼五，第1315页，中华书局。

4 （明）李东阳等奉敕撰、申时行等奉敕重修：《大明会典》卷二百一·工部二十一·织造、器用。

5 万历重修《大明会典》卷八二·郊祀二。

6 刘新园：《明宣宗与宣德官窑》，《南方文物》2011年第1期。

7 （清）昆冈等修：《钦定大清会典事例》卷四五〇·礼部·祭器。

8 “其牲齐器皿之数，牲用牛一、羊五、豕五……竹木之器三百八十有四，笾二百四十有八，篚三，俎百三十有三。陶器三，瓶二，香炉一。”出自（明）宋濂等撰：《元史》卷七十六·志第二十七·祭祀五，第1893页，中华书局。

9 陕西省考古研究院：《西安南郊大朝刘黑马墓发掘简报》，《考古与文物》2015年第4期。

10 西安市文物保护考古研究院：《西安曲江缪家寨元代袁贵安墓发掘简报》，《文物》2016年第7期。

11 甘肃省博物馆、漳县文化馆：《甘肃漳县元代汪世显家族墓葬（简报之一）》，《文物》1982年第2期。

12 （明）宋濂等撰：《元史》卷七十二·志第二十三·祭祀一，第1781页，中华书局。

13 西安市文物保护考古所：《西安南郊元代王世英墓清理简报》，《文物》2008年第6期。

14 洛阳市第二文物工作队：《洛阳道北元墓发掘简报》，《文物》1999年第2期。

15 马志祥、张孝绒：《西安曲江元李新昭墓》，《文博》1988年第2期。

16 洛阳市博物馆：《洛阳元王述墓清理》，《考古》1979年第6期。

17 洛阳市铁路北站编组站联合考古发掘队：《元赛因赤答忽墓的发掘》，《文物》1996年第2期。

18 陕西省考古研究院、西安市文物保护考古研究院、陕西历史博物馆：《蓝田吕氏家族墓园》，文物出版社，2018年。

19 图自：陕西省考古研究院、西安市文物保护考古研究院、陕西历史博物馆：《蓝田吕氏家族墓园》第1160页，文物出版社，2018年。

20 （清）庞钟璐：《文庙祀典考》卷三，第279页，中国礼乐学会，1977年。

21 （清）庞钟璐：《文庙祀典考》卷五，第343页，中国礼乐学会，1977年。

22 图自：（清）庞钟璐：《文庙祀典考》卷首，第58页，中国礼乐学会，1977年。

23 钱穆：《国史大纲》第662页，商务印书馆，2010年。

Historical Origin of Porcelain Ritural Utensils in Ming and Qing Dynasties

Tang Xuemei

Abstract

Ritual utensils physically manifest etiquette system of a country. Being the last two imperial dynasties of Chinese traditional society, Ming and Qing inherited political and etiquette system from the previous generations, and in particular, utenstils that represented the system, with no exeption, followed their predecessors. Findings of documentations indicate that porcelain ritual utensils played a significant role in various ritual activities in the Ming and Qing Dynasties. Scholarly discussions on porcelain ritual utensils during this period have also been relatively fruitful. If we look into their origin, however, it's clear that it was highly related to the etiquette system and the rules of using ritual utensils in the Yuan Dynasty, while Yuan's ritual system once again was influenced by the Song and Jin Dynasties. Therefore, the present article, taking documentations, archaelogical finds and relics as foundation, explores the origin of ritual utensils during the Ming and Qing Dynasties. In the light of a clear outline of such exploration, the article examines how ritual utensils were used in the Yuan Dynasty so as to prove its impact on the Ming's and Qing's ritual system. Once again, setting off from the Yuan Dynasty, the article furtherly discusses how the ritual system in the Song and Jin Dynasties affected the Yuan Dynasty.

Keywords

ritual utensils, etiquette system

附录：陶瓷相关知识链接

吕成龙

磁山文化陶器

磁山文化属于新石器时代中期文化。因首先于1972年在河北省武安县（1988年撤县建市）磁山村被发现而得名。遗址总面积约14万平方米。1976年～1978年对部分区域进行了科学考古发掘，发掘面积6000平方米，出土陶器、石器、骨角器、蚌器、动物骨骸、植物标本等遗物6000余件。其中陶盂及陶支架、石磨盘及磨棒堪称磁山文化最具代表性的器物。据碳-14法测定其年代，距今约8000年至7600年，与1977年在河南省新郑县裴李岗村发现的裴李岗文化的年代大体相当。磁山文化的陶器均为手工制作，用泥条盘筑法和捏塑法成型，绝大部分属于夹砂红褐陶，少部分为泥质红陶，以素面为主，烧成温度在700℃～930℃左右。

仰韶文化陶器

仰韶文化因1921年首次发现于河南省渑池县仰韶村而得名，属于分布在黄河中、下游地区最重要的新石器时代文化。1921年10月，经中国政府批准，受聘为中国政府农商部矿政顾问的瑞典地质学家安特生、中国地质学家袁复礼等对仰韶村遗址进行了首次发掘，证实此处为新石器时代的文化遗存。遗址先后经过三次发掘，出土大量陶器、石器、骨器等遗物，在国际上引起极大轰动。仰韶村遗址遂成为中外史学界、考古界向往的“文化圣地”。由于遗址中还发现了非常精美的彩陶，因此，过去有人称之为“彩陶文化”。据碳-14法测定其年代，仰韶文化距今约7000～5000年，先后经历了约2000年的发展历程。仰韶文化陶器质地有泥质陶和夹砂陶两种，造型有盆、罐、钵、壶、尖底瓶、盒、鼎等。普遍采用泥条圈筑法或泥条盘筑法成型，小件器物则直接用手捏制而成。

马家窑文化陶器

马家窑文化因1924年最初发现于甘肃省临洮县马家窑村而得名。一般认为马家窑文化是黄河中游仰韶文化庙底沟类型的进一步发展，过去亦有人称之为“甘肃仰韶文化”。据碳-14法测定其年代，距今5000年左右。马家窑文化主要分布于甘肃、青海地区，可分为石岭下、马家窑、半山、马厂四个类型。马家窑文化陶器造型主要有钵、瓮、盆、双耳罐等。陶器质地有泥质红陶、灰陶、夹砂红陶等。马家窑文化的彩陶特别发达，与仰韶文化彩陶相比，马家窑文化彩陶图案具有显著的旋动特征，其旋动的方式丰富多样，或交错盘旋，或来往反复，使人感到变化莫测，回味无穷。

青莲岗文化陶器

青莲岗文化属于新石器时代中期文化，因1951年首先在江苏省淮安市楚州区宋集乡青莲村发现而得名。该文化主要分布在鲁中南和苏北地区，据碳-14法测定其年代，青莲岗文化距今约7400～6400年。出土陶器主要有鼎、釜、甑等炊器，豆、碗、钵等饮食器。青莲岗文化彩陶多用红、褐、紫红彩描绘纹饰，纹饰有双弧线纹、水波纹、八卦纹、十字纹及圈点纹等。青莲岗文化遗址的发现，在我国新石器时代考古中具有重大意义，它把东南沿海地区的原始文化同中原黄河流域的诸原始文化有机联系起来，在地域上连成一片，形成了我国新石器时代文化考古的完整体系。

大汶口文化陶器

大汶口文化是黄河下游地区新石器时代文化，因1959年首先在山东省宁阳县堡头村和泰安市郊大汶口镇发现而得名。主要分布在山东省和江苏省北部。据碳-14法测定其年代，大汶口文化距今约6000～4200年。大汶口文化陶器按质地可分为泥质陶和夹砂陶两类，按颜色可分为红陶、灰陶、白陶、橙黄色陶等，白陶出现于大汶口文化晚期。陶器造型主要有鼎、豆、罐、壶、杯、盉、鬶、背壶等。背壶是大汶口文化所特有的器物。大汶口文化也有非常精美的彩陶。

龙山文化陶器

龙山文化泛指黄河下游地区新石器时代晚期的一种文化。因1928年首次发现于山东省章丘县（1992年撤县建市）龙山镇而得名。龙山文化可分为山东龙山文化（或称典型龙山文化）、庙底沟二期文化、河南龙山文化、陕西龙山文化、龙山文化陶寺类型等几种类型。山东龙山文化是大汶口文化的延续，据碳-14法测定其年代，距今约 4500 ~ 4000 年。龙山文化陶器有黑陶、灰陶、红陶、黄褐陶和白陶等，造型有鼎、碗、罐、甗、鬶、盆等，制陶工艺水平比仰韶文化有很大提高。黑陶是该文化最具代表性的作品，尤以“蛋壳黑陶”最为精美，以致有人曾将该文化称为“黑陶文化”。龙山文化薄如蛋壳的黑陶，是陶工用快轮拉坯法制作而成。龙山文化黑陶的呈色是在烧成后期用烟熏法进行渗碳的结果。

齐家文化陶器

齐家文化继承马家窑文化发展而来，是黄河上游地区新石器时代晚期至青铜时代早期的一种文化，因 1924 年首先发现于甘肃省广河县齐家坪而得名。据碳-14 法测定其年代，距今 4100 年左右。遗址主要分布在青海、甘肃等地。齐家文化陶器大致可分为泥质红陶和夹砂红陶两类，造型有鬲、斝、甗、罐、盆、盉、碗、豆等，以罐最为多见。罐有单耳、双耳、三耳者，其中最具特征的是双耳大罐。

唐代著名青瓷窑——越窑

越窑这一名称最早见于唐人陆龟蒙的《秘色越器》诗，诗中有“九秋风露越窑开，夺得千峰翠色来”句。今人所谓越窑，系对浙江东北部宁波、绍兴一带北宋以前瓷窑的统称。越窑制瓷渊源可以上溯至商周时期的原始瓷生产，自东汉创烧成熟青瓷后，其制瓷业不断发展，先后经历了三国、两晋、南北朝的大发展时期和唐、五代、北宋早期的全盛期，至北宋中期衰落。唐、宋时期越窑为宫廷烧造过贡瓷。越窑所产瓷器始终以青瓷为主，汉至南朝还烧造少量黑釉瓷。唐至北宋时期的越窑秘色瓷代表越窑青瓷的最高水平。

越窑瓷器除了行销全国各地以外，从唐代开始还大量外销亚、非各国。

唐代著名白瓷窑——邢窑

邢窑的中心窑场位于今河北省内丘县、临城县，因这一地域在唐代隶属邢州管辖，故名。始烧于北朝，唐代为繁荣期。盛产白瓷，胎质细腻，釉色洁白。唐代陆羽《茶经》中有邢瓷“类银”“类雪”的记载。唐代邢窑白瓷曾一度被朝廷纳为贡品。唐代李肇《唐国史补》曰：“内丘白瓷瓯，端溪紫石砚，天下无贵贱通用之。”说明邢窑白瓷在当时深受人们喜爱。

陶瓷釉面开片

陶瓷釉面开片又称“纹片”，是陶瓷器因胎、釉膨胀系数不同所导致的釉面开裂现象。绝大多数陶瓷器的釉面均有不同程度的开片，这本是一种工艺缺陷，但宋代官窑、汝窑、哥窑等工匠却巧妙地利用这种开片美化器物，创烧出釉面开片不但有大、有小，而且片纹颜色有深、有浅的瓷器，可谓自然天成、精美绝伦。后人根据瓷器釉面开片颜色和形状的特点，曾赋之以“鱼子纹”“百圾破”“金丝铁线”等美称。

浇黄釉瓷

我国传统低温黄釉是一种以氧化铁（Fe_2O_3）为着色剂，以氧化铅（PbO）为助熔剂的单色釉。由于这种黄釉瓷器的施釉方法是将釉浆直接浇在素烧过的涩胎上，故称“浇黄釉瓷”。明代自洪武朝至万历朝、清代自顺治朝至宣统朝，浇黄釉瓷的烧造从未间断。从传世品及出土物看，宣德、成化时期的浇黄釉瓷器已很精致，但以弘治、正德时期的黄釉瓷器受到的评价最高。特别是弘治浇黄釉瓷，颜色纯正，色调均匀一致，釉面平整，犹如涂抹的鸡油，恬淡娇嫩，透彻明亮，达到历史上最高水平，故人们又赋之以“娇黄”之美称。

郎窑红釉瓷

高温颜色釉瓷名品之一。系因康熙四十四年（1705 年）至五十一年（1712 年）江西巡抚郎廷极（1663 ~ 1715 年）在景德镇设窑烧造、进贡朝廷而得名。是在模仿明代宣德鲜红釉瓷基础上而创烧的一种高温铜红釉瓷。其釉色浓艳者，被称作“牛血红”；釉色浅淡者，被称作“鸡血红”。郎窑红釉的着色剂主要为氧化亚铜胶体粒子。郎窑红釉瓷系生坯挂釉后，入窑经 1300℃ 以上的高温在强还原气氛中焙烧而成。因烧成时釉中氧化铜对窑内气氛、温度等技术指标要求极为严格，故烧造一件成功的作品非常困难，常常是百里挑一甚至千里挑一。当时有民谚曰：“若要穷，烧郎红。”由此可知郎窑红釉瓷器烧造难度之大。

豇豆红釉瓷

豇豆红釉瓷系康熙晚期景德镇窑创烧的一种著名的高温铜红釉瓷，属于各种铜红釉瓷中最精妙的一种。因淡红色釉面上分布有深红色斑点，酷似豇豆粒的颜色，故名“豇豆红”。豇豆红釉带有窑变性质，有通体红者、有类似豇豆粒颜色者、有泛绿点或绿斑者，人们据此赋予其“大红袍”“美人醉”“桃花片”“娃娃脸”等美称。康熙朝豇豆红釉瓷常见造型有太白尊、苹果尊、莱菔瓶、塑贴绿蟠螭瓶、菊瓣瓶、柳叶瓶、锹锣洗、印泥盒等，基本都是小件文房用具，无大件器。

胭脂红釉瓷

系以金为着色剂的低温单色釉瓷，亦称“金红釉瓷”。因这种釉是在清代康熙年间从欧洲传入我国，故又称“西洋红”或“洋金红”。釉烧温度约为 800℃ ~ 850℃。在康熙朝珐琅彩瓷上已见应用，但将其作为一种颜色釉单独用来装饰瓷器，则始于康熙六十年（1721 年）。雍正、乾隆两朝，胭脂红釉瓷成为皇帝喜爱的名贵单色釉瓷。胭脂红釉中的金大约占万分之二，足见金的发色能力之强。胭脂红釉呈色有深浅之分，浓重者称“胭脂紫”，稍淡者称“胭脂水”，最淡者称“淡粉红”。

蚯蚓走泥纹

钧窑瓷器釉面特征之一。即钧窑瓷器釉面呈现的类似于蚯蚓在雨后细泥上爬过的不规则痕迹。“蚯蚓走泥纹”系胎体施釉后晾干时釉层产生不规则开裂、然后入窑烧成所致。也就是说，在器物施釉后晾干时，釉面上已现出“蚯蚓走泥纹”的雏形。现代科学实验表明，形成“蚯蚓走泥”的关键是控制好两个因素，即胎体的素烧温度（一般为980℃ ~ 1000℃）和釉浆的颗粒细度。素烧温度过高、过低或釉浆的颗粒过粗、过细均不会形成“蚯蚓走泥纹”。现在仿钧窑瓷器完全可以做到人为控制“蚯蚓走泥纹”的有无。

枢府釉瓷

系对元代景德镇窑创烧的“卵白釉”的另一种称谓。因元代卵白釉印花盘、碗等器物的内部常见有同时模印的对称“枢”“府”二字，因此人们有时将这种釉称作“枢府釉”。其实，元代卵白釉印花盘、碗上的铭文不只有“枢府”二字，除此之外，尚见有“太禧”“东卫”“福禄”“白王”等铭文。更多的则不带铭文。“枢府”是元代最高军事机构“枢密院”的俗称，带有这种铭文的卵白釉瓷专供枢密院使用。

卵白釉瓷的特点是釉层较厚，呈失透状，色泽如鸭蛋壳之色，故被称作卵白釉瓷。元代景德镇窑卵白釉瓷的创烧，为明代永乐、宣德时期甜白釉的发明奠定了基础。元代卵白釉瓷在元代墓葬、窖藏、沉船和元大都遗址中均有发现。1984年安徽省歙县元代瓷器窖藏曾出土109件卵白釉瓷，而且均带有“枢府”铭文，是一次性出土“枢府”铭卵白釉瓷最多的一次。经综合排比研究后得知，卵白釉瓷约在元代大德年间（1297 ~ 1307年）就已经烧造，并且终元一代盛烧不衰，一直到明代早期还在烧造，时间长达一个世纪左右。

明、清两代青花瓷的演进

青花瓷是人们对白地蓝花瓷的称谓，属于高温釉下彩瓷器。它是明、清两代景德镇瓷器中的主流产品。虽然青花瓷均以天然钴土矿加工成的“钴料”来装饰，但由于各个历史时期人们的审美趣味不同、青花料来源不同，致使各个时期青花瓷的艺术风格各异，呈现鲜明的时代特征。如典型明代永乐、宣德青花瓷使用的是进口“苏麻离青”（亦称“苏泥渤青”）料，典型成化、弘治青花瓷使用的是产于江西省乐平县的平等青（亦称“陂塘青”）料，典型嘉靖、隆庆、万历青花瓷使用的是产于江西省上高县的“石子青”与从国外进口“回青”的混合料，清代典型康熙青花瓷器使用的是国产“浙料”或“珠明料”。由此形成永乐、宣德青花之浓丽凝重，成化、弘治青花之明净素雅，嘉靖、隆庆、万历青花之浓重艳丽，康熙青花之亮丽明翠等。虽风格有异，却有异曲同工之妙。

珐琅彩瓷

彩瓷品种之一。系清代康熙晚期在康熙帝授意下，将从欧洲传入的铜胎画珐琅技法成功移植到瓷胎上而创烧的彩瓷新品种。以雍正、乾隆时期的产量最大，乾隆以后即少有制作。乾隆时期，宫中收藏的珐琅彩瓷器曾集中存放在端凝殿，据档案记载有400多件。按清代宫廷档案记载和珐琅彩瓷原盛匣之标识，得知珐琅彩瓷之正式名称应为“瓷胎画珐琅”。珐琅彩瓷是专供皇帝玩赏的艺术珍品，宫廷控制极为严格。制作它所需要的白瓷胎系由景德镇御窑厂提供，运送到宫廷后，在皇帝的授意下，于内务府造办处珐琅作由宫廷画师精心彩绘，宫廷写字人题写诗句、署款，最后入炉经600℃左右焙烧而成。

珐琅料是一种人工烧炼的特殊彩料，雍正六年（1728年）以前需依赖从欧洲进口，自雍正六年开始，清宫造办处已能自炼20余种珐琅料，而且色彩种类比进口彩料更为丰富，遂使珐琅彩瓷器的生产获得突飞猛进发展。

康熙时期的珐琅彩瓷器多以胭脂红、淡黄和蓝色作地，还有一类特有的在宜兴紫砂胎上画珐琅彩的器物。典型雍正、乾隆时期的珐琅彩瓷成为诗、书、画、印相结合的艺术珍品，是中国古代彩瓷工艺臻达顶峰时期的产物。那些形状看似普通的珐琅彩盘、碗等，已摆脱被用作餐具的功能，属于能给人视觉带来美好享受的艺术珍品。

五彩瓷和斗彩瓷的区别

五彩瓷按工艺技法可分为两类：一类是纯釉上五彩瓷；另一类是釉下青花和釉上诸彩相结合的青花五彩瓷。斗彩瓷也是釉下青花与釉上诸彩相结合的一种彩瓷，从广义上说，斗彩属于青花五彩之范畴。但两者又有区别。斗彩强调的是先在已做好的生坯上用青花料双钩图案轮廓线，或在此基础上描绘图案局部，施透明釉经高温烧成后，再在釉上按青花轮廓线填涂红、黄、绿、紫等各种色彩。而青花五彩则是先在做好的生坯上以青花料描绘图案局部，施透明釉经高温烧成后，再在釉上勾线，并施以红、黄、绿、紫等各种色彩，凑齐整个图案。

粉彩瓷

彩瓷品种之一。系康熙晚期景德镇御窑厂在烧造五彩瓷器的基础上、受珐琅彩瓷器工艺影响而创烧的一种低温釉上彩瓷新品种。因采用西洋绘画技法描绘纹饰，故亦名“洋彩”。盛烧于雍正、乾隆时期，其后延续烧造。官、民窑均有烧造。制作时，先在经高温烧成的白瓷上用墨线起稿，然后在图案内以含砷的“玻璃白”打底，再将所需的色料用芸香油调匀，在玻璃白上进行渲染，最后入炉焙烧而成。由于彩料中掺入粉质，致使每一种颜色都可形成深浅、浓淡的变化，改变了五彩单线平涂的生硬色调，给人一种粉润柔和之感，故有“粉彩”之称。其装饰效果显得秀美、优雅、富丽。雍正、乾隆以后粉彩工艺极为盛行，成为瓷器釉上彩的主流。

锦上添花

清代乾隆朝创烧的一种瓷器装饰工艺。乾隆朝御窑瓷器装饰崇尚华丽繁缛，此时出现一种新的工艺技法，即在珐琅料色地上用一种状如绣针的工具划出或用毛笔蘸彩料画出细如毫芒、宛如凤尾状的锦纹或花卉纹，此种工艺俗称“轧道”，在轧道以外再加绘洋花，构成一种新颖的锦地花卉装饰。景德镇称这种工艺为“耙花”，清代宫廷档案则称之为“锦上添花”。

此种工艺非常复杂，有如铜胎画珐琅的艺术效果。乾隆以后各朝瓷器上仍有使用，但均不如乾隆朝产品工艺精湛。

剔花

陶瓷装饰技法之一。其做法是通过减地形成胎色与釉色的色差对比来衬托图案花纹。品种主要有白釉剔花、青釉剔花、黑釉剔花、酱釉剔花、绿釉剔花等。其中白釉剔花、绿釉剔花均需先在坯胎上施一层洁白的黏土，俗称“化妆土”。剔花工艺可分为留花剔地和留地剔花两种。前者是剔去花纹以外的空间，保留花纹；后者是保留花纹以外的空间，剔去花纹。

剔花技法主要流行于北宋、金、元时期的河南修武当阳峪窑、河北磁州窑及山西诸窑瓷器上。因这些地方的瓷土都比较粗糙，很适合施化妆土后以剔花技法进行装饰。特别是北宋当阳峪窑剔花瓷器，化妆土洁白如雪，胎色棕褐，颜色对比鲜明，剔花技艺娴熟，代表了当时剔花瓷器的最高水平。

剔花常与划花技法结合使用，称之为“剔划花”。

刻花

陶瓷装饰技法之一。系指以竹、骨、木或铁制刀具在已成型的陶瓷坯体上通过直刀和斜刀的灵活运用刻出图案花纹。刻花技法最早见于新石器时代陶器上，以后各朝陶瓷器上均有使用，但以宋代瓷器上使用最为普遍。宋代耀州窑、定窑、磁州窑、越窑、龙泉窑、景德镇窑等烧造的刻花瓷均各具特点。其中以耀州窑刻花青瓷受到的评价最高，所刻花纹下刀较深，刀锋犀利洒脱，具有浅浮雕般立体感，被推为宋代各窑瓷器刻花之冠。

刻花技法常与划花技法结合使用，被称作“刻划花”。

划花

陶瓷装饰技法之一。系指以竹、骨或铁制的锥或针在已成型的陶瓷坯体上划出图案花纹。早在新石器时代陶器上已有使用，此后直至今日都在使用，从未间断。历史上最著名的划花瓷器是五代耀州窑划花青瓷、北宋越窑划花青瓷和明清时期景德镇御窑划花瓷。其划花线条流畅，细如发丝，图案清晰，显示出高超水平。明、清时期景德镇窑瓷器上的划花技法亦被称作“锥拱”。

印花

陶瓷装饰技法之一。系指用带有花纹的印戳或印模在已成型的半干坯体上印出纹饰，印戳或印模一般用瓷泥制作而成。这一技法曾在西晋、隋代青瓷和宋、金时期定窑、耀州窑瓷器，以及宋、元以后景德镇窑瓷器上广泛使用。尤其是宋、金时期定窑印花瓷器，花纹清晰，构图严谨，堪称中国古代印花瓷器之冠。

高岭土

高岭土（矿物实验式：$Al_2O_3 \cdot 2SiO_2 \cdot 2H_2O$）俗称瓷土，制瓷用主要原料之一。是一种主要由高岭石或多水高岭石组成的软质黏土。其生成类型主要有两种：一种是地壳深处的“中低温热液蚀变形”；另一种是地壳上层的“风化型”，长石经完全风化以后，生成高岭石、石英和可溶性盐类，随雨水、河川漂流于它处后，可溶性盐类已分离，沉积下来的即为含有石英的高岭石，称作高岭土。

高岭土主要由小于2微米的微小片状、管状、叠片状等高岭石簇矿物（高岭石、地开石、珍珠石、埃洛石等）组成，另外还含有蒙脱石、伊利石、叶腊石、石英和长石等其他伴生矿物。高岭土的主要化学成分为Al_2O_3、SiO_2，另含有少量Fe_2O_3、TiO_2和微量K_2O、Na_2O、CaO、MgO等。纯净高岭土外观呈白色或浅灰色，含杂质时呈黄、灰、青、玫瑰等色。原矿呈致密块状或疏松土状，质软，有滑腻感，比重2.4～2.6。耐火度高，可达1770℃～1790℃。

高岭土不能单独用来制作瓷胎。1869年德国著名地理学家、地质学家李希霍芬（Ferdinand von Richthofen，1833～1905年）访问景德镇后，著文介绍景德镇以东约45公里高岭村边的山上所产高岭土，并根据汉语读音译成“Kaolin”，从此以后，“高岭”成为国际上通用的矿物学专有名词。

我国高岭土的储量大、分布广、品种繁多。已探明的矿点约700余处，储量约30亿吨。其中比较著名的有江西星子高岭、江苏苏州高岭、湖南大德高岭等。高岭土不仅是当今必不可少的制瓷原料，而且也是造纸、橡胶、化工、涂料、医药和国防等几十个行业所必需的矿物原料。高岭土的发现和使用，曾对景德镇的制瓷业产生过极为重要的影响，在世界陶瓷史上也堪称具有划时代意义的事件。

瓷石

瓷石是一种用来制造瓷器的坚硬或半坚硬天然石质矿物原料。通常呈灰色或灰白色。瓷石不是单一的矿物岩石，而是多种矿物的集合体。其矿物和化学组成都比较复杂，性质差别很大。一般瓷石的矿物组成以石英、长石、绢云母为主，还含有少量高岭石、碳酸盐等。其矿物组成的含量大致为：石英 40% ~ 60%、长石 0% ~ 37%、绢云母 16% ~ 38%、高岭石 0% ~ 12%、方解石 0.1% ~ 4%，还含有少量黄铁矿或磁铁矿、微量金红石、白钛矿、磷灰石、榍石、锆石和黑云母等。

瓷石的化学组成一般为：SiO_2：70% ~ 80%、Al_2O_3：12% ~ 18%、Fe_2O_3：0.38% ~ 1.36%、CaO：0.2% ~ 1.75%、MgO：0.06% ~ 0.5%、K_2O：1.6% ~ 4%、Na_2O：0.09% ~ 4.18%、H_2O：1% ~ 4%。虽然其化学组成中二氧化硅和氧化钾含量较高，氧化铝含量较低，但因其含有构成瓷胎的基本组分，而且经粉碎加水调和后，具有一定的可塑性和干燥强度，故某些瓷石可以单独用来制作瓷胎。早在距今约三四千年前的夏商时代，我国烧造原始瓷时就已经使用单一瓷石作胎。

二元配方

系指景德镇瓷业生产中将瓷石和高岭土两种矿物按适当比例配合用作制胎原料。瓷石和高岭土是两种性质不同的制瓷原料，二者在瓷胎中的作用亦各不相同。优质瓷石本身即含有构成瓷胎的各种化学成分，故可被单独用于制作瓷胎；而高岭土则必须与瓷石配合使用方能用来制作瓷胎。科学检测的结果表明，元代以前景德镇瓷器采用瓷石一种原料制胎，从元代开始，随着浅层瓷石和优质瓷石的缺乏，采用深层瓷石或劣质瓷石单独制胎，易造成瓷器烧成后产生严重变形，于是导致在瓷石中加入适量高岭土所谓“二元配方”的出现。这是中国陶瓷发展史上的一次革命性变化。由于高岭土中氧化铝（Al_2O_3）的含量约为 35%，因此将其引入瓷胎后，提高了瓷胎中氧化铝的含量，使制品的烧成温度范围拓宽，变形减少，成品率得以提高，并能烧造出颇有气势的大件器物。

白不（dǔn）

景德镇方言之一。系对将高岭土直接淘洗或将瓷石经粉碎淘洗后制成的长方砖大小的料坯的称谓。瓷石不的传统制作方法是：将采来的瓷石先靠人工用铁锤敲至鸡蛋大小的块状，放入碓坑中，藉溪流利用水碓将其击打成粉末，然后经过淘洗、沉淀去渣、稠化浓缩，放入预制好的具有一定尺寸规格的木模内，脱模后即成为长方砖大小的坯泥，再经过干燥，即成为瓷石“白不”。高岭土经直接淘洗后，亦可制成高岭土“白不”。将这两种“白不”运到瓷厂后，按一定比例配合化浆，再经过淘洗、沉淀去渣、稠化浓缩，即成为制作瓷器的胎泥。

胎泥制备

元代以来，景德镇瓷器一直采用高岭土不和瓷石不两种原料混合制成胎泥。通常是通过试烧用这两种原料按比例混合后制成的“照子”来调整并最终确定二者的配比。不同的制品对胎泥工艺性能的要求也不相同，一般为瓷石七分、高岭土三分；或瓷石六分、高岭土四分。确定了二者的配比后，即可开始配料，因为每块不子的重量都是一定的（一般每块重约 2 公斤），所以操作上均以不子的块数计算，对于未成块的不子碎料，则以重量计算。将不子在化浆池化浆混合后，经过淘洗、过筛除去粗颗粒和杂质，将得到的细泥浆滤去水分，俟泥料自然干燥至含水率 25% 左右时，即移入泥房陈腐。陈腐过的泥料经练泥后方可用来成型。

釉果

景德镇瓷器配釉用的主要原料。亦称釉石，是一种风化程度较轻或未经风化的瓷石。外观呈致密的岩石状。多产于景德镇以东的瑶里乡。釉果的开采和加工，与制胎用瓷石相同，亦需制成不子备用。

釉灰

景德镇传统瓷器配釉用原料之一。其制作方法是：先将石灰石烧成生石灰，运至炼灰场堆放，使其自然吸潮消解粉化成熟石灰备用。在铺放成一定厚度的狼萁柴（亦称“凤尾草”）上筛布一定厚度的熟石灰，然后再铺一层狼萁柴，其上再筛布一层熟石灰，如此依次叠加成一长方堆。沿底脚周围将狼萁柴点燃，经煨烧后，耙平拌匀。将得到的混合物再如前法与狼萁柴堆叠煨烧，经过三次煨烧后，再陈放均化数日，得到的即是釉灰成品。然后即可将其运至窑场备用。

配釉

景德镇传统瓷器的釉料，历来都是以釉果为基础，加入釉灰配合而成，俗称灰釉。釉灰在釉料中所占比重约为 7% ~ 20%。因釉灰的主要成分是碳酸钙，釉果系由绢云母、石英、长石和少量碳酸盐矿物组成，所以景德镇传统瓷釉属于石灰石—石英—绢云母质釉。配釉时，先将釉果不泥和釉灰分别加水在木桶内化成浆，并将二者配成同等浓度，然后依拟制瓷之种类，按一定容量比例用特制的铁锅分别舀出，倾倒入同一个木桶中混合搅匀，再加水调至适当浓度备用。

玉堂春瓶

清宫用于赏赐的瓶式之一。俗称“赏瓶”。创烧于雍正朝。基本形体为撇口、长颈、圆腹、圈足。乾隆朝以后历朝相袭。主要有 3 个品种，即青花、粉彩和祭蓝釉金彩。其中青花玉堂春瓶可分为两种，一种是肩部无凸起弦纹，另一种是肩部凸起 4 道弦纹。粉彩和祭蓝釉金彩玉堂春瓶仅见于光绪、宣统两朝。

红拂传

“红拂传”或称“风尘三侠”。相传故事出

自唐代杜光庭小说《虬髯客传》。描写隋炀帝杨广下扬州，令越国公杨素留守京城。三原布衣李靖往见，杨慕其才欲留用。杨素府中歌姬红拂女张凌华敬慕李的才华，趁黑夜逃出杨府，投奔李靖馆舍，同李结为夫妇，乘夜离开都城。一日，路上遇见大侠虬髯客张仲坚，三人谈心，志趣相同，遂结为挚友，并约定同往太原访谒李世民。李靖决心留下辅佐李世民，张见李世民后，自知难于争胜，遂将家财尽赠李靖后，飘然而去，浪迹天涯。

清代宫廷对黄釉瓷的管控

中华民族素以炎黄子孙著称于世，炎帝、黄帝是传说中的中原各民族共同的祖先，因此，黄色被冠以皇族的象征，由此对黄色的使用也有严格限制。早在唐代，各级官员的服装颜色就已形成制度，规定天子着黄袍，其他人不得穿用。清承旧制，对此有更为详细的规定，即浇黄釉瓷是皇家独享的器物，是身份尊贵的象征，不准流入民间，即使是次色浇黄器也要随大运瓷器运输至京入库备赏。因此，浇黄釉瓷属于清宫控制最为严格的一类瓷器。

据清代宫廷档案记载，乾隆七年（1742 年），督陶官唐英曾接到内务府造办处传来谕旨："嗣后脚货不必到京，即在本处变价，钦此。"对此，唐英在奏折中回复称："惟是国家分别等威，服物采章，俱有定制，故厂造供御之瓷，则有黄器及锥拱彩绘、五爪龙等件。此等器皿，非奉赏赐，凡在臣下，不敢珍藏擅用，以滋违制之戾……奴才愚昧之见，请将此落选之黄器、五爪龙等件，照旧酌估价值，以备核查，仍附运进京，或备内廷填补副余，或供赏赐之用，似可以尊体制而防亵越。"唐英在此强调了黄釉瓷器和饰有五爪龙瓷器的重要性。乾隆皇帝见到唐英奏折后，朱批曰："黄器如所请，五爪龙者外边常有，仍照原议行。"由此可见，黄釉瓷器比饰有五爪龙的瓷器还要尊贵。

清代后妃制度

中国古代皇帝实行一夫多妻制，皇帝的正妻为皇后，皇后统率后宫，地位极崇，皇后以下设妃、嫔、常在、答应等，分享不同待遇。此制度起源于后周，据《礼记》载："古者天子后宫立六宫、三夫人、九嫔、二十七世妇、八十一御妻。"意思是帝王身边需要有一大群妻妾，且要有等级高低之分。至秦代，开始建立内廷后宫，人数远远超过以前朝代的规模。汉代，后妃有十四个等级，规模庞大。隋唐时期这项制度趋于定型，设有皇后、夫人、嫔、世妇等多个等级，此后历代相承。至清代，随着封建制度的发展，后妃制度得到进一步确立和健全，"清太祖努尔哈赤 1616 年正式即汗位统"，"筑城三层，启建楼台"，"宫闱未有位号，但循国俗称福晋"。

清朝建立以后，皇太极对封建帝制进行了改革，其改革反映到宫中，就是要建立一套封建后妃制度与之相适应，于是"五宫并建，位号即明，等威渐辨"。

清朝入关后，加强了这方面建设，《世祖实录》载："顺治十五年十一月庚子，礼部等衙门会议宫闱女官名数、品级及供事宫女名额。乾清宫设夫人一人，秩一品；淑仪一人，秩二品；婉侍六人，秩三品；柔婉二十人、芳婉三十人，俱秩四品。慈宁宫设贞容一人，秩二品；慎容二人，秩三品；以下勤秩无定数，无品级。又设女官，设六局一司。"康熙以后典制大备，后宫号位定制严明。"皇帝尊圣祖母为太皇太后，尊圣母为皇太后，居慈宁、寿康、宁寿等宫。奉太妃、太嫔等位随居。皇后居中宫，主内治。皇贵妃一位、贵妃二位、妃四位、嫔六位，分居东西十二宫，佐内治。自贵妃以下封号，俱由内阁恭拟进号，钦定册封。贵人、常在、答应俱无定位，随居十二宫，勤修内职。"

大运瓷器

所谓大运瓷器从字义上解释就是指大批运输的瓷器，从实际烧造情况看，系指御窑厂每年底在清宫内务府奏销，按年例不用皇帝另外下旨、按固定瓷样定式烧造且统一运至京城、交付清宫瓷库的器物。现常被称作传统品种。大运瓷器中的琢器一类，系指不能仅靠陶车拉坯一次成型、需要多道工序加工而成的瓷器。大多被用作赏赐或陈设。

同治皇帝大婚用瓷

同治十一年（1873 年）二月，内务府遍召满蒙大臣的女儿入宫，为年满 17 岁的同治皇帝选皇后。同治帝按照慈安皇太后的旨意，选翰林院侍讲崇绮之女阿鲁特为皇后，慈禧皇太后中意的富察氏为慧妃，并于九月举行大婚之礼。为举办这次婚礼，从国库拨 1100 万两白银用于造办大婚用物品，其中即包括景德镇御窑厂烧造的 1 万余件大婚用瓷。同治六年（1867 年）三月初十日朝廷下达烧造命令，同治八年全部烧造完并运至京城后，被认为"均烧造粗糙，不堪应用"，遂命负责烧造的九江关监督景福照数赔补。景福于同治十一年十一月才补造完毕并解运至京城，未赶上同治皇帝大婚典礼。

清代宫廷祭祀

清代在后金、天聪时期，尚无宗庙之制，当时满洲只是依其旧俗，设"堂子"祭天和举行萨满祭祀活动。清太宗时逐渐接受和学习汉文化，于天聪十年（1636 年），朝廷在盛京（今沈阳）德盛门外和内治门外建圜丘坛（即天坛）、方泽坛（即地坛），祭告天、地。

顺治元年（1644 年），清朝定都燕京（今北京），在正阳门外南郊建圜丘坛，在安定门外北郊建方泽坛。按照清制，每年冬至祀圜丘、夏至祀方泽。另外，凡皇帝登极、皇帝和太后皇后上尊号、万寿节、册封皇后、册立太子、亲征命将、岁旱祈雨等，都要祭告天、地。而且凡遇有大事，像康熙年间朝廷平定"三藩"叛乱，也要祭告天地。在紫禁城内还保留满洲原有的萨满祭祀旧俗，其地点设在奉先殿、坤宁宫等处。

大雅斋

“大雅斋”是挂于长春宫后殿怡情书室内的匾额。据档案记载，咸丰五年（1855年），宫中写挂新匾“大雅斋”两面，分别挂在平安室和圆明园“天地一家春”殿内。平安室为皇帝寝宫养心殿的西耳房，咸丰年间，懿嫔（即慈禧）随侍时曾居于此处。此匾后被移挂至长春宫后殿怡情书室内东间的东托枋上。

“天地一家春”位于圆明园九洲清晏内，是后妃随皇帝驻跸御园时的居所。《圆明园考》载：“所谓天地一家春，乃孝钦后所居。”孝钦后即慈禧皇太后。

大佛堂

位于紫禁城内廷外西路，是慈宁宫的后寝殿。建于明代嘉靖十五年(1536年)，清沿明制，于顺治十年（1653年）重修。清代为太后、太妃礼佛之所，堂内陈设有佛像、龛座和五供等。

《国朝宫史》

清乾隆七年（1742年）大学士鄂尔泰、张廷玉等奉敕编纂，乾隆三十四年（1769年）成书。全书分6门36卷，其中训谕4卷、典礼6卷、宫殿6卷、经费3卷、官制2卷、书籍15卷。

训谕一门收录了从顺治朝至雍正朝圣训、乾隆皇帝御旨，以昭垂内廷法制。典礼一门，备著内廷典礼、仪节、规制、冠服、舆卫之制，充分体现宫中封建伦理纲常关系。宫殿一门，分外朝、内廷、景山、西苑和雍和宫等区域，详列规模。经费一门，详细记载内廷年例、日月、典礼、筵宴的花费等规定。官制一门，俱载太监职事级职与其功罪赏罚等。书籍一门，主要汇集这一时期官修重要书籍的名称、编书缘起、内容梗概和御制诗文等。

《钦定满洲祭神祭天典礼》

成书于乾隆十二年（1747年），乾隆帝钦定书名并作序，由庄亲王允禄等奉敕修纂。此书收集、诠释、整理满族各种祭祀仪式、祝辞，进行详细考订，并将祭祀中使用的祭器等绘成图。此书是满族萨满信仰礼俗的总结，也是研究清代宫廷萨满祭祀的重要资料。

米万钟

米万钟（1570～1631年），字仲诏，号友石、湛园、漫园漫士、勺海亭长、海淀渔长、莲花中人、宛香居士、文石居士、石隐庵居士、烟波钓叟等，陕西安化（今甘肃省庆阳市庆城县）人，后徙居燕京（今北京）宛平。系北宋著名书画家米芾（1051～1107年）后裔。明代万历二十三年（1595年）进士，先后任永宁、铜梁、六合县令，转任浙江承宣布政司右参赞、江西布政使、山东右布政使等职。政声好，得民心。为人刚正不阿。后被魏忠贤党所污，遭革职。崇祯元年（1628年）被起用为太仆少卿。卒于北京。一生喜爱山水花石，爱石成癖，工书画，擅诗词，行草得米家法，绘画以北宗为楷模，花卉宗明代画家陈淳（1483～1544年）。与董其昌（1555～1636年）齐名，遂有“南董北米”之誉。其书法成就很高，与董其昌、邢侗、张瑞图并称“明末四大书家”。

米万钟多才多艺，除了诗词、书画，还擅长蹴鞠、击丸、营造园林等。尤其受人称道的是其曾在北京先后营造过三座著名私家园林，即湛园、勺园和漫园。

从实物资料看，米万钟还喜爱瓷器，曾以私家名义在景德镇订烧过瓷器。故宫博物院收藏一件口沿下青花双方框内署“天启年米石隐制”款花觚，即是其中一件。从花觚腹部所绘折枝花托藏传佛教八吉祥之轮、螺、伞、盖看，还应有一件下落不明的绘折枝花托花、罐、鱼、肠的同样造型的花觚与之配对。据考证，米氏崇信佛教，其私家园林里曾建有佛堂，这种花觚应是供其插花供佛所用。由于天启四年至五年，米氏曾任江西按察使分守饶南，官位五品，驻饶州府，距景德镇不足百公里，因此，这为其在景德镇订烧瓷器提供了便利。这种花觚应是米氏在这期间所订烧。

明代万历三十五年（1607年）以后随着社会剧烈变革，景德镇御器厂停烧，民营瓷业跃居主导地位，国内市场上，缙绅阶层成为高档瓷器的主要消费群体。在追求奇趣品位思潮影响下，瓷器正式成为缙绅阶层所追求的展示个性的物品，主要标志是在所订烧瓷器上书写姓名或署以斋堂名号。据考证，米万钟是目前已知最早在瓷器上署以字号和私家园林名字的文人。这一标志性事件，为明末清初文人意趣与陶瓷艺术紧密融合开启了先声，而且此例一开，蔚然成风，引领了这一时期具有转型意义、主要供缙绅阶层使用的清新雅致风格高档细瓷发展的潮流。

郎廷极

郎廷极（1663～1715年），字紫衡、紫垣，号北轩，奉天广宁（今辽宁北镇）人。康熙朝官吏、学者。康熙四十四年（1705年）至五十一年（1712年）郎氏任江西巡抚期间曾在景德镇创立瓷窑，世称“郎窑”。从与郎廷极同时代人刘廷玑《在园杂志》和许谨斋诗稿看，郎窑的主要成就是擅仿明代各朝御窑瓷器，尤其是所仿宣德、成化朝御窑瓷器，水平高超，足以乱真。传世瓷器上见有署“御赐纯一堂”者，还见有将“御赐纯一堂珍藏”“大清康熙年制”同署于一件器物上者，因“纯一堂”系康熙皇帝赐给郎廷极的堂号，故这类瓷器无疑是郎窑制品。郎窑瓷器曾进贡朝廷，主要为康熙皇帝60岁万寿庆典而烧造。郎窑瓷器代表了康熙晚期景德镇瓷器的烧造水平。

唐英

唐英（1682～1756年）字俊公（亦作隽公），又字叔子，号蜗寄，奉天（今辽宁沈阳）人。出自满族家奴之家。隶汉军正白旗。康熙三十六年（1697年），年仅16岁的唐英开始供役于宫中养心殿，扈从圣祖康熙皇帝20余年。雍正元年（1723年）42岁的唐英授内务府员外郎衔，负责每月稽查内务府造办处伙计房各作当差匠役，画押办事，承造伙计，领取钱料。因办事干练，雍正六年（1728年）秋八月，47岁的唐英被派驻景德镇，协助时任内务府总管、管理淮安关税务监管景德镇御窑厂务的年希尧（？～1738年）督理御窑厂务。从乾隆元年（1736年）开始，唐英先后任淮安关、九江关监督，并监理景德镇御窑厂务（乾隆十五年[1750年]至十六年一度赴广东任粤海关监督），直到乾隆二十一年（1756年）离职、谢世。由于唐英的苦心经营，景德镇御窑厂在仿古创新方面均取得巨大成就。在勤于实践的基础上，唐英撰写了《陶务叙略》《陶成纪事》《陶冶图说》《陶人心语》等陶瓷工艺专著。唐英堪称我国历史上成绩最为卓著的一位督陶官，同时也是一位画家、文学家。人们习惯将乾隆年间由他督理的景德镇御窑称作“唐窑”，实际上，“唐窑”应从雍正六年（1728年）算起，直至乾隆二十一年（1756年）。

熊希龄

熊希龄（1870～1937年），字秉三，湖南省凤凰县人。近代著名政治家。光绪十八年（1892年）参加会试，成贡士；光绪二十年（1894年）补殿试，成庶吉士。光绪三十年（1904年）受湖南巡抚端方委派，赴日本考察实业，到过东京、大阪等地，并特意到日本瓷厂进行过考察。光绪三十一年，在他发起下，湖南省政府拨库银18000两，于姜湾创办湖南瓷业学堂，熊氏出任经理，聘日本人为教师，培养制瓷技术人才。光绪三十二年，熊氏又集商股5万银元，创建湖南瓷业公司，聘请景德镇名师向工人传授烧造细瓷之技艺。自此，醴陵瓷业才由乡村发展到城市，由粗瓷发展到细瓷。湖南瓷业公司的突出成就是在反复试验下，创烧出前所未有的釉下五彩瓷器。宣统元年（1909年）至民国四年（1915年），醴陵釉下五彩瓷器多次在国内劝业会和博览会上获奖，醴陵瓷器也因此而闻名中外。

无量寿佛

无量寿佛是无量光佛的化身，与后者一同作为西方极乐世界的主尊而广受佛教信众崇拜。无量光佛代表空间广度，无量寿佛代表时间长度，因其经典宣扬人死后可以往生西方净土的教义，致使无量寿佛广受欢迎。清代宫廷受藏传佛教影响，皇帝、皇后过生日时，经常有造瓷胎、铜胎藏传佛教式无量寿佛作为寿礼的传统，每批均以九尊或九的倍数为量，故宫博物院收藏的这类佛像数量颇丰。

三世佛

大乘佛教对原始佛教进行教义革新，在此基础上对于佛的概念进行了时间与空间上的拓展。三世佛概念的提出就是这种思想的体现，即以空间维度扩展为“横三世佛”，以时间维度扩展为“纵三世佛”。

所谓横三世佛，分别是：东方药师佛，主管东方净琉璃世界，有两位胁侍，分别为日光菩萨和月光菩萨，也被称为“东方三圣”；西方无量光佛，主管西方极乐世界，两位胁侍分别为大势至菩萨和观世音菩萨；中央为释迦牟尼佛，主管中央娑婆世界，有两位胁侍，即文殊菩萨和普贤菩萨，号称“华严三圣”。

所谓纵三世佛，系指过去燃灯佛、现世释迦牟尼佛和未来弥勒佛。燃灯佛是释迦牟尼佛之前的佛，曾在过去世预言释迦牟尼未来将成佛；现世释迦牟尼佛，在此娑婆世界以佛法救度世人。未来弥勒佛，现在还在兜率内院为菩萨，未来将于龙花树下演法救度一切众生。

景德镇

中国历史文化名城之一。位于江西省东北部，原名新平，因地处昌江东南，故又名昌南镇，北宋景德年间（1004～1007年）改称景德镇，以皇帝年号为名。景德镇地处群山环抱之中，自然资源非常丰富，历史上曾以瓷、茶而闻名中外。瓷、茶并茂，工商辐辏，促进了城市的繁荣和经济发展，曾与湖北汉口镇、广东佛山镇、河南朱仙镇并称我国古代“四大名镇”。

文献记载景德镇制瓷始于汉代，但迄今为止所发现的瓷窑遗址的年代最早为唐代。明、清以来，随着历朝皇帝在景德镇设陶厂、御器（窑）厂，专门烧造宫廷用瓷，带动了民营瓷业的发展和繁荣，于是，天下至精至美之瓷器莫不出于景德镇，景德镇也因此博得“瓷都”之美誉。

窑神碑拓片

我国古代各行各业学习业务都讲究师徒传承，因此有行业祖师，即祖师爷，俗称“行业神”。后生们都要塑其像，虔诚供奉，顶礼膜拜，以求保佑学有所成。如木工之奉鲁班，造酒业之奉仪狄、杜康，药铺之奉孙思邈，医生之奉华佗，茶叶店之奉陆羽，私塾之奉孔丘等。陶瓷行业也不例外，而且由于陶瓷烧造的成功与否，带有很大的偶然性，因此，窑工们认为冥冥之中有神灵在起作用，致使各地都很重视修建窑神庙。从目前所掌握的资料看，至迟从北宋（960～1127年）以来，在陕西铜川，河南鹤壁、修武、禹县、宜阳、密县，山西榆次、介休，山东淄博，河北邯郸、临城，江西景德镇等产瓷区都曾建造窑神庙，供奉窑神，祈求保佑烧造成功。庙里供奉的窑神有伏羲、神农、黄帝、尧、老子、雷公、山神、土神、牛马二王、金火圣母、宁封子、伯灵翁、童宾、赵慨、蒋知四、华光等。故宫博物院收藏的一批陕西、山西、河南等地的窑神碑拓本或重修窑神庙碑记拓本，反映了各地供奉窑神的情况。这些文字资料对于研究古代陶瓷文化具有重要意义。

Appendix: Ceramic Knowledge Link

Lü Chenglong

Pottery of the Cishan Culture

Cishan culture is a mid-Neolithic culture. It is named after the village of Cishan, the first excavated site of this culture, which was discovered in 1972 in Wu'an County, Hebei Province (the county was made into a city in 1988). The total area of the site is about 140,000 square meters. From 1976 to 1978, archaeological excavations were carried out in some regions, with an area of 6,000 square meters. More than 6,000 relics, including pottery, stoneware, bone tools, mussel tools, animal bones, and plant specimens, were discovered. Among them, pottery bowls, furniture, stone saddle-querns, and stone rollers are the most representative of the Cishan culture. According to radiocarbon dating, the site dates back to ca. 8000-7600 years ago, which is around the same age as the Peiligang culture discovered in Peiligang Village, Xinzheng County, Henan Province in 1977. The pottery of Cishan Culture is handcrafted by coiling and kneading. The majority is reddish-brown pottery mixed with sand, while some are red pottery made of fine clay. The surface is mostly plain, and the firing temperature is between 700 ℃ and 930 ℃ .

Pottery of the Yangshao Culture

Yangshao Culture is named after the village of Yangshao, the first excavated site of this culture, which was discovered in 1921 in Mianchi County, Henan Province. It is the most important Neolithic culture in the middle and lower Yellow River region. In October 1921, the Swedish geologist Johan Gunnar Andersson and Chinese geologists, including Yuan Fuli, were hired, with the approval of the Chinese government, as Mineral Consultants of the Ministry of Agriculture and Commerce of the Chinese government. They conducted the first excavation of the site and confirmed that it was a cultural relic of the Neolithic period. With three excavations, a large amount of pottery, stoneware, bone tools, and other relics were unearthed. The discovery caused a great international sensation. The Yangshao site has thus become a "cultural pilgrimage site" for historians and archaeologists at home and abroad. Since exquisitely painted pottery was also found here, the site used to be called "painted pottery culture". According to radiocarbon dating, the Yangshao culture spanned about 2000 years from ca. 7000 to ca. 5000 years ago. The Yangshao culture pottery has two types: pottery made of fine clay and pottery mixed with sand. The shapes include basins, jars, bowls, pots, pointed-bottom bottles, boxes, tripods, etc. The majority are made with clay-strip forming technique or coiling technique, while small objects are directly made by hand.

Pottery of the Majiayao Culture

Majiayao culture is named after the village of Majiayao, where the culture was discovered in 1924 in Lintao County, Gansu Province. It is generally considered to be a further development of the Miaodigou phase of the Yangshao culture in the middle Yellow River region. It was thus called "Gansu Yangshao culture" in the past. According to radiocarbon dating, the site dates back to ca. 5000 years ago. The culture is mainly distributed in Gansu and Qinghai and can be divided into four types: Shilingxia, Majiayao, Banshan, and Machang. Pottery from the Majiayao culture mainly includes bowls, urns, basins, and jars with two handles. The texture of pottery includes red pottery made of fine clay, grey pottery, and red pottery mixed with sand. Painted pottery of the Majiayao culture is especially developed. Compared with that of the Yangshao culture, the pattern of Majiayao painted pottery has a distinctive swirling feature in its pattern. The diverse swirls that are sometimes interlaced and sometimes repeated bring endless fascination and intrigue.

Pottery of the Qingliangang Culture

Qingliangang culture is a mid-Neolithic culture. It is named after the village of Qinglian, where the culture was discovered in 1951 in Songji town, Chuzhou District of Huaian, Jiangsu Province. The culture spreads throughout central and southern Shandong and northern Jiangsu. According to radiocarbon dating, the site dates back to ca. 7400-6400 years ago. Excavated pottery includes cooking vessels such as 鼎 (Ding), 釜 (Fu), and 甑 (Zeng) as well as food vessels such as 豆 (Dou), 碗 (Wan), and 钵 (Bo). Painted pottery of the Qingliangang culture is often decorated with red, brown, and purple-red ornaments that include patterns such as double-arc, wave, eight trigrams, cross, and dots. The discovery of the site of the Qingliangang culture is of great significance in the Neolithic archaeology of China. It serves as an organic connection between the prehistoric cultures of the southeast coast and those of the Central Plain area of the Yellow River. It completes the archaeological system of the Neolithic cultures of China.

Pottery of the Dawenkou Culture

Dawenkou culture is a Neolithic culture in the lower Yellow River region. It is named after the town of Dawenkou, where it was discovered in 1959 in Baotou Village and the suburban area of Tai'an, Ningyang County, Shandong Province. The culture spreads throughout the Shandong Province and northern Jiangsu Province. According to radiocarbon dating, the culture dates back to ca. 6000-4200 years ago. In terms of texture, pottery of the Dawenkou culture can be divided into two types: pottery made of fine clay and pottery mixed with sand. According to colour, it can be divided into red pottery, grey pottery, white pottery, orange pottery, etc. White pottery appeared in the late phase of the culture. Pottery shapes include 鼎 (Ding), 豆 (Dou), 罐 (Guan), 壶 (Hu), 杯 (Bei), 盂 (Yu), 鬶 (Gui), 背 壶 (Bei Hu) 等 , etc. *Bei Hu*, water jar with two tape holes, is distinctive of the Dawenkou culture. Exquisitely painted pottery can also be found here.

Pottery of the Longshan Culture

Longshan culture is a late Neolithic culture in the lower Yellow River region. It is named after the town of Longshan, where it was discovered in 1928 in Zhangqiu County (the county was made into a city in 1992), Shandong Province. The culture includes several types: Shandong Longshan (also known as the typical Longshan culture), Maodigou II, Henan Longshan, Shaanxi Longshan, and Longshan Taosi. As a further development of the Dawenkou culture, the Shandong Longshan culture dates back to ca. 4500-4000 years ago, according to radiocarbon dating. Pottery of the Longshan culture includes black pottery, grey pottery, red pottery, yellowish-brown pottery, and white pottery. The shapes include 鼎 (Ding), 碗 (Wan), 罐 (Guan), 甗 (Yan), 鬶 (Guī), 盆 (Pen), etc. The level of skill in pottery making in Longshan is much improved compared to that of the Yangshao culture. The most characteristic of this culture is the production of black pottery, among which the "eggshell black pottery" is most exquisite. The culture is thus sometimes referred to as the "black pottery culture". The Longshan black pottery, with its wall as thin as an eggshell, is made by moulding with the fast wheel. Colouration is achieved by smoking the pot at the later stage of firing to allow carbon to seep through.

Pottery of the Qijia Culture

A successor of Majiayao culture, the Qijia culture is a late Neolithic to early Bronze Age culture distributed around the upper Yellow River region. It is named after the Qijiaping site in Guanghe County, Gansu Province, where it was discovered in 1924. According to radiocarbon dating, the culture dates back to ca. 4100 years ago. Qijia culture spreads throughout Qinghai and Gansu. Pottery from the Qijia culture can be roughly divided into two types: red pottery made of fine clay and red pottery mixed with sand. The shapes of vessels include 鬲 (Li), 斝 (Jia), 甗 (Yan), 罐 (Guan), 盆 (Pen), 盉 (He), 碗 (Wan), 豆 (Dou), among which jars are the most common. Jars may come with a single handle, double handles, or triple handles, though double-handled jars are the most characteristic.

Yue Kiln: The Famous Celadon Kiln of the Tang Dynasty

Yue kiln is first recorded in the poem *Mi Se Yue* Ware by the Tang poet Lu Guimeng, "the autumn wind revealed the Yue kiln, where thousands of Yue wares appeared like viridescent mountain ranges. " Today, Yue kiln widely refers to pre-Northern Song kilns in northeastern Zhejiang and the Ningshao region. Yue kilns originated from the production of primitive porcelain in the Shang and Zhou Dynasties. Since the creation of celadon in the Eastern Han Dynasty, the production of Yue wares developed through the Three Kingdoms period, the Jin Dynasty, and the Northern and Southern Dynasties. The Tang Dynasty, the Five Dynasties, and early Northern Song Dynasty mark the peak of Yue ware production, although the decline started in the mid-northern Song, Yue kilns also produced wares that would be paid as tributes for the court. Though Yue wares are predominantly celadon, a small number of black-glazed wares were also produced from the Han Dynasty to the Southern Dynasty. *Mi Se* ware ("Oliver Green Porcelain") produced from the Tang to Northern-Song Dynasty represented the peak of Yue ware quality.

On top of being traded nationwide, Yue ware has also been exported to Asian and African countries since the Tang Dynasty.

Xing Kiln: The Famous White Porcelain Kiln of the Tang Dynasty

The centre of Xing kiln lies in the Neiqiu and Lincheng County, Hebei Province. The kiln takes its name from Xing, the jurisdiction of the region during the Tang Dynasty. The production of Xing ware began in the Northern Dynasties and flourished in the Tang Dynasty. The Xing kiln is famous for the production of white porcelain with a smooth body and white glaze. *The Classic of Teas* by the Tang writer Lu Yu described Xing wares as "like silver" and "like snow". The court once accepted the white porcelains of Xing kiln in the Tang Dynasty as tributes. Tang writer Li Zhao wrote in *Supplement to the History of Tang*, "white porcelain bowls from Neiqiu and purple inkstones from Duanxi are used by both the noble and the base," which shows that Xing white porcelain was highly popular at the time.

Crackled Glazes of Ceramic

Kai Pian, crackles in glazes, also known as "Wen Pian (crazes)," is a pattern caused by the unequal expansion of body and glaze. Crazes of various degrees can be found on most glaze surfaces. They used to be a defect in craft. However, potters of the Guan kiln, Ru kiln and Ge kiln from the Song Dynasty skillfully took advantage of the phenomenon of crazing and created glaze with deliberate crackles of various sizes and shades. The effect looks natural yet exquisite. Based on the characteristics of the colour and shape of the crackled glaze, people also called it "fish pattern, " "*Bai Ji Po*, " and "gold thread and iron wire".

Bright Yellow-Glazed Porcelain

Traditional Chinese lower-fired yellow glaze is a monochrome glaze that is coloured with Fe_2O_3 and fluxed with PbO. Since the making of yellow-glazed wares requires pouring the liquid glaze directly onto the biscuit, they were called "pouring-yellow-glazed porcelain". The making of yellow-glazed wares spanned the Ming Dynasty from the reign of Hongwu Emperor to the reign of Wanli Emperor. Judging from handed-down objects and archaeological artefacts, yellow-glazed porcelain from the Xuande and Chenghua period is already well-crafted. However, the ones from the Hongzhi and Zhengde period are the most esteemed. Hongzhi yellow-glazed porcelain, in particular, is renowned for its clear glazes, even colouring, and polished surfaces, the effect of which is a chicken-oil-like delicacy, translucency, and brightness, making it the highest quality of all time. The Hongzhi yellow-glazed porcelain also gained the name "bright yellow" ("*jiao huang*") for its bright colour.

Lang Kiln Red-glazed Porcelain

Lang kiln red-glazed porcelain is one of the most famous high-fired glazed porcelain. It is known as porcelain that was fired at a kiln built by the Jiangxi governor Lang Tingji (1663-1715) in Jingdezhen and presented as tributes to the court from the 44th to the 51st year of Kangxi (1705-1712). It is a high-fired copper-red-glazed ware that took after the Xuande bright-red-glazed porcelain of the Ming Dynasty. Heavy-coloured glazes are called "ox blood red," while light-coloured ones are called "chicken blood red". Lang kiln red glazes are coloured with colloidal particles of copper oxide. After glazing, the piece would be fired in the kiln at 1300℃ in a reducing atmosphere. Since the copper oxide in the glaze required strict control of technical indicators such as atmosphere and temperature, it was challenging to produce a piece successfully. The success rate was often one in a hundred or even one in a thousand. As the saying goes, "he who wants to be poor should fire Lang wares," which is a great indication of the difficulty of producing Lang kiln red-glazed porcelain.

Kidney-bean-red-glazed Porcelain

Kidney-bean-red-glazed porcelain is a famous high-fired copper-red-glazed porcelain created by Jingdezhen in the late Kangxi period. It is the most exquisite copper-red-glazed porcelain. Its light-red glaze surface is filled with dark red spots that resemble kidney beans, thus the name "kidney-bean red". Kidney-bean-red glazes often experience *Yao Bian* ("furnace transmutation"). Some pieces turn out all-red, while others turn out with green spots or flecks. Names such as *Da Hong Pao* ("big red rope"), *Mei Ren Zui* ("drunken beauty"), *Tao Hua Pian* ("peach blossom petal"), *Wa Wa Lian* ("baby face") were given accordingly. Typical kidney-bean-red-glazed wares include small-sized study-room objects such as beehive waterpot (*Tai Bai Zun*), apple-shaped jar, turnip-shaped bottle, vase with applied *chi* dragon design, chrysanthemum-petal-shaped bottle, willow-shaped bottle, gong-shaped washer, and seal paste box, none of which is large-sized.

Crimson-pink-glazed Porcelain

Crimson-pink-glazed porcelain is lower-fired monochrome porcelain coloured with gold. It is also known as "gold-red-glazed porcelain". Since the glaze was introduced to China from European countries during the Kangxi period of the Qing Dynasty, it was also called "Western red" or "foreign gold red". Firing temperature is about 800-850℃. Crimson-pink glaze has been used in the decoration of cloisonné enamel wares far earlier than the 60th year of Kangxi (1721), when it started to be used as a monochrome glaze. During the Yongzheng and Qianlong periods. Crimson-pink-glazed wares became the Emperors' favourite precious monochrome-glazed wares. The proportion of gold in the crimson-red glaze is only about two in ten thousand, which is evidence of the strong pigmentation ability of gold. Crimson-red glaze comes with different shades. Rich ones are called "rouge purple," lighter ones are called "liquid blush," while the lightest ones are named "light pink".

Earthworm Mark

Earthworm mark is a characteristic of the Jun kiln porcelain glaze that has marks like irregular tracks left by the earthworm climbing in the mud after rain. The earthworm mark is a result of the irregular cracking of the glaze when the piece is dried after glazing and then fired in the kiln. In other words, the nascent form of the earthworm mark should already have appeared on the glaze surface when the piece is dried. A scientific experiment shows that the keys to the formation of earthworm mark are the firing temperature of the biscuit (generally between 980℃ and 1000℃) and the grain size of the glaze slip. When the firing temperature of the biscuit is too high or too low, or the grain size of the glaze slip too coarse or too fine, the earthworm mark would not be formed. Nowadays, the formation of earthworm on imitated Jun kiln porcelain can be completely controlled.

Shufu Porcelain

Shufu porcelain is another name for the "egg-white glaze" that was produced in Jingdezhen in the Yuan Dynasty. Since the Yuan egg-white-glazed wares such as printed plates and bowls often had symmetrical marks of the characters "shu" and "fu," they were sometimes called "*shufu* glaze". In fact, the inscriptions on the Yuan egg-white-glazed printed plates and bowls include words other than "shu fu," such as "tai xi," "dong wei," "fu lu," and "bai wang," though inscriptions are absent on most wares. "Shufu" refers to the highest military institution of the Yuan Dynasty, "the Privy Council," and egg-white-glazed porcelain with such inscription is for the exclusive use of the Privy Council.

Egg-white-glazed porcelain is characterized by its thick, opaque, and duck-eggshell-like glaze, hence the name "egg-white-glazed porcelain". The creation of egg-white-glazed wares by the Jingdezhen kilns in the Yuan Dynasty laid the foundation for the invention of sweet-white glaze in the Yongle and Xuande periods of the Ming Dynasty. Yuan egg-white-glazed porcelain was discovered in tombs, cellars, shipwrecks and the Yuan Capital City (Yan Da Du) Wall Ruins. In 1984, 109 pieces of egg-white-glazed wares were excavated in the Yuan porcelain cellars in She County, Anhui Province. All unearthed objects bear the "shufu" inscription. It was an excavation with the most egg-white-glazed wares with the "shufu" inscription. A comprehensive comparative study confirmed that egg-white-glazed wares were fired as early as the Dade period of the Yuan Dynasty (1297-1307). Its production flourished throughout the late Yuan Dynasty and continued until the early Ming Dynasty, spanning around a hundred years.

The Evolution of Blue-and-White Porcelain of the Ming and Qing Dynasties

Blue-and-white porcelain refers to white porcelain decorated with blue patterns with the underglaze method. It was the most popular product of the Ming and Qing Dynasties. All blue-and-white porcelain is decorated with pigment made from the natural material of cobalt oxide. However, the difference in aesthetic preferences from different periods and the variance in material sources resulted in distinctive porcelain styles that bear characteristics of each era. Typical Yongle and Xuande blue-and-white porcelain from the Ming Dynasty, for instance, were made of imported Sumani blue (also known as Sumatra blue). Chenghua and Hongzhi porcelain were usually made of *pingdeng qing* (also known as *Po-Tang qing*) from the Leping County in Jiangxi Province. Typical Jiajing, Longqing and Wanli porcelain were painted with a mixture of "stone blue" (*shizi qing*), produced in the Shanggao County, Jiangxi Province, and imported "Mohammedan blue" (*hui qing*). Kangxi porcelain from the Qing Dynasty was typically painted with locally produced "Zhe material" or "Zhuming material". Accordingly, Yongle and Xuande blue-and-white wares are known for their richness and imposingness, while brightness and elegance are characteristics of Chenghua and Hongzhi wares. Jiajing and Wanli wares are sumptuous and bright-coloured, while Kangxi porcelain has an air of vibrancy and lucidity. Despite the difference in styles and approaches, those wares are equal in beauty and charm.

Porcelain Painted in Cloisonné Enamels

Porcelain with cloisonné enamels is a variety of overglaze polychrome porcelain. In the late Qing Dynasty, under the instruction of Emperor Kangxi, the technique of European painted enamels on copper was adopted and applied to porcelain. Production of porcelain painted in cloisonné enamels flourished in the Yongzheng and Qianlong period. Few were produced after Qianlong. During the Qianlong period, porcelains with cloisonné enamels collected by the court were stored together in Duan Ning Hall. The archive recorded more than 400 pieces. According to Qing court documents and labels on the original containers of porcelain with cloisonné enamels, the official name of those wares is "Painted Cloisonné Enamels on White Porcelain". Cloisonné enamel wares was produced for the exclusive use and pleasure of the emperor. Production was strictly controlled by the court. Glazed white porcelain body were provided by the imperial kilns at Jingdezhen and transported to the court. Cloisonné enamels would then be painted by court painters from the Ministry of Internal Affairs according to the desire of the emperor. After the court writer has added a poem and signed, the piece would be fired in the furnace at about 600 ℃ .

Cloisonné enamel is a special manmade paint. Before the 6th year of the Yongzheng era (1728), all enamels were imported from Europe. After 1728, court workshops were able to produce more than twenty kinds of cloisonné enamels with colours more abundant than imported ones. This greatly facilitated the development of the production of cloisonné enamel wares.

Cloisonné enamel wares in the Kangxi period was mostly in rouge, light yellow, and blue. There was also a unique ware that was made by applying enamels on biscuit made of Yixing purple clay. Porcelain in the Yongzheng and Qianlong periods is an artistic treasure that combines poetry, calligraphy, painting, and printing. It is a product of the peak of ancient Chinese painted porcelain technique. Those seemingly ordinary enamel porcelain plates, bowls, and bottles have been deprived of their function as tableware and have instead been treated as pure art that brings pleasure and satisfaction.

The Difference between *Wucai* and *Doucai* Porcelain

Wucai ("five-colour") porcelain can be divided

into two types in terms of technique: pure glaze with overglaze polychrome enamels and underglaze blue with overglaze polychrome enamels. *Doucai* ("contending-colours") porcelain is also decorated with a combination of underglaze blue and overglaze polychrome enamels and therefore belongs in the category of *wucai* in a broad sense. However, differences still exist between the two. In *doucai*, the design would be either entirely or partly outlined with blue pigment on the biscuit. After translucent glaze has been applied and the piece has been fired, the outlined area would be filled with colours such as red, yellow, green, and purple. *Wucai*, on the other hand, involves applying blue underglaze on the biscuit only for parts of the design. After the piece is glazed and fired, the design would be outlined and completed with colours such as red, yellow, green, and purple.

Famille Rose Enamel Ware

Famille rose enamel ware is a variety of overglaze polychrome porcelain created by the imperial kilns at Jingdezhen in the late Kangxi period. It is a new variety of lower-fired porcelain that is based on *wucai* porcelain and inspired by the polychrome enamel overglaze technique. Since its decoration is drawn with the European painting technique, it is also known as yangcai ("foreign colours"). Production of *famille rose* enamel wares flourished in the Yongzheng and Qianlong periods and continued thereafter. They were fired at both official and private kilns. The production process starts with ink sketches on high-fired white porcelain body, after which the pattern would be first filled with an opaque white pigment that contains arsenic. The rest of the pigments needed would then be mixed with rue oil and applied on top of the opaque white pigment. Finally, the piece is fired in a furnace. Since the pigments were mixed with powder, each colour could come with different shades and thickness that neutralized the harshness of *wucai* palette, adding a subtle softness. Famille rose ware is thus called *fencai* ("soft colours"). The effect achieved by such decoration is charming, elegant, and sumptuous. Famille rose ware flourished after the Yongzheng and Qianlong period. It gradually replaced the dominance of *wucai* ware and became the most popular porcelain.

Jin Shang Tian Hua —— Painted Cloisonné Enamels on Sgraffiato Ground

"*Jin Shang Tian Hua*" is a form of porcelain decoration created in the Qianlong period of the Qing Dynasty. Since the Qianlong imperial kilns sought to create lavish and elaborate patterns, a new technique was developed. It involved using an embroidery-needle-like tool to create brocade or floral patterns with strokes as thin as a hair and as delicate as phoenix feather. The technique is commonly known as *zhadao* ("the way of rolling"). After *zhadao*, exotic flowers would be added to create a new floral decoration against a brocaded ground. Jingdezhen named the technique *bahua*, while the Qing Ministry of Internal Affairs called it "*Jin Shang Tian Hua*".

This extremely complicated technique creates a similar effect as cloisonné wares. It continued to be used on porcelains after the Qianlong period, though none were as exquisite as those of the Qianlong period.

Cut Decoration

Cut decoration is a decoration technique of ceramics. The pattern is achieved by cutting away parts of the surface layer to create colour contrast between the body and the glaze. Varieties of resist-decoration wares include cut decoration on white glaze, cut decoration on blue glaze, cut decoration on black glaze, cut decoration on russet glaze, and cut decoration on green glaze. Among them, both white and green-glazed wares require applying a layer of white slip on the body before applying cut decorations, commonly known as "makeup slip". The cut decoration can be used in two ways: either cutting away the layer to reveal the design pattern or cutting away the design pattern and retaining the remaining space.

The cut decoration was widely used in the Dangyangyu kiln in Henan Xiuwu, the Cizhou kiln in Hebei, and numerous kilns in Shanxi during the Northern Song, Jin, and Yuan Dynasties. Since the clay in these regions is relatively coarse, the application of white slip and the cut decoration is well-suited. Porcelain from the Dangyangyu kiln in the Northern Song period, in particular, has snow-white slip and brown body. Its strong contrast of colours is an indication of the skilful exercise of the cut decoration, making it a representation of the pinnacle of ancient Chinese porcelain with cut decorations.

Cut decoration (*Ti Hua*) is often used in combination with the carving technique (*Hua Hua*), which is called "*Ti Hua Hua*" (cut and carved decoration) today.

Carved Decoration

One of the decoration techniques of ceramic is carving. The pattern is achieved by the flexible use of knives made of bamboo, bone, wood, or iron at a perpendicular or inclined angle on the ceramic body. The carving technique appeared as early as the Neolithic period and continued to be used in successive dynasties, though the most common use was on the Song Dynasty porcelain. Carved porcelain from each Song kiln, such as Yaozhou kiln, Ding kiln, Cizhou kiln, Yue kiln, Longquan kiln, and Jingdezhen kiln, has its own characteristics. Among all Song kilns, Yaozhou kiln produced the most well-received carved blue porcelain. Its carved pattern is characterized by the deep, sharp, and precise blade that creates a three-dimensionality that reminds one of bas-relief. The Yaozhou kiln is undoubtedly the best among all Song kilns in terms of carving skill.

The carving technique (*Ke Hua*) is often used in combination with the incising technique (*Hua Hua*). Together, they are called "*Ke Hua Hua*"(carved and incised decoration).

Incised Decoration

Incising is one of the ceramic decoration techniques that involves carving patterns on the ceramic body with needles or awls made of bamboo, bone, or iron. The technique appeared as early as the Neolithic period and was continually used to date. The most famous porcelains with incised decoration in history are the Yaozhou kiln celadon wares in the Five Dynasties, the Yue kiln celadon wares in the Northern Song Dynasty, and the wares produced by Jingdezhen imperial kiln in the Ming and Qing Dynasties. The smoothly incised patterns that are as thin as a hair and the clarity of decorations are of superb quality. The incising technique of the Jingdezhen porcelain during the Ming and Qing dynasties was also called "*zhui gong*".

Impressed Decoration

One of the ceramic decoration techniques is impressing. With this technique, patterns are stamped into the semi-dry surface of the clay body. The stamps or moulds are often made of porcelain clay. The technique was widely used on celadon wares of Western Jin and Sui Dynasties, porcelain of the Ding kiln and Yaozhou kiln in the Song and Jin Dynasties as well as Jingdezhou wares after the Song and Yuan Dynasties. Porcelains with impressed decoration in the Song and Jin period, in particular, show clear patterns and well-designed composition and can be regarded as the best of its kind.

Kaolinite Clay

Kaolinite clay (chemical composition: $Al_2O_3 \cdot 2SiO_2 \cdot 2H_2O$), commonly known as porcelain clay, is one of the main raw materials for making porcelain. It is a soft clay mainly composed of kaolinite or halloysite. Kaolinite clay can be formed either by "medium and low temperature hydrothermal deformation" in the deeper crust or by the chemical weathering of feldspar in the upper part of the crust.

Completely weathered feldspar will generate kaolinite, quartz, and soluble salts that will be separated and washed away by rainwater and river. The remaining sediment is kaolinite stone with quartz, also known as kaolinite clay.

Kaolinite clay is mainly composed of flaky, tubular, or lamellar kaolinite cluster minerals (kaolinite, dickite, perlite, halloysite, etc.) less than 2 micrometer large. It also contains other associated minerals such as montmorillonite, illite, Pyrophyllite, quartz, and feldspar. The main chemical components of kaolinite are Al_2O_3, SiO_2, small amount of Fe_2O_3 and TiO_2, as well as traces of K_2O, Na_2O, CaO, and MgO, etc. Pure kaolinite appears to be white or light gray, while impure kaolinite could be yellow, gray, green, or rose. Raw ore is in the form of dense lump or loose soil. It is soft and smooth, with a specific gravity of 2.4 to 2.6 and high refractoriness, which is up to 1770-1790℃.

Kaolinite alone cannot be used to make porcelain body. After a visit to Jingdezhen in 1869, the well-known German geographer and geologist Ferdinand von Richthofen (1833-1905) wrote about the *kaolin*ite produced on the hillside of Kaolin village about 45 kilometers east of Jingdezhen and transliterated the Chinese word kaolin into English. "Kaolinite" has since then become an internationally used proper name in mineralogy.

Chinese kaolinite clay is not only large in quantity and variety but also widely distributed. More than 700 proven mine sites have been found, with reserves of about 3 billion tons of kaolinite. Well-known kaolinite clay sites include Xingzi in Jiangxi, Suzhou in Jiangsu, and Dade in Hunan. Today, kaolinite clay is a raw material not only indispensable for porcelain making but also essential for plenty of industries such as paper making, rubber manufacturing, chemical industry, paints and coatings, medicine, and national defense. The discovery and use of kaolinite clay had an extremely important impact on the porcelain making industry of Jingdezhen. It is also an epoch-making event in the world history of ceramics.

China Stone

China stone is a hard or sometimes semi-hard mineral rock used to make porcelain. It is usually grey or light grey. China stone is not a single mineral rock but an aggregate of multiple minerals, which have a relatively complex chemical composition and varying properties. China stone is mainly composed of quartz, feldspar, and sericite, while it also contains a small amount of kaolinite and carbonate. Its mineral composition is as follows: 40%-60% quartz, 0%-37% feldspar, 16%-38% feldspar, 16%-38% sericite, 0%-12% kaolinite, 0.1%-4% calcite, with small amount of limonite or magnetite as well as traces of rutile, white titanium, apatite, sphene, zircon, biotite, etc.

The chemical composition of china stone is as follows: 70%-80% SiO_2, 12%-18% Al_2O_3, 0.38%-1.36% Fe_2O_3, 0.2%-1.75% CaO, 0.06%-0.5% MgO, 1.6%- 4% K_2O, 0.09%-4.18% Na_2O, and 1%-4% H_2O. Although china stone has a high content of silica and potassium oxide and low content of alumina, it contains the basic components that make up the porcelain body as well as a certain amount of plasticity and drying intensity after being crushed and mixed with water. Therefore, certain china stone can be used alone to produce porcelain body. As early as the Shang Dynasty about 3,000 years ago, China has already employed single china stone as porcelain body when firing primitive wares.

Binary Formula

The binary formula refers to the use of two minerals—china stone and kaolinite clay—in proper proportions as raw materials for the production of porcelain in Jingdezhen. China stone and kaolinite clay are two kinds of materials with different properties. Their roles in the making of porcelain body are also different. High-quality china stone itself contains various chemical components that make up the porcelain body. Therefore, it can be used alone to make the porcelain body. Kaolinite clay, on the other hand, must be used in combination with china stone to produce porcelain body. Scientific tests show that only china stone was used to make Jingdezhen porcelain before the Yuan Dynasty. With the shortage of both china stone from the shallow layer and high-quality china stone since the Yuan Dynasty, the making of porcelain body had to rely on china stone from the deeper layer or low-quality china stone, resulting in severe deformation of the porcelain body after firing. This prompted the development of the so-called "binary formula," which involves combining china stone with a certain amount of kaolinite clay. This is a revolutionary change in the history of Chinese ceramics. Since the alumina (Al_2O_3) content in kaolinite clay is about 35%, the alumina in the reformulated porcelain body also increased, which broadened the temperature range of firing, decreased the rate of deformation, increased product yields, and made the production of large-sized imposing wares possible.

Bai Dun——White Briquette

Bai dun is a term in the Jingdezhen dialect. It refers to a rectangular brick-sized blank made by washing the kaolinite clay directly or crushing and washing the china stone. The traditional production process of *dun* is as follows: the collected china stone is first hammered to the size of an egg by hand and then placed in a pit where it would be beaten into powder by a pestle powered by stream water. After washing, sedimentation, and thickening, it would be put into a tailored wooden mould where it would take the shape of a rectangular brick after demolding. The sludge is then dried and turns into a *bai dun*. Kaolinite clay can also be made into a *bai dun* directly after washing. The two kinds of *bai dun* would then be transported to the porcelain factory where they will be mixed with chemical pulp according to a certain proportion. Through washing, precipitation, and thickening, a porcelain body is made.

Formulation of the Porcelain Paste

Since the Yuan Dynasty, Jingdezhen has always used porcelain clay made of kaolinite clay *dun* and china stone *dun*. The formula was usually created by the trial firing of *zhaozi* made by mixing these two raw materials in proportion to adjust and finally determine the ratio. Different products have different requirements on the performance of the porcelain clay. The usual formula is composed of 70% china stone and 30% kaolinite clay or 60% china stone and 40% kaolinite clay. After determining the ratio, one can start mixing the ingredients. Since each *dun* has a fixed weight (usually 2kg), the ingredient is determined in terms of the number of *dun*, Non-block fragments of *dun* are calculated in terms of weight. After mixing the *dun* in the pulp pond and washing and removing particles and impurities, filter the water from the remaining fine mud. When the mud has been naturally dried to a moisture content of about 25%, move it to a mudroom too let it decay. After processing, the decayed mud can then be used for shaping.

Youguo

Youguo, also known as glaze stone, is the main ingredient for the glaze of Jingdezhen porcelain. It is a light-weathered or unweathered porcelain stone of dense and rocky appearance. It is mostly produced in Yaoli Town, east of Jingdezhen. The mining and processing of *youguo* are the same as that of the china stone used for making porcelain body. It also needs to be made into *dun* to be used.

Glaze Powder

Glaze powder is one of the ingredients for traditional Jingdezhen glazes. Its production method is as follows: first, burn limestone into quicklime and pile it up in the ash smelting yard. Let it absorb moisture naturally to dissolve and pulverize into slaked lime for use. Sift a certain amount of slaked lime on a layer of phoenix-tail fern. Then, place another layer of phoenix-tail fern on top and sift another layer of slaked lime. Repeat the above steps until they form a rectangular stack. Light the phoenix-tail fern around the bottom of the stack. After burning, rake and mix it well. Layer the obtained mixture with phoenix-tail fern as in the steps mentioned above and burn it for three times. Age and homogenize it for several days to obtain the finished glaze powder, which can then be transported to the porcelain factory for use.

Formulation of Glaze

The formulation of traditional Jingdezhen porcelain glaze has always been based on *youguo*, added with glaze powder, commonly known as *huiyou*. Glaze powder makes up about 7-20% of the glaze. Since the glaze powder is mainly composed of calcium carbonate while *youguo* is composed of sericite, quartz, feldspar and a small number of carbonate minerals, traditional Jingdezhen glaze is limestone-quartz-sericite glaze. To formulate the glaze, first mix *youguo dun* mud and glaze powder respectively with water to form a slurry in a wooden barrel. The two should be made into the same concentration. With a special iron pot, scoop out the slurries in a certain ratio according to the type of porcelain and pour them into the same wooden bucket and mix well. Then add water to adjust to the appropriate concentration for use.

Yutangchun Bottle

The *yutangchun* bottle is one of the bottle styles used as rewards in the Qing court. It was created in the Yongzheng period. Its shape is characterized by a lip, a long neck, a round belly, and a circular base. The *yutangchun* bottle was continuously produced since the Qianlong period. It has three main varieties: blue and white, famille rose, and gilded sacrificial blue glaze. Among them, the blue and white *yutangchun* bottle can be divided into two types: the shoulder without raised string pattern, or the shoulder with two raised strings. Famille rose and gilded sacrificial-blue-glazed *yutangchun* bottles were only found in the Guangxu and Xuantong periods.

Romance of Red Dust

The Romance of Red Dust ("*Hong Fu Zhuan*"), also known as *The Three Musketeers*, is adapted from the novel *The Man with the Curly Beard* by the Tang fiction writer Du Guangting. In the story, Emperor Yang Guang of Sui is travelling to Yangzhou and leaves the Duke of Yue, Yang Su, in charge of the capital. When Li Jing, a commoner from Sanyuan visits Yang Su, the latter is impressed by Li' s talent and wants to keep him. The Hongfu girl Zhang Linghua, a singer and entertainer at Yang Su' s house, is also overcome with Li' s talents and runs away from Yang' s house at night and flees to Li' s place. They get married and leaves the capital at night. One day, they meet Zhang Zhongjian, the hero with the curly beard, on the road. After a conversation, the three find that they share the same interests. They become close friends and agree to go to Taiyuan to see Li Shimin. After visiting Li Shimin, Li Jing is determined to stay and assist Li Shimin. Knowing that she will not change his mind, Zhang leaves all her property to Li Jing and wanders away.

The Control of Yellow-Glaze Porcelain by the Qing Court

The Chinese people is known as descendants of Yan and Huang. The Yan Emperor and the Huang Emperor ("Yellow" Emperor) are the legendary ancestors of all ethnic groups in the Central Plains. Therefore, the colour yellow is crowned as a symbol of the royal family and strict restrictions are enforced on the use of yellow. As early as the Tang Dynasty, the system of clothing colours was formed, according to which the emperor shall wear a yellow robe and no one else should wear it. Having inherited the old system, the Qing Dynasty made more detailed regulations on the use of colour, which specified that bright-yellow-glazed porcelain is for the exclusive use of the imperial household. It is a symbol of noble status and is not allowed to be used by commoners. Even those that did not meet standards should be transported with *dayun* (mass production) porcelain to the capital as spare tributes. Thus, bright-yellow-glazed porcelain is the most strictly controlled porcelain by the Qing court.

According to Qing court records, in the seventh year of Qianlong (1742), Governor Tang Ying received a decree from the Office of the Ministry of Internal Affairs: "According to the order of the Emperor himself, low-quality goods do not have to go to the capital, that is, they can be sold". In response, Tang Ying replied in a memorial: "Only the country imposes hierarchy strict regulations on clothing and articles. Now that the factory produces porcelain such as yellow wares, incised polychrome wares, and wares with decoration of dragon with five claws, for the imperial household. If these wares are not awarded to me by the Emperor, I do not dare to keep or use them lest I break the law...In my humble opinion, these yellow wares and five-clawed-dragon wares that did not meet standards should still be appraised for records and shipped to the capital as spares or tributes. Thus, the system can be preserved, and crimes can be prevented." In this response, Tang Ying emphasized the importance of yellow wares and polychrome wares with decoration of dragon with five claws. When Emperor Qianlong saw Tang Ying's memorial, he commented in red, "Yellow wares can be handled as your request. Five-clawed-dragon wares, however, are commonly seen outside, so the decree shall be enforced as planned". This shows that yellow-glazed porcelain is even more valuable than polychrome five-clawed-dragon porcelain.

The Concubine System of the Qing Dynasty

Ancient Chinese emperors practiced polygamy. The principal wife of the emperor was the queen. The queen ruled the harem and had high status. Below the queen were *fei* (consorts), *pin* (imperial concubines), *changzai* (ady-in-waiting), and *dayin* (responders), each of which were treated differently. This system originated in the late Zhou Dynasty. As recorded in the *Book of Rites*, "The ancient emperor had six harems, three *furen* (wives), nine *pin*, twenty-seven *shifu*, and eighty-one *yuqi*," which means that there was a large group of women with different ranks by the emperor's side. The inner court harem was established in the Qin Dynasty. The number of people far exceeded the size of the previous dynasty. In the Han Dynasty, the concubine came with fourteen ranks and was also huge in size. During the Sui and Tang Dynasties, the system started to come into shape and included multiple ranks such as the queen, wife, imperial concubine, and *shifu*. The system was passed down through successive dynasties. In the Qing Dynasty, with the development of the feudalism, the concubine system was established and perfected. "The first Qing Emperor Nurhachi established the Khan dynasty in 1616". "Three layers of city wall were built and houses were constructed". "The residence of concubines did not have *weihao*, but according to customs of the country, they are called "Fu Jin".

After the establishment of the Qing Dynasty, Huang Taiji reformed feudalism, whose influence extended to the palace. A feudal concubinage was established corresponding to the reform. "Build five palaces to establish *weihao* and determine ranks".

After the Qing Dynasty entered the strategic pass, the aforementioned construction was strengthened. As recorded in *Veritable Records of Taizu*, "The 15th year of Shunzhi, government offices such as the board of rites held meetings to discuss the number and rank of concubines and the number of ladies-in-waiting in the palace. The Qianqing Palace assigned one *furen*, first rank, one *shuyi*, second rank, six *wanshi*, third rank, and twenty *rouwan* and thirty *fangwan*, fourth rank. The Cining Palace assigned one *zhenrong*, second rank, and two *shenrong*, third rank; the rest are indefinite in number and have no ranks. There were also the position of palace woman and relevant regulatory bodies." After Kangxi, and the harem system was strictly adhered to. "The Emperor regarded his holy grandmother as the grand empress dowager and his mother as the empress dowager. They lived in the palaces of Cining, Shoukang, and Ningshou, with other concubines and consorts. The empress lived in the central palace and governs internal affairs. The first-rank imperial concubine, two second-rank imperial concubines, four third-rank concubines, and six fourth-rank concubines lived in twelve palaces of the east and west and assisted in internal affairs. Those below the second-rank imperial concubine were given their title by cabinet. Concubines of the fourth rank, ladies-in-waiting, and responders did not have titles. They also lived in the twelve palaces and managed household affairs".

Dayun Porcelain

The so-called "dayun porcelain" refers literally porcelains that are transported in large volumes. Based on situations of firing, it refers to porcelains that are produced in fixed models and transported to the capital to be stored in the imperial warehouse without the Emperor's order or instruction. Commonly regarded as traditional ware *Dayun* porcelain is a type of carved vessel (*zhuoqi*), which refers to wares that can only come into shape with the help of not only the potter's wheel but also multiple production processes. They are mostly used as gifts or for display.

The Imperial Wedding of Tongzhi

In February of the 11st year of Tongzhi (1873), the Ministry of Internal Affairs summoned the daughters of the ministers of Manchu and Mongolian into the palace to select an empress for the 17-year-old Emperor Tongzhi. According to the wish of Empress Dowager Ci'an, Tongzhi chose Arute, the daughter of Chongqi who was a literary official in the Hanlin Academy, as the empress. Fucha, who won the favour of Empress Dowager Cixi, was chosen as *Hui Fei* (consort). The imperial wedding ceremony was held in September. For this wedding, 11 million pieces of silver were allocated from the state treasury to purchase wedding items, including more than 10,000 pieces of large-scale wedding porcelain fired by the Jingdezhen imperial kiln factory.

Ritual Vessels of the Qing Court

In the Houjin and Tiancong periods of the Qing Dynasty, the system of ancestral temple did not exist. At that time, Manchuria followed old customs to set up "Tangzi" to worship the sky and hold shamanic sacrificial rituals. The Qing Emperor Taizong gradually accepted and studied the Han culture. In the tenth year of Tiancong (1636), the court built the Yuanqiutan (the Temple of Heaven) and the Fangzetan (the Temple of Earth) outside the Desheng Gate and the Neizhi Gate in Shengjing (present-day Shenyang) to offer sacrifices to heaven and earth.

In the first year of Shunzhi (1644), the Qing Dynasty set its capital in Yanjing (present-day Beijing) and built the Yuanqiutan in the southern suburbs outside the Zhengyang Gate and the Fangzetan in the northern suburbs outside the Anding Gate. According to the Qing system, Yuanqiu should be worshiped on the winter solstice while Fangze should be worshiped on the summer solstice each year. In addition, worships to the heaven and earth should also be made during events such as enthronement of the Emperor, the granting of the title of dignity to the Emperor and Empress, the Wanshou Festival, the appointment of the Empress and the Prince,the year-long draught and prayer for rain ,etc. Moreover, worships to heaven and earth should also be made in case of major events, such as the suppress of the Revolt of the Three Feudatories during the Kangxi period. Traditional shamanic ritual customes of Manchuria were preserved by the inner court of the Palace of Forbidden City. Ritual locations were set in Fengxian Hall and Kunning Palace.

Dayazhai

Dayazhai is a plaque hung in the Yiqing study room in the back hall of the Changchun Palace. According to archives, in the fifth years of Xianfeng (1855), two new plaques of "Dayazhai" were made in the palace to be hung in the Pingan Room and the "*Tian Di Yi Jia Chun*" Hall of Yuanmingyuan. The Ping' an Room is the west room of the palace where the Emperor sleeps and rests. During the Xianfeng period, Yibin (Cixi) once lived here as an attendant. This plaque was later moved onto the east ridge of the east of the Yiqing study room in the back hall of the Changchun Palace.

The hall of "*Tian Di Yi Jia Chun*" is located in Qingyan, Jiuzhou, in the Yuanmingyuan, which was the residence of the concubine when the Emperor was stationed here. As recorded in A Study on *Yuanmingyuan*, "The so-called '*Tian Di Yi Jia Chun*'is the residence of Empress Xiaoqin". Empress Xiaoqin is Empress Dowager Cixi.

The Great Buddha Hall

The Great Buddha Hall is in the inner court of the Outer Western Section of the Forbidden City. It is the back dormitory of the Cining Palace. Built in the fifteenth year of Jiajing in the Ming Dynasty (1536), the Great Buddha Hall was renovated in the Qing Dynasty, which followed the traditions of the Ming Dynasty. In the Qing Dynasty, it was the place where the Empress Dowager and the Concubine made worships to the Buddha. The hall is equipped with Buddhist statues, niches, and five-piece altar set (*wugong*), etc.

The History of the National Palace

The history of the seventh Year of Qianlong in the Qing Dynasty (1742) was compiled by scholars Feng Ershi and Zhang Tingyu of the inner court. The manuscript is divided into six chapters and 36 volumes, including four volumes of instruction, six volumes of ceremony, six volumes of the palace, three volumes of finance, two volumes of official regulation, and 15 volumes of books.

The volumes of instruction contain imperial decrees from the Shunzhi to Yongzheng period and the imperial rescript of Emperor Qianlong to elucidate the palace system. The ceremony volumes record palace ceremony, etiquette, regulations, costume, and military system, which reflect the feudal ethics and morality. The volumes of the palace are divided into the outer court, the inner court, Jingshan palace, Xiyuan palace, Yonghe Palace, etc., whose scales are detailed. The volumes of finance exhaustively record costs for the New Year, Ri Yue (the sun and the moon), ceremonies, and banquets of the inner court. The volumes of official regulation document the positions of eunuch and their awards and punishment. The volumes of book compile the titles, origins, and outlines of important books of official training of the period as well as imperial poems.

The Manchu Ritual Ceremony Organized by the Emperor

The book *The Manchu Ritual Ceremony Organized by the Emperor* was completed in the 12th year of Qianlong (1747). Emperor Qianlong gave the title of the book and wrote the preface, which was edited by Prince Yunlu of Zhuang and others. This book collects, interprets, and sums up various Manchu ritual ceremonies and congratulatory speeches, which are examined in detail. Sacrificial utensils used in the ritual are also drawn in this book. A summary of Manchu shamanistic beliefs and customs, the book is an important material for studying the shamanic sacrifices in the Qing court.

Mi Wanzhong

Mi Wanzhong (1570-1631), courtesy name Zhongzhao, pen name Youshi, Zhanyuan, Manyuanmanshi, Shaohaitingzhang, Haidianyuzhang, Lianhuazhongren, Wanxiangjushi, Wenshijushi, Shiyinanjushi, Yanbodiaosou and so on. He was from Anhua, Shaanxi (present-day Qingcheng County, Qingyang City, Gansu) and later moved to Yanjing (now Beijing) Wanping. A descendant of the famous Northern Song Dynasty painter and calligrapher Mi Fu, Mi Wanzhong became a *Jin Shi* in the twenty-third year of Wanli in the Ming Dynasty (1595) and served successively as the district magistrate of Yongning, Tongliang, and Liuhe. He was also appointed to the positions of the Provincial Administration Commissioner Assistant of Zhejiang, Provincial Administration Commissioner of Jiangxi, and Provincial Administration Commissioner of Shandong. An upright and impartial person, Mi had good political reputation and wide popular support. However, he was latter set up by Wei Zhong Xian fractions and dismissed from his position, after which he worked as deputy director of Taipusi from the first year of Chongzhen (1628). He passed away in Beijing. Throughout his life, Mi had a great passion on landscape and flowers, and a slavish addiction to stones. He was also a practitioner of calligraphy and painting and was good at composing poems. H adopted the method of Family Mi for his semi-cursive script, took Northern Song paintings as models for his own, and appreciated the flowers drawn by the Ming painter Chen Chun (1483-1544). Of comparable reputation, Mi and Dong Qichang (1555-1636) were respectfully described as "South Dong North Mi". With his great achievement in calligraphy, Mi, along with Dong Qichang, Xing Dong and Zhang Ruitu, was called "the four great calligraphers in the late Ming Dynasty".

In addition to poems, calligraphy, and painting, the multitalented Mi Wanzhong was also good at Cuju, Jiwan, and designing gardens. His construction of three private gardens in Beijing, namely Zhan Yuan, Shao Yuan and Man Yuan, were especially praised.

Based on existing documents, Mi Wanzhong was also passionate about porcelain. He once commissioned porcelains in Jingdezhen under his own name, one of which is a piece of beaker with inscription "Under the private commission of Mi Shi in the year of Tianqi" inside a blue-and-white double-square below the rim. Above the flower sprays decoration, there are the wheel, conch, parasol, and canopy of the Eight Auspicious Signs of Tibetan Buddhism painted on the body. There should be another undiscovered piece of beaker painted with the lotus flower, water bottle, golden fish, and knotted cord as a pair. According to verifiable sources, Mi was devoted to Buddhism and built a Buddhist hall in his private garden. The abovementioned beaker is likely a vessel for flower arrangement to make offerings. Since Mi served as rank-five Secretary Commissioner of Jiangxi in Raonan from the fourth to the fifth year of Tianqi, and Raonan, where he stationed, was less than 100 km from Jingdezhen, a convenient place for commissioning porcelain, this beaker was likely ordered by Mi during this period.

With drastic societal change from the fifteenth year of Wanli (1607), the Jingdezhen imperial kiln stopped producing porcelain and the industry of private porcelain came to a dominant position. In the domestic market, the *jinshen* class became the main consumer of high-end porcelain. With a widespread trend of pursuing curiosities, porcelain became objects for the *jinshen* class to demonstrate personalities and tastes, an evidence of which is the signature on the commissioned wares. According to verifiable sources, Mi Wanzhong is the earliest known literati to sign his name and private garden on the porcelain, which served as a precursor for the integration of ceramic art and the aesthetic taste of literati in the late Ming and early Qing period and started a transformational trend of the use of elegant and fine porcelain by the *jinshen* class.

Lang Tingji

Lang Tingji (1663-1715), courtesy name Ziheng and Ziyuan, pen name Beixuan, was from Guangning, Fengtian (present-day Beizhen, Liaoning). He was an official and a scholar in the Kangxi Dynasty. During his tenure as the governor of Jiangxi from the 44th to the 51st year of Kangxi (1705-1712), Lang founded a porcelain kiln in Jingdezhen, which is known as the "Lang kiln". Judging from the *Zaiyuan Magazine* written by Lang's contemporary Liu Tingji and the poems by Xu Jinzhai, a major achievement of the Lang kiln was its imitation of the imperial wares of the Ming Dynasty, especially those from the Xuande and Chenghua period. Its exceptional skill of imitation made it hard to tell spurious ones from authentic ones. Surviving examples include wares with inscription "Yu Ci Chun Yi Tang" and with both "Yu Ci Chun Yi Tang Zhen Cang" and "Made in the Kangxi period of the Great Qing Dynasty". As "Chun Yi Tang" was the title granted by Emperor Kangxi to Lang Tingji, these wares are undoubtedly produced by the Lang kiln. The Lang kiln porcelains were used as tributes to the court and represent the firing skills of Jingdezhen in the late Kangxi period.

Tang Ying

Tang Ying (1682-1756), courtesy name Jun Gong, also known as Shuzi, pen name Woji, was born into a Manchu slave family of the Plain White Banner of the Han army in Fengtian (present-day Shenyang, Liaoning). In the 36th year of Kangxi (1697), Tang Ying, who was only 16 years old, began to serve in the Yangxin Hall (Hall of Mental Cultivation) and attended Emperor Kangxi for over 20 years. In the first year of Yongzheng (1723), the 42-year-old Tang Ying was given the title of *Yuan Wai Lang* of the Imperial Household Department and was responsible for the monthly inspection of craftsmen on duty of the Imperial Workshop of the Department, which included assessing documents, human resources, and warehouse management. Due to his high capabilities, in August of the sixth year of Yongzheng (1728), the 47-year-old Tang Ying was stationed in Jingdezhen, assisting Nian Xiayo (?-1738), the then General Manager of the Imperial Household Department, who also managed the Tax Bureau of the Huai'an Customs and supervised the Jingdezhen imperial kiln, in supervising the imperial kiln. Starting from the first year of Qianlong (1736), Tang Ying served as the supervisor of Huai'anguan and Jiujiangguan successively, and supervised the kiln factory in Jingdezhen (from the fifteenth year of Qianlong (1750) to the sixteenth year, he went to Guangdong to serve as the supervisor of the Guangdong Customs), until Qianlong resigned and died in the 21st year (1756). Thanks to Tang Ying's effective management, the Jingdezhen imperial kiln Factory made great achievements in imitate antiques and innovation. Diligent in putting his ideas in practive, Tang Ying wrote many ceramics monographs, including *Tao Wu Xu Lue, Tao Cheng Ji Shi, Tao Ye Tu Shuo, Tao Ren Xin Yu*. Tang Ying is not only a painter and writer but also regarded as one of the most outstanding officials in Chinese history. People used to call the Jingdezhen imperial kiln under his supervision in the Qianlong period "Tang kiln". In fact, the "Tang kiln" should be counted from the 6th year of Yongzheng (1728) to the 21st year of Qianlong (1756).

Xiong Xiling

The famous modern politician Xiong Xiling (1870-1937), courtesy name Bingsan, was from Fenghuang, Hunan. He participated in the Metropolitan Examination in the eighteenth year of Guangxu (1892) and became a Gongshi, after which he resat in the Palace Examination in the twentieth year of Guangxi (1894) and became a Shujishi. In the thirtieth year of Guangxu (1904), he was appointed by the Hunan Governor Duanfang to go on a study tour to Japan. He visited areas such as Tokyo and Osaka to inspect Japanese porcelain factories. In the 31st year of Guangxu, under Xiong's sponsorship, the Hunan Government allocated 18,000 *liang* of silver and established the Hunan Porcelain Academy, which appointed Xiong as the manager and hired Japanese as teachers, to train ceramics skills. In the 32nd year of Guangxu, Xiong set up another 50 thousand silver to establish the Hunan Porcelain Company and hire Jingdezhen masters to teach skills of firing fine porcelain. Since then, the Liling porcelain industry developed from suburbs to the urban area and from coarse to fine porcelain. An outstanding achievement of the Hunan Porcelain Company was the creation of unprecedented underglaze polychrome porcelain after numerous trials and failures. From the first year of

Xuantong (1909) to the fourth year of the Republic of China (1915), Liling underglaze polychrome porcelain was awarded several times at domestic industry and fairs and became reputed both at home and abroad.

Amitayus Buddha

Amitayus Buddha (Buddha of Boundless Life) is the incarnation of Amitabha (Buddha of Immeasurable Splendor). Together, they are worshipped by Buddhist followers as principal Buddhas of the Western Pure Land. Amitabha represents the breadth of space while Amitayus stands for the length of time. Since its scriptures promote that people will be able to go to the Western Pure Land after death, Amitayus is widely accepted. Under the influence of Tibetan Buddhism, the Qing court had the tradition of making porcelain and copper statues of Amitayus as birthday gifts for the emperors and empresses. The number of statues in each group was always nine or multiple of nine. The collection of the Palace Museum has a large number of these types of Buddhist statues.

Trikala Buddhas

Mahayana Buddhism reformed the doctrine of primitive Buddhism and expanded the concept of Buddha in terms of time and space. An embodiment of this idea is the concept of the Trikala Buddhas, which expands spatially into "Horizontal Trikala Buddhas" and temporally into "Vertical Trikala Buddhas".

The so-called "Horizontal Trikala Buddhas" are as follows: the Bhaisajyaguru of the East (the Buddha of Medicine), who is in charge of the Vaidūryanirbhāsā world, with two servants, Suryaprabha and Candraprabha, also known as the "Three Oriental Sages"; the Amitayus Buddha of the West, who is in charge of the Pure Land of the West, with two servants, Mahasthamaprapta and Avalokitesvara; in the centre is Shakyamuni, who is in charge of the Saha world, with two servants, Manjusri and Samantabhadra, also known as the "Shakyamuni Trinity".

The so-called "Vertical Trikala Buddhas" are Dipamkara Buddha of the past, Shakyamuni of the present, and Maitreya Buddha of the future. Dipamkara Buddha, who predicted in the past that Shakyamuni would become a Buddha in the future, is the Buddha before Shakyamuni. Shakyamuni, the Buddha of the present saves the world by Dharma. Maitreya Buddha of the future, who is still a bodhisattva in Tushita in the present, will teach Dharma under a Mesua ferrea tree to save all beings in the future.

Jingdezhen

Jingdezhen is one of the most famous historical and cultural sites in China. It is located in the northeast of Jiangxi Province, formerly known as Xinping. Since it is located in the southeast of Changjiang, it is also known as Changnan Town. It was renamed Jingdezhen after the era name during the Jingde period of the Northern Song Dynasty (1004-1007). Surrounded by mountains, Jingdezhen is rich in natural resources. Historically, its production of porcelain and tea are famous both at home and abroad. Porcelain, tea, and industrial and commercial development have brought about prosperity and economic development of the city. It was once called the "Four Famous Towns" in ancient China, together with Hankou Town in Hubei, Foshan Town in Guangdong, and Zhuxian Town in Henan.

According to historical documents, the porcelain production of Jingdezhen began in the Han Dynasty, though the earliest porcelain kiln site was discovered as early as the Tang Dynasty. Since the Ming and Qing dynasties, with the establishment of pottery factories and imperial kiln factories in Jingdezhen by emperors of the past dynasties, Jingdezhen has specialized in the burning of porcelain for the palace, which drove the development and prosperity of the private porcelain industry. It is said that all the most exquisite porcelains are from Jingdezhen. Thus, Jingdezhen has won the reputation of the "Porcelain Capital".

Kiln God Tablet Extension

In ancient China, the succession of mentorship and apprenticeship were emphasized in all walks of life. Therefore, the founder of each industry was regarded as the "industrial god". Later generations should make statues of their founder to worship with devotion and pray for success. For instance, wood-workers worship Luban, wine makers worship Yidi and Dukang, pharmacists worship Sun Simiao, medical practitioners worship Huatuo, tea-vendors worship Luyu, while educators worship Kongqiu. The ceramic industry is no exception. Since successful firing of ceramics was usually fortuitous, kiln workers believed that it was governed by gods and therefore placed great importance on the construction of kiln temples in all regions. According to existing documents, at the latest since the Northern Song Dynasty (960-1127), kiln temples were built in porcelain-producing areas such as Tongchuan in Shaanxi, Hebi, Xiuwu, Yuxian, Yiyang, and Mixian in Henan, Yuci and Jiexiu in Shanxi, Zibo in Shandong, Handan and Lincheng in Hebei, as well as Jingdezhen in Jiangxi, for people to make offerings to kiln gods and pray for success in firing. Enshrined kiln gods include Fuxi, Shennong, Huangdi, Yao, Laozi, Leigong, Shanshen, Tushen, Niu Ma Er Wang, Jin Huo Shen Mu, Ning Fengzi, Bolin Weng, Tong Bin, Zhao Cai, Jiang Zhisi, and Huaguang. The collection of kiln god steles and inscriptions from areas such as Shaanxi, Shanxi, Henan in the Palace reflects the dedication of kiln gods all around the country. These written materials are of great significance for the study of ancient ceramic culture.

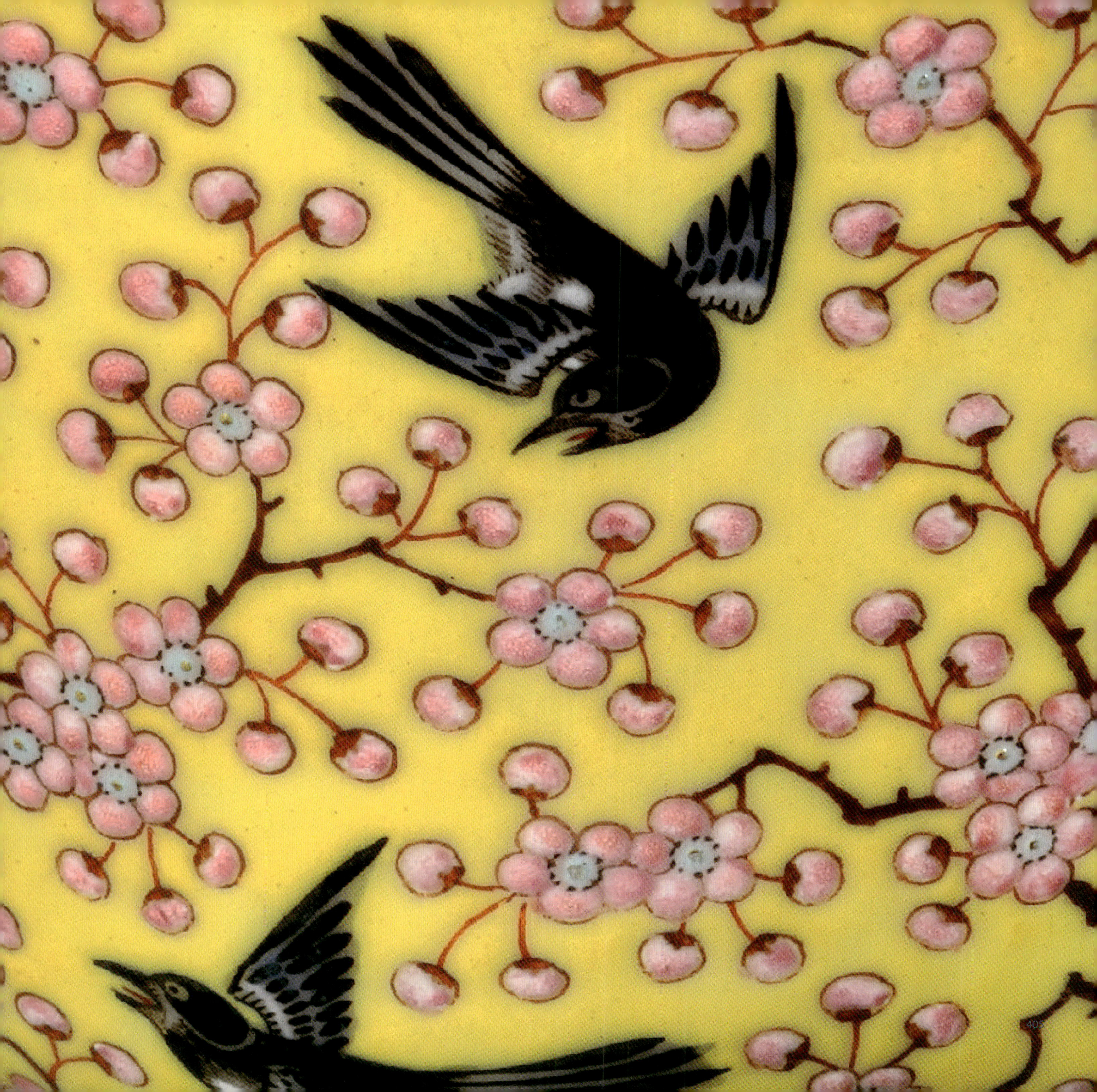

后记

2020 年是紫禁城建成 600 年，也是故宫博物院成立 95 周年。在故宫博物院 95 年的发展历程中，曾举办过大量内容丰富的各类文物展览，其中 1952 年开始创办的“陶瓷馆”所代表的陶瓷类文物展，以其琳琅满目的陶瓷展品、设计新颖的展出形式、深入浅出的文字内容，吸引数以千万计的国内外观众前来参观，受到广泛喜爱和好评。

经过两年多的筹备，最新改陈的“陶瓷馆”即将在武英殿区域与观众见面。在主体建筑武英殿及其后殿敬思殿和中间穿廊组成的“工”字形建筑内，将展示自约七八千年前新石器时代磁山文化至民国时期（1912 ~ 1949 年）的陶瓷器，向观众呈现中国陶瓷延绵不断的发展历程。武英殿东、西配殿分专题展出清代宫廷进膳、陈设和赏赐、大婚、万寿、祭祀、宗教用瓷，院内西北平台上的浴德堂专门展示外销陶瓷。另外，原设于延禧宫西配殿的“中国古陶瓷窑址标本展”和“古陶瓷资料观摩室”亦将分别移至武英殿东、西配殿之北值房。总之，武英殿区将成为紫禁城内集中展示陶瓷类文物的常设展馆，以满足不同观众的参观需求。

在本次陶瓷馆改陈和图录编辑出版过程中，故宫博物院领导、专家、学者、同事付出了辛勤劳动。

故宫博物院研究馆员耿宝昌先生担任学术顾问，并为本书惠赐宏文。

故宫博物院院长王旭东先生在百忙中为本书作序。

故宫博物院副院长任万平女士、副院长闫宏斌先生、副院长王跃工先生等主抓展览内容和展陈形式设计。

故宫博物院器物部主任、研究馆员吕成龙先生撰写展览大纲、为本书惠赐大作并修改书中全部文物定名和文字介绍。

器物部徐巍、赵小春、赵聪月、董健丽、王光尧、黄卫文、高晓然、郑宏、李卫东、陈润民、郭玉昆、韩倩、冀洛源、孙悦、陈志鸿、张涵、单莹莹、唐雪梅、蒋艺、王照宇、董彦卿、王振宇、于英洲、冯贺军、达微佳、王全利、梁勇、赵芸格、施磊同志等，宫廷部李中路、鲍楠、安静同志等在配合展品遴选、摄影、布陈以及本书文物说明撰写、英文翻译、文字校对等工作中，均投入了大量时间和精力。

展览部张光耀主任、薄海昆、朱继伟、李怀玉、胡博、高冉同志等，为展览的形式设计付出了大量心血。

外事处李绍毅处长、袁宏副处长、李月莎、杨若晨、汪辰菲、汪予同志等负责展厅文字英文翻译和审校工作。

资料信息部苏怡主任、于壮副主任统筹安排展品拍摄和影像加工提取以及宣传推介工作。余宁川同志负责本书部分文物摄影，孙竞同志负责本书全部影像提用，司冰、张云天、李小龙、肖弋同志等负责展览宣传视频拍摄制作，郭珽、庄颖、张林、李睦麟同志等负责“微故宫”宣传和“故宫陶瓷馆”APP 及小程序开发。

文保科技部于子勇主任统筹安排文物保养、维护和科技检测工作。王五胜、高飞、纪东歌、杨玉洁、于子雅、李亚非同志等，负责部分文物的修复、保养、加固工作。李合、丁银忠、侯佳钰、康葆强同志等，负责部分文物无损科技检测工作。

故宫出版社万钧、方妍、张志辉、李园明同志等为本书的编辑出版付出了辛劳。

展览筹备和图录编辑工作中，还得到院办公室、文物管理处、宫廷部、古建部、宣传教育部、修缮技艺部、财务处、保卫处、消防处、安全技术处、开放管理处、工程管理处、行政处等院内各部门的大力支持。

在此，一并表示衷心感谢！

编辑委员会

2020 年 12 月

Afterword

2020 is the 600th anniversary of the establishment of the Forbidden City and the 95th anniversary of the Palace Museum. In the 95-year history of the Palace Museum, a large number of exhibitions of various cultural relics have been held. Among them, exhibitions of the ceramics collection since 1952 have attracted millions of visitors at home and abroad with the richness of exhibits, innovative exhibition design, and the presentation of complicated ideas in simple terms, and were widely enjoyed and praised.

After more than two years of preparations, the newly renovated ceramics exhibition will meet visitors in the Hall of Military Prowess (*Wuying dian*). In the I-shaped space composed of the main building, the Hall of Martial Valor, the rear building, the Hall of Respectful Thoughts (*Jingsi dian*), and a corridor connecting the two, ceramics ranging from those of the Cishan Culture in the Neolithic period, about seven to eight thousand years ago, to those of the Republic of China (1912-1949) will be exhibited to present a continuous development of Chinese ceramics. The east and west sides of the Hall of Military Prowess are divided into themed exhibitions of Qing court porcelain dinner services, porcelain for display and reward, porcelain for longevity and wedding, as well as porcelain for rituals and religion. The Hall for Cultivating Virtues (*Yude tang*) on the northwest terrace of the courtyard is specifically for the display of export ceramics. In addition, the Specimens of Ancient Chinese Kilns exhibition and the archive room of ancient ceramics, which were originally located in the west warehouse of the Palace of Prolonged Happiness (*Yanxi gong*), will be moved respectively to the east and west side hall of the Hall of Military Prowess. In short, the area of the Hall of Military Prowess will become a permanent exhibition space for the concentrated display of ceramic relics in the Forbidden City to satisfy different visitors.

In the process of revising the ceramics exhibition content and editing and publishing the catalogue, the leaders, experts, scholars and co-workers of the Palace Museum have put in hard work and effort.

Mr Geng Baochang, researcher at the Palace Museum, served as an academic advisor and contributed greatly for this book.

Mr Wang Xudong, director of the Palace Museum, composed the preface of this book in his busy schedule.

Ms Ren Wanping, Mr Yan Hongbin and Mr Wang Yuegong, deputy directors of the Palace Museum, contributed to the content and design of this exhibition.

Mr Lü Chenglong, director and researcher of the Department of Objects and Decorative Arts at the Palace Museum, wrote the exhibition outline and made great contributions to this book by revising the names and descriptions of cultural relics.

Members of the Department of Objects and Decorative Arts, including Xu Wei, Zhao Xiaochun, Zhao Congyue, Dong Jianli, Wang Guangyao, Huang Weiwen, Gao Xiaoran, Zheng Hong, Li Weidong, Chen Runmin, Guo Yukun, Han Qian, Ji Luoyuan, Sun Yue, Chen Zhihong, Zhang Han, Shan Yingying, Tang Xuemei, Jiang Yi, Wang Zhaoyu, Dong Yanqing, Wang Zhenyu, Yu Yingzhou, Fe Hejun, Da Weijia, Wang Quanli, Liang Yong, Zhao Yunge and Shi Lei, Members of the Department of Palace Life and Imperial Ritual, including Li Zhonglu, Bao Nan and An Jing, all invested a lot of time and effort in the selection of exhibits, photography, cloth presentation, the writing of cultural relics descriptions, and translation and proofreading.

Zhang Guangyao, director of the Exhibition Department, and Bo Haikun, Zhu Jiwei, Li Huaiyu, Hu Bo, Gao Ran etc., contributed greatly to the form of exhibition design.

Director Li Shaoyi and Deputy Director Yuan Hong of the Foreign Affairs Office and Comrade Li Yuesha, Yang Ruochen, Wang Chenfei and Wang Yu are responsible for reviewing the English translation of the exhibition.

Director Su Yi and Deputy Director Yu Zhuang of the Department of IT, Imaging, and Digital Media coordinated exhibit shooting, image processing and extraction, and promotion. Yu Ningchuan was responsible for the photography of part of the cultural relics in this book. Sun Jing is responsible for the extraction of all the images in this book. Si Bing, Zhang Yuntian, Li Xiaolong and Xiao Yi are responsible for the production of the exhibition promotion video. Guo Ting, Zhuang Ying, Zhang Lin, and Li Mulin are responsible for the promotion of *Weigugong* and the planning of the "Ceramics Gallery of the Palace Museum" APP.

Yu Ziyong, director of the Department of Conservation Science, coordinated conservation of cultural relics, maintenance and technological examination. Wang Wusheng, Gao Fei, Ji Dongge, Yang Yujie, Yu Ziya and Li Yafei are responsible for the restoration, conservation and consolidation of some cultural relics. Li He, Ding Yinzhong, Hou Jiayu, Kang Baoqiang, etc., are responsible for the non-destructive technological examination of some cultural relics.

Wan Jun, Fang Yan, Zhang Zhihui and Li Yuanming of the Forbidden City Publishing House have worked hard to edit and publish this book.

The preparation of the exhibition and the editing of catalogues have also gained support from departments including the Director's Office, Collection Management Department, Department of Palace Life and Imperial Ritual, Department of Architectural Heritage, Department of Publicity and Education, Department of Heritage Architectural Technologies, Finance Office, Security Department, Fire Department, Department of Information Security, Public Services Department, Department of Construction Management, and the Office of Administrative Supervision.

We sincerely express our gratitude to all contributors!

Editorial Board
December 2020

学术顾问

耿宝昌

编辑委员会

主任

王旭东

委员

王旭东　都海江　娄　玮　任万平　朱鸿文　闫宏斌　赵国英　王跃工　罗先良
吕成龙　曾　君　严　勇　张　楠

主编

吕成龙

副主编

韩　倩　董彦卿　徐　巍

本卷主编

赵聪月

本卷副主编

唐雪梅

展览协调

任万平　王跃工　吕成龙　张光耀　李永兴　严　勇　于子勇
苏　怡　于　壮　徐　巍

展览主持

吕成龙

展览工作组

吕成龙　徐　巍　赵小春　赵聪月　董健丽　王光尧　黄卫文　高晓然　郑　宏　李卫东
陈润民　郭玉昆　韩　倩　冀洛源　孙　悦　陈志鸿　张　涵　单莹莹　唐雪梅　蒋　艺
王照宇　董彦卿　王振宇　于英洲　冯贺军　达微佳　王全利　梁　勇　赵芸格　李中路　鲍　楠　安　静

展品保养维护

王五胜　高　飞　纪东歌　杨玉洁　于子雅　李亚非

展品无损检测

李　合　丁银忠　侯佳钰　康葆强

展览形式设计

张光耀　薄海昆　朱继伟　李怀玉　胡　博　高　冉

展览英文翻译

李绍毅　袁　宏　李月莎　杨若晨　汪辰菲　汪　予　施　磊

本卷英文翻译

张淳淳

摄影

余宁川

影像加工

孙竞

展览宣传视频拍摄制作

司　冰　张云天　李小龙　肖　弋

“微故宫”宣传、“故宫陶瓷馆”APP及小程序开发

郭　珽　庄　颖　张　林　李睦麟

Academic Adviser

Geng Baochang

Editorial Board

Director

Wang Xudong

Members

Wang Xudong　Du Haijiang　Lou Wei　Ren Wanping　Zhu Hongwen
Yan Hongbin　Zhao Guoying　Wang Yuegong　Luo Xianliang
Lü Chenglong　Zeng Jun　Yan Yong　Zhang Nan

Chief Editor

Lü Chenglong

Associate Editors

Han Qian　Dong Yanqing　Xu Wei

The Chief Editor of The Volume

Zhao Congyue

The Associate Editor of The Volume

Tang Xuemei

Exhibition Coordination

Ren Wanping　Wang Yuegong　Lü Chenglong　Zhang Guangyao　Li Yongxing
Yan Yong　Yu Ziyong　Su Yi　Yu Zhuang　Xu Wei

Exhibition Conductor

Lü Chenglong

The Exhibition Work Group

Lü Chenglong　Xu Wei　Zhao Xiaochun　Zhao Congyue　Dong Jianli　Wang Guangyao　Huang Weiwen　Gao Xiaoran　Zheng Hong　Li Weidong　Chen Runmin
Guo Yukun　Han Qian　Ji Luoyuan　Sun Yue　Chen Zhihong　Zhang Han　Shan Yingying　Tang Xuemei　Jiang Yi　Wang Zhaoyu　Dong Yanqing　Wang Zhenyu
Yu Yingzhou　Feng Hejun　Da Weijia　Wang Quanli　Liang Yong　Zhao Yunge　Li Zhonglu　Bao Nan　An Jing

Exhibits Maintenance

Wang Wusheng　Gao Fei　Ji Dongge　Yang Yujie　Yu Ziya　Li Yafei

Exhibits Nondestructive Testing

Li He　Ding Yinzhong　Hou Jiayu　Kang Baoqiang

The Design of Exhibition Form

Zhang Guangyao　Bo Haikun　Zhu Jiwei　Li Huaiyu　Hu Bo　Gao Ran

Exhibition English Translators

Li Shaoyi　Yuan Hong　Li Yuesha　Yang Ruochen　Wang Chenfei　Wang Yu　Shi Lei

English Translation of The Volume

Zhang Chunchun

Photography

Yu Ningchuan

Image Processing

Sun Jing

Shooting and Making Promotional Videos for the Exhibition

Si Bing　Zhang Yuntian　Li Xiaolong　Xiao Yi

"Weigugong" Promotion, " Ceramics Gallery of the Palace Museum" APP and Small Program Development

Guo Ting　Zhuang Ying　Zhang Lin　Li Mulin

图书在版编目（CIP）数据

故宫陶瓷馆. 卷五，专题 / 故宫博物院编. — 北京 ：故宫出版社，2021.1
（古代陶瓷经典）
ISBN 978-7-5134-1369-5

Ⅰ. ①故… Ⅱ. ①故… Ⅲ. ①古代陶瓷－中国－图录 Ⅳ. ①K876.32

中国版本图书馆CIP数据核字(2020)第237460号

故宫陶瓷馆
卷五・专题

故宫博物院编
主　　编：吕成龙
本卷主编：赵聪月
责任编辑：方　妍　李园明
装帧设计：北京气和宇宙艺术设计有限公司
责任印制：常晓辉　顾从辉
出版发行：故宫出版社
　　　　　地址：北京市东城区景山前街4号　邮编：100009
　　　　　电话：010-85007800　010-85007817
　　　　　邮箱：ggcb@culturefc.cn
印　　刷：北京雅昌艺术印刷有限公司
开　　本：889毫米×1194毫米　1/12
印　　张：34.5
版　　次：2021年1月第1版
　　　　　2021年1月第1次印刷
印　　数：1～2500册
书　　号：ISBN 978-7-5134-1369-5
定　　价：560.00元